THE SPECTRE OF RACE

The Spectre of Race

How Discrimination Haunts Western Democracy

Michael G. Hanchard

PRINCETON UNIVERSITY PRESS
PRINCETON AND OXFORD

Requests for permission to reproduce material from
this work should be sent to
Permissions, Princeton University Press

Published by Princeton University Press,
41 William Street, Princeton, New Jersey 08540

In the United Kingdom: Princeton University Press,
6 Oxford Street, Woodstock, Oxfordshire OX20 1TR

press.princeton.edu

Jacket design by Amanda Weiss

ISBN 978-0-691-17713-7
Library of Congress Control Number: 2017956528

British Library Cataloging-in-Publication Data is available

This book has been composed in Adobe Text Pro and Gotham.

Printed on acid-free paper. ∞

Printed in the United States of America

10 9 8 7 6 5 4 3 2 1

In Memoriam:

Mark Q. Sawyer (January 10, 1972–March 26, 2017)

Que Vaya Bien, Hermano . . .

CONTENTS

ACKNOWLEDGEMENTS

As is the case with most book projects, a community of disparate people helped me along the way. Several former and current students from the Johns Hopkins University and the University of Pennsylvania provided invaluable research assistance at different stages of manuscript preparation and development. At the Johns Hopkins University, Lauren Bovard, Casey McNeill, and Katherine Bonil helped with translation, tracking down primary materials, citations, and endnotes. Special thanks goes to Karina Christiansen, primary research assistant from the project's beginning to its completion. I am grateful for the competence, care, and companionship she provided during this process. At the University of Pennsylvania, Gabriel Salgado and Augusta Irele provided timely assistance in the final stage of manuscript preparation.

Given the range of primary sources and scholarly debates traversed in a project such as this, I am grateful for the helpful suggestions and critiques from colleagues in several disciplines. Colleagues at the Johns Hopkins University provided valuable insights and criticisms at several stages of the manuscript's development. Special thanks to historians Todd Shephard, Gabe Paquette, Nathan Connolly, Ken Moss, and Sara Berry. Ariane Chebel d'Appollonia of Rutgers University helped me through some of the conceptual stakes in the French case and provided detailed comments on the earliest version of the manuscript. Thanks to Jane Guyer of the anthropology department for her insights into the subfield of political anthropology, and for her abundant wisdom and good humor.

Three anonymous reviewers for Princeton University Press, specialists on Britain, the United States, and classical Athens, helped me avoid several mistakes in my handling of empirics. Several workshops, speaker series, and forums provided an opportunity for feedback on the relationship between the larger claims of the book and available historical evidence. Thanks to Jennifer Brody, director of the Center for the Comparative Study of Race and Ethnicity at Stanford University, Vaughn Rasberry, Grant Parker, and workshop participants in attendance. The Multicultural Center at the University of Santa Barbara and the Center for International Studies at UC Davis provided opportunities to present portions of the manuscript. Thanks to longtime friends and supportive colleagues, Edward Telles and Howard Winant (UCSB), and Kamal Sadiq and Cecelia Lynch (UC Davis) for the opportunity. An early version of the chapter on E.A. Freeman and comparative politics was delivered as part of the W.E.B. Du Bois Lectures in 2014 at the Hutchins Center of Harvard University. Thanks to Henry Louis Gates Jr. for the opportunity to present my work to a larger audience.

Kathleen Thelen of MIT and Robert Vitalis of the University of Pennsylvania provided generous comments on chapter 2 as well as suggestions for situating Freeman within the context of the comparative politics genealogy. Ira Katznelson provided useful suggestions for broadening my argument in early versions of chapters 2 and 3. I am thankful for a close reading by George Reid Andrews at the University of Pittsburgh, who pointed out the connections between the development of a discipline of comparative politics and the development of the discipline of history. Zita Nunes provided helpful suggestions on several drafts of the manuscript and led me to the implications of comparative methodologies in the realm of literature.

Thanks to Abdoulaye Gueye, of the University of Ottowa, for the suggestion that I incorporate some discussion of independent black political organizations and social movements in France after World War II. Stephen Small, sociologist at UC Berkeley, traveling and teaching companion in Brazil and elsewhere, helped clarify the empirics in my interpretation of France and Britain, and as a result made the comparisons across cases sharper and better delineated. Historian Tessie Liu at Northwestern University introduced me to the intense debates within France during the French Revolution about the institution of slavery and colonialism. Her comments on the chapter on difference and polity and additional references for suggested readings helped me understand the layers of complexity in the French case that I was previously unfamiliar with.

My 2014–2015 sabbatical year at the Institute for Advanced Study in Princeton provided an ideal opportunity to develop this project in an extremely supportive and energizing environment. IAS faculty at the School of Social Science were generous with their time, encouragement, and rigor. Joan Scott and Danielle Allen buoyed my spirit and encouraged me to sharpen the contours of my argument with increased historical nuance of materials on the French and Haitian Revolutions, classical Athens, and the gendered dimensions of racialized dynamics. Didier Fassin provided incisive, probing suggestions and counterarguments. Sophia Rosenfeld and Jennifer Morgan, members of my 2014–2015 cohort, provided detailed suggestions on several chapters of the manuscript in addition their comments within our seminar on Egalitarianisms led by Danielle Allen. Nolan McCarty, corridor neighbor and fellow political scientist, provided generative insights and counterarguments about democracy with respect to the literatures in political science and the US case in particular.

Political theorist Demetria Kasimis' cautionary suggestions about the complexities of slavery and citizenship in classical Athens after the Persian Wars helped me avoid errors in fact and interpretation. Jill Frank, political theorist at Cornell University, was extraordinarily generous in providing much needed contextualization in my treatment of citizenship in classical Athens. Thanks to you both for your time and expertise.

Robert Heubeck of the Gilman School in Baltimore, thanks for the inspiration. Mitch Duneier has been an extraordinarily generous friend and colleague, beginning with the suggestion that I return to Princeton University Press, my first academic publisher, and reunite with Peter Dougherty, my first editor. Eric Crahan has been an attentive, meticulous editor who, along with one of the anonymous reviewers, convinced me that my book was as much about the history of political inequality in democracy as it was a book about comparative politics.

Thanks to my immediate family, Zita Nunes, Mattias Hanchard, and Jenna Hanchard for their abiding love and support, and my extended family of Nathan Connolly, Shani Mott, and Elijah, London, and Clarke Connolly for making me part of their own.

THE SPECTRE OF RACE

Introduction

HOW DISCRIMINATION HAUNTS
WESTERN DEMOCRACY

This book is principally intended for two audiences, one within the discipline of political science, and a broader audience interested in understanding the interrelationship of racism, institutions, and modern politics. One central concern is the importance of comparison as a fundamental endeavor in human deliberation. Another is the implications of comparative analysis for both scholarship and public deliberation about the capacity for people in diverse societies to convene productively and creatively in a political community. Goethe, the great German writer, once proclaimed that idiots compare, his way of contrasting in-depth assessment of a singular event to produce universal meaning with what he considered a superficial gloss on a range of disparate phenomena. Goethe's proclamation notwithstanding, however, people across the spectrum of human intelligence necessarily engage in some form of comparison as a means to identify an object on its own and to distinguish that object from other objects.

In political science, comparative politics is the field that specializes in identifying, classifying, and distinguishing the myriad forms of political life. Many students of comparative politics trace the origins of the field to Aristotle. He, along with Plato, Herodotus, Thucydides, and Socrates, were among the first students of politics to compare and contrast forms of political community and render judgments about them. Their conclusions had normative implications along with scholarly and analytic ones. Comparisons were also judgments that produced hierarchies of value—in determinations regarding the best form (or forms) of political community and in the distinction between political and social subjects. The ancient philosophers also had a personal stake in protecting their polity from outsiders who, if granted access to citizenship, would lessen its value for the polity's original citizens and their descendants.

Athenian leadership recognized that democracy had to be nurtured, and it had to be protected from both exogenous and endogenous threats. Foreigners, whether through invasion or peaceful settlement, could negatively impact Athenian civic culture if they grew too powerful in economic and political life. Athens fought off several invasions by outsiders, most notably the Persian Army. Within Athens itself, metics (foreigners), along with Athenian women, were restricted from full participation in the polity. After the fifth-century Greco-Persian Wars, restrictions upon citizenship acquisition were tightened for Athenian women and foreigners. Before these wars, neither foreigners nor women held the right to vote, though they could participate in formal public rituals. After the Persian Wars, autochthony became a requirement for citizenship, even though its premise—that citizens could only be male descendants of original Athenian males who literally sprang from the soil—was entirely mythical. In this sense, the citizenship regime of Athens after the Persian Wars was a gendered, ethno-national regime, with a myth of autochthony (male descendants who were, figuratively, of the soil) as the first order criterion for political membership.

Among the ancients, Socrates, Aristotle, and Plato rendered judgments about the capacity for diverse peoples to forge political communities based on their sociocultural priorities and emphases. The views of the ancients on the best form of government and polity were summoned by modern thinkers to justify the importance of culture, education, and positive political socialization in human development, but also to compare and contrast civilizations, societies, and polities and their relative capacities and potential for modern governance. David Hume, John Stuart Mill, Jean Jacques Rousseau, Adam Smith, Marx, and most famously Thomas Hobbes compared and contrasted various human communities. Hierarchy, however, was comparison's companion, usually lurking in the background, just a few steps or sentences behind.

Despite the restrictions imposed upon their political participation, metics and Athenian women had a least some political rights, public duties, and responsibilities. The enslaved had none. Slavery was rationalized as a necessary institution that allowed citizens to fully participate in civic life without material constraints. Slavery, according to its proponents, made Athenian democracy practicable.

The complexities of Athenian democracy, citizenship, and civic culture require far more detail and expertise than this author can provide, and in any case, are not the focus of this book. Nevertheless, important lessons can be extracted and ultimately, abstracted, from these facts of Athenian citizenship and democratic practice before and after the Greco-Persian wars; these lessons are relevant not only for the book but for a better understanding of the relationship between the practice of democracy and political inequality in the contemporary world. Despite the absence of historical, cultural, and social continuities between the *demos* of classical Athens and contemporary democratic polities, there are nevertheless certain political continuities. Gender, nation ethnicity, and nationality mattered in the constitution of Athenian citizenship and voting rights. Citizenship, like democracy itself, was not static, but underwent permutations and transformations in moments of crisis, whether in the city-states of the ancient world now associated with the West or in the nation-states of the contemporary world system.

Part of my contention is that autochthony, designed to naturalize and restrict membership in the Athenian polity, became a prototypical form of differentiation intended to rationalize limitations upon citizenship or formal membership in the political community. This political mythology served to naturalize citizenship, making it inaccessible to those who could not prove that they descended from Athenian soil. Additionally, since citizenship descent was patrilineal, a woman, even one descended from autochthonous parents, could not become a citizen. Thus, a law designed to exclude male foreigners from acquiring and deploying citizenship consequentially excluded women who were actually (rather than figuratively) born in Athens. In this sense, autochthonous criteria for political membership also served as a form of immigration policy that excluded the majority of non-Athenians from citizenship after 451 BC.

In sum, although the Athenian polity was constituted by its citizens, Athenian society (to the extent it could be considered a society in any contemporary sense) contained not only citizens, but foreigners, women, and slaves (noncitizens). Given the disparity between the number of polity members and the number of social subjects, Athenian elites were faced with a series of questions with political import that resonate in the contemporary world: How should democratically empowered citizens interact with members of their society who are not citizens, namely foreigners, minorities (both women and men), and in some (not all) instances, women? How does a democratic polity (namely, relations between government and the governed that are premised upon democratic principles) exist within a society that is not founded upon democratic principles, but upon hierarchies? Must its laws, norms, and rules of exclusion be deliberated upon by the excluded, as well as those included, in the demos, for those laws to be truly democratic? In ancient Athens as well as in modern political communities of Western nation-states, groups of people were excluded from political participation through law, normative reprobation and, when necessary, coercion. The legal, juridical, and institutional empowerment of citizens has been dynamically related to limiting second class citizens or prohibiting noncitizens from access to citizenship, as well as certain key economic and political institutions. In classical Athens, no less than in contemporary nation-states founded upon democratic principles, democratic institutions and practices coexist with antidemocratic ones.

An inquiry into the history of politics—any politics—requires an understanding of the practices of human actors and the institutions they seek to forge or dismantle, not just comprehension of the ideas and concepts that inspired or revolted them. Part of this book's mission is to represent democracy not only as a concept and ideal, but as a practice, a particular combination of norms, institutions, and actors. One of the key questions this book explores is how the practice of democracy produces—and is affected by—political inequality.

Democratic institutions and practices of classical Athens were often in tension with tyrannical, oligarchic, and imperial tendencies within its polity. Athenian democracy did not exist in a bubble, but in a larger geopolitical context with internal and external threats to its existence. Thus, democracy has not evolved in isolation, but in relation to other forms of social organization and administration that have often been fundamentally unequal, but nonetheless part of the same social ecology. The Athenian polis relied heavily upon slave labor for citizen subsistence and wealth. Territorial expansion and subjugation of non-Athenian populations (what we would now refer to as colonization), along with the threat of invasion, also influenced how democracy and, most importantly, differential citizenship regimes developed. The most robust, long-standing democratic polities in the contemporary world—France, Britain, and the United States—have been housed in societies that have profited from slave labor, empire, and colonialism.

A fuller appreciation of the legacy of the Athenian democratic polis in contemporary democratic polities requires the recognition of the polyarchic character of ancient Athens as well as the contemporary societies categorized as liberal democratic polities. Common to both is how emphasis on distinctions and variations in human collectivities were rendered politically salient. A core concern of this book is how difference, figured as race, was rendered politically salient in modern politics.

As sociologists have reminded us, race, like power, is a relational concept. A so-called race is invariably defined in distinction to other presumed races. Where racial reasoning and the practice of comparison have combined in modern politics is in the rendering of judgments about the relative merits of groups of people distinguished by race, and subsequently, through the codification of categories and the attempt at regulation of populations, especially their interactions. In essence, apartheid and other forms of segregation can be boiled down to this more abstract formulation. Comparison, judgment, codification, hierarchy, and ultimately, inequality are the keywords that help characterize the process and relationship between the race construct, politics, and institutions in modernity.

In a more dynamic understanding of the relationship between democratic and nondemocratic institutions in societies with democratic polities, we can also explore how those excluded from citizenship in both ancient and modern eras sought and in some cases demanded participation in the democratic polities around them, or alternatively, sought to create polities of their own. Political and economic exclusion is often manifested in laws, norms, and coercive sanctions that delimited or outright prohibited noncitizen populations (slaves, women, serfs, and peasants among them) from participating in formal civic life. The combination of formal and informal institutions designed to limit political participation of the excluded can be conceptualized as mechanisms or institutions of political inequality.

Most contemporary scholarship on inequality has focused on economic manifestations and disparities in life expectancy, health care, education, and stress-related diseases. Known as "the social question" in the 18th century in the aftermath of the French and US revolutions, the roots of social inequality are often traced to the economic sphere. While not discounting the economic and material sources of social inequality, many aspects of social inequality have political roots. Gendered disparities are perhaps the most obvious manifestations of inequality. Neither the socially constituted character of gender roles, and certainly not nature, can explain why women, across the ages and spaces, have been subordinated in economic, social, and material relations. The ability to own property and access to wealth, education, and suffrage have their origins in law and custom that have privileged males in most societies.

Political and social inequality are often dynamically related, insofar as exclusionary and inclusionary criteria for citizenship formation and participation invariably emanate from the same source: state power. Yet one of the core lessons of this book is that political inequality is not simply an epiphenomenal feature of social and economic inequality. Instead, political inequality is often the result of deliberate decisions to exclude specific groups from participation in a polity and to deny their access to the same social and economic opportunities afforded to members of dominant groups. Whether by gender, social class, ethno-nationality, religion, or other forms of distinction, the administration and management of political inequality has varied by society and regime, and it has been based upon distinct criteria depending upon the marginalized groups in question and their demands for inclusion.

Racial, gendered, religious, and ethno-national chauvinism are among the forms of evaluative differentiation which, when embedded in political institutions, provide an interpretive means for governments to codify their preferences in law, edicts, and constitutions that then regulate people and their interactions. Moreover, these forms of differentiation, functioning as informal and formal institutions, have impacted the practice of democracy in three Western polities in particular: France, Britain, and the United States. Part of my contention in this book is that such forms of political inequality are not anomalous features of certain Western polities, but rather are the modern manifestations of the combination of democracy, difference, and inequality first invented and implemented in classical Athens.

The Race Concept, Institutions, and Politics

One of the claims in this book is that the race concept became the modern equivalent of the Athenian myth of autochthony in many Western and Western-influenced nation-states. Athenian autochthony and the race concept both emphasize a mythology of origins. In the realm of modern politics, the race concept enabled political actors to project the need for homogeneity among a citizen populace, making race an organizing principle for governments and popular movements alike.

A key distinguishing feature of the race concept's application within the nation-state system in modernity was its portability and not, as in the case of the ancient idea of autochthony, its sedentariness. Autochthony linked a specific territory to a particular set of rights. Nations, or more precisely, nationalities, were identified with a particular territory, but also by traditions, culture, and language, all portable. By the 19th century, race became a marker of portability as well as origins. An Anglo-Saxon could be an Anglo-Saxon whether they resided in Saxony or not. A Negro was a descendant from Africa, even though there is no Negroland in Africa (or anywhere else) and human species originated in Africa.

Where races were once treated as nations—the terms were often used interchangeably—through a combination of language, culture, territorial fixity (the land of . . .), and often associations of kinship (blood), the race concept grew detached from territory to denote populations regardless of their location in the world, with an emphasis on appearance (phenotypical and somatic traits).

For those who believed in a world organized by races and by implication, polygenesis, populations displayed their alleged "racial" characteristics wherever they appeared. They believed superior races such as the Teutonic or Aryan were predestined to rule, especially in the presence of lesser races, whether they were in Germany, England, the United States, or Africa and South America. Thus, an Italian, for example, determined through racist judgment to be of inferior stock, was doomed to either outright exclusion or circumscribed citizenship status in countries other than Italy, especially if the Italian lived among races judged to be his or her so-called racial superior.

Taken to its extreme, the belief in a world racial order articulated by the Third Reich, in its propaganda and prosecution of war domestically and internationally, constituted a threat to the very idea of a nation-state system with discrete entities composed of sovereign states, national populations, and territory. Hannah Arendt identified the threat that race-thinking posed not only for the internal composition of an individual nation-state, but of the nation-state system as a whole: "Racism deliberately cut across all national boundaries, whether defined by geographical, linguistic, traditional or any other standards, and denied national-political existence as such."[1] Arendt's conclusion about the spectre of race in Western politics urges readers to consider the relationship between race-thinking, modernity, and politics more broadly, not as a fascist anomaly but as constituting the body politic of Western nation-states.

The emergence of fascism—and the Third Reich its most virulent manifestation—is generally considered to one of the major crises in Western politics in the 20th century and a fundamental crisis of political modernity. The brutal emphasis on racial singularity in Nazi politics and society threatened the very idea of national populations created from a diversity of peoples. If not contained, the Nazis' ruthless quest for racial homogeneity could have had disastrous consequences for minority populations the world over.

Hannah Arendt's broader commentary on the spectre of race and racism in Europe, however, warns against treating Nazi policy as the only case of conjoining racism to state power in Europe. Other nation-states, even Allied ones, utilized state power to formulate and implement policies designed to differentiate populations according to racial and ethno-national criteria in their own societies, and in places under their territorial dominion (colonies, protectorates, or even other nation-states). Indeed, as this book will demonstrate, many Western democratic nation-states, as well as states in Latin America and Asia, devised racial and ethno-national regimes that combined selective immigration controls, literacy, birth, and wealth requirements designed to limit the access of specific groups to political life.

Upon close examination, traces of the Athenian practice of combining *ethnos* (naturalized political membership) with democracy (a set of institutions and practices) can be found in the laws of the most prominent democratic societies. In these societies, racial and ethno-national hierarchy provided the rationalization for the institutionalization of political inequality, based on the premise that racially and ethno-nationally divergent groups could not share the same state.

There is a dearth of comparative politics research on the role of ethno-national and racial subordination in the formation of Western polities, ideas, and practices of citizenship. There are several notable exceptions to this tendency.[2] These exceptional works notwithstanding, however, laypersons and specialists alike could be forgiven for assuming that the relationship between racial and ethno-national hierarchy and political institutions has never been central to the study of comparative politics. And yet, as I will demonstrate, the earliest developments in the creation of a comparative politics method in the modern era were devoted to marshaling evidence proving that racial and ethno-national hierarchy was central to modern political development and institutions.

A dust encrusted treasure chest of the field and discipline's history begs to be dusted off by students of comparative politics. Its lid has barely been lifted since the last quarter of the 19th century, more than three generations removed from the field's formal founding in the 1950s. Edward Augustus Freeman, Oxford historian and Euro-Aryan advocate, devised the first methodology for the comparative study of ancient and modern political institutions, in a series of 1873 lectures titled *Comparative Politics*.

In Freeman's view of politics both modern and ancient, the idea of race was central to political life; to the formation of a polis, commonwealth, and institutions; and ultimately, to the conjuncture of nation and state. The power of race lay not in its biological provenance, but in commonly held beliefs and assumptions shared by groups of people who join to form political communities. Freeman's influence is evident in the development of seminars and Ph.D. programs devoted to the study of political institutions in the late 19th and early 20th centuries, and in the scholarship and policy recommendations of Woodrow Wilson, 28th president of the United States.

For Freeman and his interlocutors, the race concept—alternating between historical and biological definitions—was central to understanding the development of political institutions and their variations. Freeman, like the Johns Hopkins University historian Herbert Baxter Adams, believed that presumed racial origin and nationality were fundamental factors in assessing group prospects for the development of a modern political community and ultimately, the modern state. Race, then, was a key variable in understanding political modernity, the capacity for self-rule, and institutional developments among the world's populations. Racial homogeneity was considered central to political development and democracy. As comparativists, Freeman, Baxter Adams, and other members of the Teutonic or Euro-Aryan school believed that racial difference enabled students of comparative politics to identify correlations, if not draw inferences, between populations and their political development.

The first formal seminar at a US research institution devoted to what was then referred to as "historical and political science," founded and taught by Johns Hopkins University professor Herbert Baxter Adams, combined an emphasis on the development of research methodologies for the examination of political and social institutions, with an empirical focus on the administration and management of subordinate, often servile, populations. The Teutonist explanation of differences in the capacity of distinct populations to produce democratic political communities and institutions can be understood as a midway point between biologically determinist arguments and culture-based explanations of distinctions among the political cultures of the modern world.

Up to now, there is no disciplinary or field account of these developments in the study of comparative politics on the cusp of the 19th and 20th century. Among several objectives in this book is to connect comparative politics' preprofessional past to the official narrative of its formation and subsequent development. Common to the 19th century and mid–20th century discussions about comparative politics was a core preoccupation: how could distinct peoples with varying capacities for self-governance participate in the same polity? A cursory examination of political events in the second decade of the 21st century will reveal to the interested observer that this question is a recurrent one, on the minds of state and nonstate actors throughout the West and other parts of the world.

Three Iterations of a Comparative Politics Discipline

This book provides the first assessment of comparative methodologies for the study of politics that encompasses the neglected period of 19th century innovation. With a broader, more historically sensitive view of comparative politics as method and field, this study has three identifiable moments or iterations of a comparative politics discipline: the late 19th century, the mid–20th century, and the cusp of the 20th and 21st centuries. As will be detailed across several chapters, comparative politics' preprofessional past has continued relevance for the study of comparative politics. In all three eras, nationalism, ethnicity, xenophobia, migration, and the rights of minority groups figured prominently in world politics, if not so prominently on the research agendas of leading practitioners of the field.

The book's chapters account for the three iterations of comparative politics across these epochs. The first iteration in the development of a method for the comparative study of politics was part of a broader movement among linguists and students of comparative literature, anthropology, and the natural sciences in the late 19th century, which explored the possibilities for cross-spatial and cross-temporal comparison. By the late 19th century, scholars across the social sciences and humanities began devising and deploying what were then considered more scientific approaches to the study of human phenomena across space and time. In this "prehistorical" era, students of comparative politics were not motivated by professional dictates; comparativists could not be members of a profession (political science) that did not yet exist. Research questions (however spurious) drove methods, not the other way around. Perceived crises and problems, whether in the study of language, a people, a bureaucracy, law or set of norms, prompted the development of comparative studies. In this sense, a discipline of comparative politics predated the field of comparative politics, as well as the profession of political science.

The second iteration in the history of comparative politics is the inaugural moment of formal recognition and legitimation of the field of comparative politics within the discipline of political science. Comparativists in political science appropriated concepts, methods, and scholarly literature from history, sociology, anthropology, and psychology as the basis for a seemingly new field of concentration. The Social Science Research Council's (SSRC) Committee on Comparative Politics was founded in 1955 at a moment when political scientists had direct experience with world war, the subsequent Cold War, and the rise of nationalism in the areas of the world that were once under Western colonial domination. Along with social scientists from other disciplines, the committee became a pivotal cross-disciplinary research nucleus known as "the politics of the developing areas." The SSRC initiative was important not only for its legitimation of a new field, but in its material support for affiliated research initiatives and the institutionalization of core thematic interests in civic foundations and governmental agencies. Governmental agencies would prove critical in the funding of regional specialization (area studies) and language training for social scientists of the era who were interested in conducting research in the so-called developing areas. During this epoch, statecraft overlapped significantly with scholarly trends.

Political scientists like Sidney Verba and Gabriel Almond recognized the need for new concepts and approaches to explain political phenomena that were unrecognizable to them in under-studied parts of the world, and the need to rid political science and comparative politics in particular of Eurocentric and Anglo-American biases. By the mid–20th century, race all but disappeared as a key theme in the study of comparative politics, despite the fact that presumed racial or ethno-national distinction was acknowledged as a key organizing principle for politics by several prominent political scientists well into the first two decades of the 20th century. Although traces of racial reasoning found their way into some cultural explanations of political behavior in both anthropology and political science, biological and essentialist understandings of race were largely absent in the conceptual and methodological tool kit of this group of social scientists. To be sure, part of the rationale for the scholarly shift in the approach to examining so-called developing areas of the world was due to an altered geo-political climate, along with a genuine shift in thinking about concepts such as race and civilization after World War II. The emergent anticolonial and nationalist movements in Asia, Africa, and parts of the Caribbean and Latin America prompted decolonization policies by the British and US governments, which ranged from peaceful, negotiated transitions to counterinsurgency and sabotage of several newly independent, sovereign governments in the so-called developing world. If Western nation-states wanted economically and politically advantageous relations with the new nation-states, they could no longer openly refer to the elites and masses of the so-called developing world as colonial minions and racial inferiors.

The third moment in the history of the field of comparative politics coincided with the collapse of the Soviet Union and subsequent reconfiguration of global politics. Known within political science as the Perestroika movement, with obvious reference to the opening and attempted transformation of Soviet politics and culture under the leadership of Mikhail Gorbachev in the waning years of the Soviet Union, historically and qualitatively minded political scientists provided a critique of the increasingly narrow and positivist approaches to the study of political phenomena. Among these critics were students of comparative politics who, having waged their own battles with positivism and behavioralism at earlier points in the field and discipline's history, joined the small but influential group of actors who sought to remind their colleagues that history, culture, language, and context (in a word, difference), remained fundamental for comprehending politics in the contemporary world.

Chapter Overview

The chapters of this book provide a chronological outline of the field of comparative politics in its three iterations. The conceptual link connecting these discrete epochs is how racial and ethno-national regimes are present—or absent—in the most significant scholarship and reviews of the field and in world politics. I have little interest in highlighting the origins of the comparative politics field in race thinking for the purpose of suggesting a distinct starting point or alternative genealogy for the study of modern comparative politics. More fruitful, in my view, is to bring the preoccupations of the three iterations in dialogical tension with one another to identify continuities and discontinuities in race-thinking among students of comparative politics.

Chapter 1 situates the genesis of a comparative politics field or discipline not in the mid–20th century, as most accounts of comparative politics do, but in the late 19th century, beginning with the writings of E.A. Freeman, Herbert Baxter Adams, and Woodrow Wilson. Freeman's pioneering efforts can be understood as the first moment in the development of a more systematic approach to the comparative study of political institutions in the social sciences and humanities.

Freeman is entirely absent, however, from the historiography of comparative politics, as well as the accounts of the history of political science as an academic profession. Despite Freeman's absence from both canonical and revisionist accounts of the subfield, however, his combination of racist ideology, cross-spatial and cross-temporal comparison, and methodological innovation reveals a set of scientific and normative concerns that have endured in contemporary politics, if not in the field of comparative politics itself. Previously ignored primary materials, normative perspectives, and methodological approaches examined in this chapter are significant for enabling current and future students of comparative politics to take a longer view of their field as a disciplinary formation.

Chapter 2 tracks the change from the first to the second iteration of comparative politics: the replacement of concepts of race with concepts of culture, what came to be known as the "politics of the developing areas." This moment in the history of comparative politics' disciplinary and professional formation is far more recognizable to students of the field. The Committee on Comparative Politics at the Social Science Research Council is generally considered the foundational moment for the instantiation of a field of comparative politics at major research institutions, in government and political science departments across the United States, and in the major foundations that provided crucial financial and institutional support for the training of graduate students and the reproduction of the profession.

The horrors of World War II, decolonization, and the geo-politics of the Cold War served as the backdrop for deliberations about the development and institutionalization of new approaches to the study of political institutions. For many Western social scientists, the new nation-states and political communities of the so-called Third World bore little resemblance to the ideal nation-states of the modern world. Culture and ethnicity were the operative concepts deployed to identify potential obstacles to political modernity in Africa and Asia, particularly in the former Western colonies that had achieved nominal independence.

The race concept and the phenomena of racial hierarchies were casualties of the positivist turn in the study of comparative politics, beginning with the politics of the developing areas movement. In anthropology and sociology, the idea of race rooted in some biological, essential form had been largely debunked by the early 20th century, even if examples of essentialist reason could be found in scholarship from both disciplines. By the 1950s, the culture concept supplanted the race concept as a key intervening variable (along with capitalism, industrialization, and modernization) for the development of non-Western nations.

The culture concept, however, as utilized by students of political development and comparative politics, was often deployed in ways similar to how the race concept was used in earlier iterations of comparative politics. While the culture concept supplanted the race concept, the associations of a people's "ways of life" with institutional variation harbored traces of E.A. Freeman's and other racialists' and nationalists' ultimately faulty correlations between people and political institutions.

Chapter 3 examines the idea of difference as a form of political distinction in democratic polities, ranging from classical Athens to the contemporary period. Students of comparative politics from the late 19th century to the present have often invoked the Greek polis as the first site or prototype for modern politics, as well as the first opportunity for speculation and support of democracy (*demos*) as the best, or least unequal, form of political practice. In this sense, Edward Augustus Freeman shares with Edward Vogelin, Charles Merriam, Gabriel Almond, Sidney Verba, David Laitin, and Robert Bates the invocation of Aristotle as inspiration and justification for a more positivist approach to the study of comparative politics and for a normative preference for democracy out of a range of possible forms of political community. Often neglected in these invocations, however, is the first-order relationship between democracy and *political* inequality, and how political inequality is both related to and distinct from social or material inequality.

Idealizations of the Greek polis as the cradle of democracy within political science and philosophy often obscure how central slaves were to the practice of freedom, and how the omission of several categories of people from citizenship and the polis required exclusionary regimes. The first documented instance of democracy was also an *ethnos*, with mechanisms and institutions designed to restrict, not universalize, political participation. While most students of contemporary and ancient democratic experiments have focused on an *ethos* of democracy, the concern here is to explore the *ethnos* of ancient and contemporary democracies, the manner in which the practice of a democratic politics, in most instances, has combined inclusionary and exclusionary regimes and value judgments regarding the prospects of citizenship for differentiated populations. Common to the city-states of the ancient and medieval worlds and nation-states of modernity was the governmental necessity of providing answers to the following questions: by what criteria do we choose citizens, and by what criteria shall we determine who shall not, or cannot, become a citizen?

Surprisingly little scholarship exists within comparative politics on the impact of slave regimes within nominally democratic societies and their political institutions. The institution of slavery influenced the institution of citizenship in classical Athens, particularly when it became clear that citizenship law would have to be changed to protect Athenian citizens who were faced with the prospect of enslavement if they could not pay their debts.

Thus, an institution founded upon and maintained by coercion influenced the development of an institution founded upon deliberation and citizen participation.

Comparative politics, on the whole, has largely invoked commentary by ancient philosophers, historians, and playwrights—intellectual commentary about Athenian democracy among classical contemporaries rather than examinations of Athenian political institutions—to render cross-temporal judgments about how democracies evolve and why they matter.[3] This chapter draws upon scholarship in political theory, American politics, comparative history, and comparative politics to further probe the nexus of slavery and democracy.

Moving from classical Athens, chapter 3 situates racial hierarchy in a line of politically salient distinctions institutionalized by Western nation-states to distinguish societal from political membership. Racial hierarchy, from the birth of the nation-state system to its present-day composition, has influenced state formation and expansion, immigration and citizenship law, interstate relations, and the conquest and withdrawal of government intervention into national and colonial societies. Leaders of national independence movements in Haiti, Gran Colombia, Brazil, and the United States all struggled with the question of slavery and the status of slaves in new republics, but also with the status of poor and nonelite whites and creoles who stood to lose the most if citizenship was not based on racial and ethno-national hierarchy. Race or color, along with gender, literacy, and property ownership, informed the criteria of citizenship in all the new republics.

With the historical and critical realignment of the comparative politics field and its range of methods in which racial and ethno-national hierarchy are fundamental factors for the study of democracy and political development, chapter 4 provides a reinterpretation of Britain, France, and the United States as polyarchies with racial and ethno-national regimes. In these and other societies with democratic politics, racial and ethno-national regimes have been responsible for the maintenance of population differentiation that enables governments and citizens to distinguish among citizens, or between citizens and noncitizens. While racial and ethno-national regimes in US political history have been identified and analyzed in the scholarship of Ira Katznelson, Desmond King, Matthew Holden, and others, rarely have these regimes been identified and analyzed within comparative politics as features of nominally democratic polities more broadly.

Much of the analysis in this chapter is a revisionist account of existing scholarship in political science, history, sociology, and anthropology, to provide further evidence of how the three countries have incorporated ethno-national and racial regimes within democratic polities. These are more contemporary examples of ethnos-based democratic polities, as in the case of ancient Athens after the Persian Wars, that have rationalized the relationship between democracy and political inequality.

Racial and ethno-national regimes did not first emerge as fully articulated, coherent, and coordinated policies. Rather, they emerged in response to the actual or anticipated encounters between dominant and minority populations (whether through marriage or sex, commerce or conflict, or sport) that prompted the creation of laws and policies to administer the relationship between citizens and noncitizens. Fears and anxieties about the presence of minoritized and racialized populations with access to both society and polity led to the earliest forms of institutional discrimination.

Immigration and resettlement of former colonial populations in the case of France and Britain, and the agitation for rights among marginalized populations in the United States resulted in many governmental crises in the post–World War II period and into the first decades of the 21st century. Each national government utilized administrative tactics and strategies to manage and in some cases to repress populations deemed threats to national security: US African Americans, particularly those engaged in civil rights and left politics; Afro-Caribbean and other black populations in Britain; and Arab populations in France during the era of anticolonial struggle. In each society, domestic unrest—youth movements, feminism, war protests, labor conflicts, civil rights struggles for nonwhite minorities—led to the reformulation of domestic and foreign policy to attend to immigration flows and to surveil protest groups. Strategies and techniques of population management, counterintelligence, and repression first deployed upon noncitizens in colonial and imperial spheres were often adapted for use in the metropole. This aspect of political management and rule further demonstrates the entanglements of democratic and antidemocratic modes of political authority, and how population categorization and classification within racial and ethno-national regimes blurs the boundaries between domestic and foreign populations, and between citizenship rights and noncitizen restrictions.

The concluding chapter, chapter 5, reviews the spectre of race in comparative politics across the three disciplinary moments outlined in this introduction and then considers their implications for how students of politics undertake comparative political analysis in the contemporary world. Moment one is the Euro-Aryan perspective on political institutions; moment two is the "politics of the developing areas" movement of the 1950s to rid

Western political science from the parochialism of its concepts and methods of inquiry. The Perestroika movement within political science is the third moment, with divergent implications for the field of comparative politics and the discipline of political science remaining unclear. After reviewing these distinct yet related moments, the chapter will elaborate upon the implications of a difference-centered approach to the study of comparative politics for contemporary students of the field and in the contemporary world.

This final chapter engages most fully with the implications of this book for an expanded research agenda within the field of comparative politics, as well as for contemporary politics. A core argument is that the contemporary iteration of comparative politics as a field within political science is also the most neglectful of the legacies of colonialism, racism, and imperialism within Western nation-states, and their combined implications for how students of comparative politics might examine racial and ethno-national regimes. Intraspatial comparison, especially in plural societies, is one of the most promising research streams for further examination of how racial and ethno-national regimes function in modern democratic polities.

In addition to a methodological emphasis on induction, interpretation, concept tracing, history, and context, this study also has implications for how students of politics understand difference as a factor or variable at the juncture of racial hierarchy and formal and informal institutions. A research topic common among 19th and 20th century students of comparative politics was pluralism in both people and politics: was it possible for distinct peoples with varying capacities for self-governance to participate peaceably in the same polity? This question has been posed by a diverse array of political actors and scholars across the ideological spectrum, including Edward Augustus Freeman, Woodrow Wilson, and Samuel Huntington, but also W.E.B. Du Bois, Indira Gandhi, and Ho Chi Minh. For Freeman and Wilson, and to a lesser extent Huntington at the end of his career, democracy and diverse populations do not mix. By contrast, the great challenge and promise of more radical and liberal visions of the nexus of cultural pluralism and democracy is to create societies, polities, and norms that allow all members of a given society to participate equally as members of the polity, to strip away barriers imposed by distinctions of gender, social class, religion, ethnicity, origin, and presumed racial distinction. Both Western and non-Western societies continue to struggle with the conflict between relatively recent egalitarian ideals and inegalitarian social and political orders designed by prior generations of government and leadership to maintain dominance of a particular ethno-national group, religion, or presumed race.

The most durable and enduring democratic polities have nurtured an ethnos within them, often at the expense of minoritized and racialized groups. The United States, France, and Britain—but also contemporary Germany, Switzerland, Belgium, the Scandinavian nations, Ghana, South Africa, Indonesia, and many other countries classified as democratic—have exhibited this tendency. The larger number of studies of these countries and the likelihood of particular groups or subgroups attaining the most preferable positions in the economy, polity, and society attest to this bias in the most democratic and societies in the contemporary world. How to make societies less ethnocentric, and more ethos-centric, is one of the great challenges of balancing cultural difference and democracy in contemporary nation-states.

1

Edward Augustus Freeman and the Dawn of Comparative Politics

The late 19th century and early 20th century was a period of tumultuous change in many parts of the world. Waning and emergent empires prompted shifts in the world's geopolitical template. Where subordinated nationalities once stood, new nation-states arose from the ashes of the Austro-Hapsburg and Ottoman empires. The scramble for Africa augured a distinct phase of European domination of human and material resources of that continent, transforming disparate African peoples into tribes and colonial subjects, and creating territorial and ethnic boundaries which, in practical terms, made more sense to colonizers than to the colonized. Amidst the swirl of imperial collapse and consolidation, self-determination, nationality, and racial and ethnic identification became important elements in the definition of what constituted a people, nation, race, and in some instances, a state.

Among the changes of this period was the deepening organization and classification of knowledge, one of the far-reaching consequences of the Enlightenment's intellectual traditions that emphasized science and reason. Increasing interaction and knowledge of peoples, norms, objects, and institutions across the globe generated the desire among a growing number of scholars to impose discipline upon forms of knowledge that had grown increasingly unruly. New genres and subject areas, ranging from the novel to mass industry and technology, made the task of information gathering and organization more difficult for all engaged in the production, translation, and dissemination of knowledge. Increasingly, scholars sought means to literally discipline new and existing information. The term *discipline* had not yet taken on the professional demarcated form now associated with academia, but in a more epistemological sense, it was a means to organize knowledge, to distinguish forms and objects of inquiry. Among the most significant changes in the organization of knowledge in the 19th century was the invention of the comparative method.

Methods of comparative analysis were utilized by a small but influential group of scholars in the late 19th century who would be considered pioneers in the development of several professional academic disciplines, including political science. Interest in the comparative method, and the subject matter that inspired it, led students of politics to create programs, seminars, and departments at places like Oxford, Smith, Cornell, Wisconsin, South Carolina, and Johns Hopkins University. Such efforts were designed to institutionally embed specific methodological approaches into one or more academic departments and disciplines.

Yet most late 19th century scholars preoccupied with making comparisons were not formally affiliated with a university, college, or specific academic discipline. Subject matter, rather than professional dictates, was the motivating force behind methodological speculation and innovation. A student of literature, religion, language or philosophy, no less than a student of history or politics, could rightfully claim the study of Western governmental constitutions as part of their disciplinary realm. For example, constitutions, particularly those of Western governments, often invoked God and divine right, thus opening them up as opportunities to study the relationship between religion and politics. The text or object in question was a site of what we would now refer to as interdisciplinarity or transdisciplinarity.

The comparative method was considered one of the greatest scholarly innovations of the century, enabling scholars to consider a novel, institution, market or language as an object on its own, independently of context or genesis. In the United States and Europe, scholars from divergent areas of interest were engaged in transatlantic conversation about the development of methods of inquiry best suited for comparative study. At this stage in the development of a dialogue about scholarly methods, thematic and topical interests were of greater significance than the professional subject position of the scholar engaged in the task of comparison.

As Natalie Melas noted, writing about comparative literature, the impact of the comparative method could be evidenced across the social sciences and humanities, providing "a comprehensive and systematic approach to the totality of objects in a given field and [replacing] the directionlessness of a merely taxonomic comparison with a positivist evolutionary teleology."[1] Regardless of subject matter, the student employing a comparative method was compelled to consider the philosophical, specifically epistemological, implications of their objects of inquiry: What are the terms and conditions of comparison? What renders certain comparisons intelligible and others incoherent? Is it possible to know and understand any object of study outside of its relation to other objects?

Several key advocates of a comparative method, especially in history, literature, and, as I will detail below, the study of politics, believed in historical immanence, the universality of all human beings despite variations in language, custom, religion, region, and appearance. Comparison would render visible seemingly disparate forms and habits of peoples across the globe, allowing for the identification of and underlying telos of the human condition. Of course, such evaluations came with judgments and determinations about the best and worst representations of the human condition—the achievements and catastrophes devised by human hands and minds.

The first known lecture utilizing the term *comparative literature* in the United States was delivered in 1871 by Chauncey Shackford at Cornell University. Shackford is considered a pioneer in the development of a method for comparing literary production from many parts of the world. In this lecture, Shackford not only described the particular benefits of a comparative method for students of literature, but placed methodological innovations in the study of comparative literature alongside a wider trend—the development and deployment of comparative methods by scholars of various subjects:

> The method in which this study can be best pursued is that which is pursued in anatomy, in language, in mythology, and recently applied by Mr. Freeman, to politics, namely the comparative. The literary productions of all ages and peoples can be classed, can be brought into comparison and contrast, can be taken out of their isolation as belonging to one nation, or one separate era.[2]

Two points in this passage are crucial for grasping the emergent use of methods of comparison in scholarly inquiry. First, Shackford declared that the study of literature utilizing a comparative method could organize distinct and varied forms of literary production under "the same aesthetic principles, the universal laws of mental, social and moral development: the same in India and in England: in Hellas, with its laughing sea, and Germany with its somber forests."[3] Thus, distinguishing features of topography, environment, or locale were no match for the ability of a comparativist to isolate, dissect, compare, and contrast forms and subjects. Further deepening the Enlightenment conceit, culture was no match for science. Second, methodological innovation in one area of knowledge could impact other areas of knowledge. The comparative method, wielding the weapons of science, became a liberator, a democratizer, of knowledge.

A second reference in Shackford's passage would, without some knowledge of the person mentioned, go unnoticed by most students of comparative politics, if not political scientists entirely: the *Freeman* referred to in his lecture is Edward Augustus Freeman, whom scholars in several fields recognized by 1871 as a methodological pioneer in the development of a comparative approach to the study of politics. It should not be surprising in a lecture on comparative literature and the comparative method that Shackford would refer to other scholars who advocated methods and approaches formally similar to his own. For a brief period roughly spanning Shackford's first mention of Freeman until the Englishman's death, Freeman enjoyed a certain notoriety in the United States, England, and Europe for his views on a variety of topics.

What is surprising, however, is that Freeman's writings on comparative politics remain virtually unknown to students within the field. Freeman devised what would appear to be the first attempt to systematize the comparative study of modern (as opposed to ancient) political institutions, texts, and language. He declared this a science and incorporated his approach into teaching and research at several key academic institutions and professions in 19th century US and England. Freeman's call for a method of comparative politics and its formal acknowledgement as a discipline was first made more than two generations before the creation of the field of "Foreign and Comparative Government" at Harvard in 1927, and eighty-four years before the creation of the Committee on Comparative Politics by the Social Science Research Council in the United States in the 1950s.

In a very influential article in 1971, "Comparative Politics and the Comparative Method," Arend Lijphart described what he characterized as Freeman's "optimism" about the field of comparative politics and its capacity, via assessment of sameness and difference, to uncover "universal laws through global and longitudinal comparison."[4] While acknowledging that the field of comparative politics might never achieve the range and depth of discoveries that Freeman had hoped for (in part due to the lack of basic information about many political systems of earlier time periods), his goals nevertheless could serve to remind students of comparative politics of "the frequent utility of extending comparative analysis both geographically and histori-cally."[5] As students of comparative politics are now well aware, Lijphart's description of Freeman's contribution to the development of the subfield implicitly frames what would become one of the key methodological de-bates in comparative politics by the 1960s, namely, delimiting the scope of comparison through concept extension and intension.[6]

Lijphart cites several passages from Freeman's lectures to underscore their shared optimism about the prospects for a comparative politics that could reveal "a world in which times and tongues and nations which before seemed parted poles asunder, now find each one its own place, its own re-lation to every other."[7] Lijphart's observations here are important not only because of the manner in which he acknowledges Freeman's contribution to the study of comparative politics, but also because his acknowledgement of Freeman's contributions points us towards an earlier period in intellectual and global history—a time when several academic disciplines in the social and natural sciences and the humanities were taking shape in the West. Besides Lijphart, however, no other student of comparative politics in the post–World War II period even cites Freeman.

Freeman's advocacy for a scientific comparative method to approach the study of political phenomena shares some uncanny similarities with arguments made by subsequent generations of comparativists in political science. Freeman believed that a science of comparative politics would free researchers from slavish attention to empirical detail, epochal and spatial boundaries, anecdotal evidence, and logical inconsistency. He advocated approaches to the study of politics that were designed to discipline other forms of knowledge, namely language and literature, and appropriated them for his new discipline. Second, Freeman invokes thinkers and institutions of ancient Athens in order to proclaim the distinctiveness of his method-ological innovation:

> In the phrase of *Comparative Politics* I wish the word *Politics* to be taken in the sense which it bears in the name of the great work of Aristotle. By Comparative Politics I mean the comparative study of political insti-tutions, of forms of government. And, under the name of Comparative Politics, I wish to point out and bring together the many analogies which are to be seen between the political institutions of times and countries most remote from one another.[8]

Freeman believed that modern politics, specifically, the forms of polity, state, administration, and institutions peculiar to the era, required its own discipline. According to Freeman, these forms were quite distinct from earlier forms of political community and administration: the Athenian polis or tribal meeting. Only with the development of a scientific method could students of modern politics reveal continuities between past and present.

In this sense, Freeman's approach to the study of politics is decidedly modern; it is tied to ideas about republicanism, a polity made up of citizens, and the conjuncture (unlike the ancients) of nation and state. On the one hand, Freeman was convinced that the comparative method provided an unprecedented means to organize and classify existing knowledge about political life and create a gateway to new insights on the similarities and dissimilarities between political institutions and actors around the world. To highlight the distinctiveness of the 19th century comparative method, however, Freeman had to consult and reference thinkers of past eras, particularly Aristotle. As noted by Habermas, Gadamer, MacIntyre, and other scholars of methods of modern philosophical inquiry, modern thinkers beginning with Descartes proceeded to make claims for the unprecedented nature of their forms of inquiry, with the assertion that most, if not all, prior forms of knowledge and inquiry were inadequate or incomplete. But to make such claims for modern science, Descartes and those who followed him were compelled to invoke the past, either for matters of contrast or continuity. In so doing, the practices called unprecedented actually had antecedents in the thoughts and actions of those living in prior times and other places.

Given the scant mention of Freeman's contributions to the study of comparative politics, it is hard to determine without further primary research why his scholarship on comparative politics has not been more widely acknowledged and utilized by subsequent generations. One possible explanation for Freeman's absence from almost every other account of the field's development and formation, however, might be Freeman's openly racialist and racist views. Even in his early lectures, Freeman makes his ultimate aims for a scientific method quite clear. The comparative method would help demonstrate that despite differences in language, geography, nationality, and even culture, Euro-Aryan political institutions share enough "likeness to show that they are all offshoots from one common stock . . . political institutions which were common to the races which hold the highest place in the history of mankind."[9]

Within his own discipline of history, Freeman is principally represented as a scholar of the Norman conquest, ancient Sicily, and Rome; secondarily as an advocate of Euro-Aryan racialism, and rarely as a methodological pioneer and practitioner of something known as a comparative method.

Evans-Pritchard, the anthropologist considered a pioneer in the development of political anthropology (whose own contributions to political science will be explored in the subsequent chapter), cites Freeman, alongside Scottish ethnologist John Ferguson McLennan, as a pioneer in the development and application of the comparative method. Nonetheless, Evans-Pritchard concludes that Freeman's broad use of comparative methods to "prove" the common racial origins and superiority of Euro-Aryan peoples "crashed in the course of time . . . against the rocks of ethnographic fact."[10]

Pioneers in any field, particularly ones who develop new ways of thinking, are remembered most for what they inspire and model for their successors, even when their initial hypotheses and conclusions are superseded by more sophisticated, more accurate, or at minimum, more ambitious formulations. Freeman, however, would appear to be the scholarly equivalent of what was once referred to as a child born out of wedlock to adulterous parents, the product of an embarrassing union of scientific ardor and normative promiscuity, credited with neither the genesis of an idea nor its disciplinary (and ultimately) institutional legitimacy. The unpleasant facts of Freeman's corpus, a combination of public lectures, journalistic writings, historical research, and methodological innovation, however, foreground how an idea of race, and the nexus of race and polity, were central themes in the earliest conceptualization of a method for comparative politics.

This chapter has three main objectives. Utilizing primary materials culled from the archives of the Johns Hopkins libraries, the first objective is to situate E.A. Freeman's pioneering scholarship in comparative politics in the genealogy of a movement and then field of comparative politics. Second, Freeman's explication of a comparative politics method—part of a broader tendency towards cross-spatial and cross-temporal analysis in the study of literature, cultures, society, and institutions—should be understood against the backdrop of the nation-state as the principal unit of political administration, organization, and recognition in the modern world, and prevailing justifications for the European powers' dominance over much of the world's people and territory. The 19th century language of race, like the language of empire in the same period, helped provide the ideological elaboration for imperial administration as well as the belief that each race or people required their own state. The fields and disciplines of the social sciences in the 19th century were saturated with ideas and beliefs of racial and ethnic hierarchy, which in turn became part of canonical formations within these fields and disciplines in the 20th century. By now, most other fields and subfields within political science, and most social science disciplines, acknowledge, however grudgingly, spectres of race and empire in their field or discipline. Comparative politics has largely ignored race's shadow.

Freeman's Aryan/Comparative Method

Freeman's six lectures at The Royal Institution in London in 1873 are a good starting point for tracing a genealogy of a scientific method for comparative politics. Comparative politics was his second vocation; his first was history. One year before delivering the lectures on comparative politics, Freeman helped found the Department of History at Oxford College. Freeman began the lectures with the assertion that "the establishment of the Comparative Method of study has been the greatest intellectual achievement of our time."[11] Systematic study of comparative politics was the most recent discipline or field, after comparative philology, mythology, and culture, to benefit from the scientific analysis of customs, ceremonies, and survival, the circulation and transformation of culture into politics. Combining analysis of culture and civilization with philology and linguistics, Freeman sought to elevate the comparative study of politics from the realm of random, idiosyncratic observations to a mode of analysis in which its objects of inquiry (political institutions, texts, rhetoric, and language) were constant.

Freeman believed that philological methods would allow scholars to piece together common linguistic threads (and thereby racial and national) in communities across the world, and bear evidence of a commonality of origins among what he and other racial theorists of the 19th century referred to as the Aryan family of Europe, or Euro-Aryans. His indebtedness to linguistic approaches of his era is evident in his emphasis on words associated with politics that recur in several languages across disparate regions and eras. For example, words such as "mill" or "king" (*rex*) appear in several languages, not merely as identifiers of particular objects (nouns), but as concepts utilized to describe the role and function of political actors and institutions. Words—as concepts—provided the means to devise imaginary and practical correlations between institutions and people. Thus, a word such as "constitution" had a political connotation, evidenced in a text that documented the existence of a specific community of people, in addition to a nonpolitical definition that could denote personal well-being or character. Words could thus be linked to specific political practices, and therefore accommodate an opportunity to examine the relationship between language, rhetoric, and politics: "By comparing together the analogous customs of various, often most remote, ages and countries, the scientific inquirer is led up to the root: he is led up to the original idea of which particular customs, ceremonies and beliefs are but the offshoots."[12]

Central to Freeman's explication of how to undertake a systematic comparison of objects of inquiry (in this instance, race, language, and nation) is the notion of origin. Freeman credited Aryans with "some of the most important steps in the march of human culture," "taken while the Aryan nations were a single people,"[13] and further down, "principles and traditions common to the whole family, but which grew up, in the several new homes of the scattered nations, into settled political constitutions, each of which has characteristic features of its own, but all of which keep enough of likeness to show that they are all offshoots from one common stock."[14] For Freeman, racial origins provided clues to gauge the existence and sophistication of political institutions.

In his view, the development of methodological instruments to systematically examine politics in comparative perspective would help prove, through the assessment of institutions, language, written and unwritten constitutions, and norms, that people of disparate nations in Europe and the Americas constituted an Aryan race, distinguished by their political sophistication wherever they resided. Freeman can be understood—simultaneously—as both a social constructivist and an essentialist.

Ideas of race and nation, together with language, served as prepolitical factors that became building blocks for the development of political community. When combined with objectives for the dominion of territory and sovereignty, these prepolitical factors could be utilized in movements toward the consolidation of state power. At several points in his six lectures (perhaps most appropriately in lecture III, "The State") Freeman proceeds inductively to chart the purported trajectory and evolution of modern/ Western/Aryan politics from the family to the clan, from clan to tribe, tribe to nation, and nation to city-state:

> The modern conception of the State is a Nation. It is perhaps not very easy to define a Nation; still the word conveys an idea which, if not always very accurate in point of philosophy, is at least practically intelligible. Whatever else a nation may or may not be, the word suggests to us a considerable continuous part of the earth's surface inhabited by men who at once speak the same tongue and are united under the same government. Anything differing from this strikes us as exceptional.[15]

Further down he asserts that "the normal nation is one where the continuous speakers of a single tongue are united under a single government;

such a nation forms the ideal of a State, whether kingdom or commonwealth, which forms the ground of all modern political speculation."[16] A political community irreducible to family, tribe, or community is, for Freeman, what distinguishes the modern nation-state from its predecessor, ancient Athens. According to Freeman, the commonwealth as practice and concept was the Anglo-Saxon and modern version of the Athenian polis.

Problems in Freeman's Comparative Method

In one sense, Freeman's motivations for a method of comparison are resolutely unscientific. He already held the answer to a loaded question: why are Euro-Aryan peoples and their politics superior to all others? In itself, this required that Euro-Aryans as a people actually existed. Thus, his central conceptual container—the Euro-Aryan—should lead readers to a conclusion similar to Evans-Pritchard's. The abstract "normal" nation, the one from which a people evolved into a state, has been, in fact, the exception rather than the rule of nation-state formation, ignoring the majority of cases wherein linguistic boundaries, whether in the United States, Germany, France, India, China, or Ghana, have often not matched territorial boundaries demarcated by a nation-state. In these and so many other cases, the unification of nation and state ultimately involved the melding, socialization, and coercion of disparate peoples into a unified, national whole.

Freeman's use of the disciplines of linguistics is at best selective. Sanskrit, by all reputable scholarship, first appeared in spoken and written form among several populations on what is now the Indian subcontinent. It is one of the first branches of the tree of human languages and the source of several generations of languages spoken in what is now Europe; Latin, Norman, Greek, and English among them. Freeman's express disinterest in Aryans outside Europe does not actually resolve the matter of Sanskrit's origins, and by implication, Euro-Aryans. The putatively common racial and national origins which Freeman attributes to Aryans and Euro-Aryans actually occurs at an earlier time in world history and in a place other than geographical Europe. Tracing this branch of human language and its attendant modes of human organization, however, would have revealed an inconvenient truth. Aryans were more Asian than European. The Euro-Aryan is, ultimately, a fiction, or at best, descended from Asia.

A second key problem in Freeman's characterization of Euro-Aryans as preternatural state makers is the problem shared by the whole of the Teutonic and racialist schools: drawing correlations between racial-national being and the making of politics. Politics, in their view, is racial and thus, ontological. There is very little mention, either in Freeman or other Teutonic accounts, of power relations and political conflict within Euro-Aryan communities, factors such as class, status, intelligence, and ideological tendencies that would complicate the image of a homologous Euro-Aryan political community whose outlines neatly corresponded to their presumed racial profile.[17]

The common origins thesis, on its own, cannot account for the subsequent variation in political processes and outcomes among the fictitious Euro-Aryan race. Why did, for example, Germany have a distinct political history from France, Britain, and the United States? Why did the monarchy exert a powerful influence until the late 19th century in British and German politics, but not in that of France or the United States? As with many arguments of this sort, a contradiction is created by resorting to a common past to explain commonalities in the present, ignoring the long interim wherein more differences than similarities in political cultures and institutions are revealed.

From Norms to Bias and from Bias to Prejudice

Advances in ethnological, forensic, and linguistic research in the last two decades of the 19th century rendered suspect Freeman's belief in the racial origins of language and politics. Linguistic specialists such as Max Muller, who once endorsed Freeman's Euro-Aryanism, cast doubt on Freeman's assertion that language and nation were coterminous.[18] Languages, no less than peoples identified as members of the same or originating group, often have multiple linguistic and dialectical sources emanating from disparate territories and human communities. Freeman's Euro-Aryan civilization was of his own making, not to be found ready made in the world. His reliance upon linguistics and etymology to demonstrate the common origins of disparate nation-states and peoples is premised upon, as we know from Wittgenstein and Otto Bauer (along with several other key scholars of linguistics and nationalism), the dubious assumption, that language, geography, and population origin could be held constant and were fundamental ordering principles of national and state formation.[19]

In his essay "Race and Language," Freeman revised his views on the relationship between language and racial origins, acknowledging that advances in linguistic and anthropological sciences rendered any direct correlation between language and racial type, and by extension, phrenology, suspect:

"The doctrine of race is an essentially artificial doctrine, a learned doctrine. It is an inference from facts which the mass of mankind could never have found out for themselves."[20]

This shift in position, however, provided Freeman with an opportunity to emphasize the race concept as a social fact, an organizing principle in society and politics: "A belief or a feeling which has a practical effect on the conduct of great masses of men, sometimes on the conduct of whole nations, may be very false and very mischievous; but it is in every case a great and serious fact, to be looked at gravely in the face."[21] The Euro-Aryan might be a fiction, but a powerful fiction with political consequences.

Freeman's changed outlook, from viewing race as a place of origin to race as a social construct, enabled the historian to shift his focus from a concern with racial origins to an emphasis on sociopolitical implications of race-thinking. His constructivist turn is evidenced in *Impressions of the United States*, a collection of essays published in *Fortnightly Review*. Freeman's outlook ranges far and wide, comparing the polyglot United States to other societies and civilizations ancient and contemporary. In a letter from New Haven, Connecticut, in 1881, Freeman wrote that the US "would be a grand land if only every Irishman would kill a negro and be hanged for it. I find this sentiment generally approved. . . . This looks like the ancient human weakness of craving for a subject race."[22] Here, Freeman found an instance where the public opinion he encountered on his travels matched his personal sentiments. One can still wonder, however, whether this "ancient human craving" was somehow intrinsic to human beings or manufactured for political and economic expediency to enable some groups to profit from the labor and misery of others.

Freeman reveals his core concerns later in the text: the prospect that members of the servile class, in this case slaves and their descendants, could potentially participate in the polity as citizens with rights, including suffrage. Freeman asserts that the United States is experimenting with a form of polity unprecedented in the history of politics both ancient and modern:

> The United States—and in their measure, other parts of the American continent and islands—have to grapple with a problem such as no other people ever had to grapple with before. Other communities, from the beginning of political society, have been either avowedly or practically founded on distinctions of race.[23]

From Freeman's perspective, what makes the United States an exceptional nation-state is not the experiment in democracy. Athens had already set that precedent. What made the US polity exceptional was its experiment with multi-racial democracy, which provided opportunities—at least in theory— for people from inferior races to acquire state power and consequently rule over their racial superiors. Freeman's anxiety on this score is clear in the following observation from a trip to Washington, DC: "I cannot help thinking that those in either hemisphere who were most zealous for the emancipation of the negro must, in their heart of hearts, feel a secret shudder at the thought that though morally impossible it is constitutionally possible, that two years hence a black man may be chosen to sit in the seat of Washington and Garfield."[24] Multiracial democracy had dire political consequences for the racially superior when subjects with different capacities for politics and institution-building not only inhabit the same territory and society but also participate in the same polity.

Writing less than two decades after the Civil War ended, Freeman refers to a constitutional possibility that was not a practical reality for blacks, Native Americans, or white women. Formal limits to suffrage (gender, race, literacy, and property requirements) and practical sanction (coercion) were among the dire rewards awaiting those minority-within-minority groups who dared try. Freeman's bigotry, expressed as irony, nonetheless underscores the possibility of black participation in the US polity as voters and as elected officials. Freeman's implicit warnings also foreground the prospect of a democratic polity with plural subjects, a people differentiated by religion, racial identification, and ethnicity but sharing a common state. Much elite and popular opinion in Europe and Latin America in the last two decades of the 19th century suggests that Freeman was not alone in his sentiments about the difficulties of race and polity, specifically, the potential dangers of black rule. White reaction to elected black officials during Reconstruction, the Haitian Revolution, and independence movements in Latin America would suggest that fear of black domination in politics helped generate support for measures to limit and circumscribe participation of former slaves in political society—the state—of many New World nation-states.[25]

If we consider Freeman's preoccupations more abstractly, however, we can glimpse questions and concerns about the relationship between racial hierarchy, institutions, and power: Should minority groups be allowed to participate in the polity? If so, how? If not, under what criteria shall they be excluded? Most fundamentally, what makes a minority group?

Freeman's Euro-Aryan vision provides innumerable examples of the ethnocentrism, national chauvinism, racialism, anti-Semitism, and outright racism that led one reviewer writing about Freeman to declare, "No man loved or admired his friends with greater heartiness, no man ever took more unreasonable dislikes or antipathies to individuals, no man who has striven to be impartial has ever shown himself more prejudiced and biased in certain directions."[26] One can assume that Freeman's Euro-Aryan chauvinism, racism, and anti-Semitism are among the "certain directions" to which the reviewer refers. Freeman's forcefully articulated prejudices were not unique. He is, in several important respects, a garden variety late 19th century racist with views on the relationship between politics and human hierarchy. What makes Freeman unique, in my view, is his elaboration of a methodology to explore how presumed racial difference, along with other forms of presumed difference, influenced the development and maintenance of political institutions. Race was central to explaining institutional variation. Politics informed, and was informed by, racial distinction.

Freeman's preoccupations as a scholar and racialist resonated in the scholarship and politics of arguably the most influential political scientist of the early 20th century—Woodrow Wilson—the 28th president of the United States. Wilson was a student in the Seminary while completing his doctorate in history at Johns Hopkins University between 1883 and 1886. Based upon available documents in the archives, Wilson took minutes for several Seminary meetings. The Woodrow-Wilson papers at the Mudd Library in Princeton and the Seminary archives at Hopkins reveal a long-standing relationship and correspondence between Wilson, Adams, and other members of the Teutonic school. Wilson and Herbert Baxter Adams in particular maintained correspondence well into Wilson's tenure as president of the United States. These archives contain no correspondence between Wilson and E.A. Freeman.

Further research would help determine whether such correspondence exists in Freeman's papers. Chronologically there was no overlap between Wilson's and Freeman's respective stints at Hopkins. Nevertheless, examination of the materials available in the Seminary archives, Wilson's published scholarship, and posthumously published lectures and letters provides evidence that Wilson's outlook on the question of nationality, race, and state was deeply influenced by the scholarship of Freeman, Adams, Thomas Carlyle, and other adherents to the Teutonic or Euro-Aryan view.

The first piece of evidence of Wilson's views on the relationship between race and democracy can be found in an unpublished manuscript on modern democracy titled "The Modern Democratic State." The editors of his papers surmise this was an early draft and foundation for his later work, *The State*, which will be examined below. In "The Modern Democratic State," Wilson cites Carlyle, Bagehot, Spencer, and others to emphasize the role of public opinion, newspapers, and public education as key elements in the development of a democratic state, through the cultivation of a citizenry capable of self-government. At the outset, Wilson details what he describes as "several all-important conditions" for the successful operation of democratic institutions.[27] Number one on his list is the:

> homogeneity of race and community of thought and purpose among the people. There is no amalgam of democracy which can harmoniously unite races of diverse habits and instincts or unequal acquirements in thought and action. . . . A nation once come into maturity and habituated to self-government may absorb alien elements, as our own nation has done and is still doing. . . . Homogeneity is the first requisite for a nation that would be democratic.[28]

Several extended passages in "The Modern Democratic State" are on the themes of homogeneity, political education, and capacity and aptitude for government among different races or nations of people; these demonstrate Wilson's grasp of empirical cases ranging from the Norman and Saxon to the Austro-Hungarian Empire and the US South after Reconstruction. At various junctures Wilson makes clear that even though US Negroes, the brighter and more ambitious among them, have the capacity for self-government, they should never under any circumstances rule over the Saxon race, as was the case during Reconstruction.[29] In this same section Wilson does acknowledge that the United States had a history of absorbing "alien" populations into its society, mainly ethno-nationalities from central and southern Europe. Racial categorization provided Wilson and other adherents of Euro-Aryanism with a homogenizing device to render the diversity of European populations in the United States under a single, unifying chromatic rubric—whiteness.

More direct evidence of Freeman and Adams' influences upon Wilson can be found in *The State*, first published in 1889. *The State* is Wilson's best known work of scholarship, a broadly comparative, historico-institutionalist interpretation of the history of governance, with assessments and comparisons of forms and institutions of governance among the world's peoples and civilizations. Revised and reissued in 1918, at the end of World War I, the book provides a clear statement of Wilson's worldview, particularly the principles of nationality and the right to self-determination, core themes during Wilson's presidency and his prototype for the League of Nations. Like Freeman and Adams, Wilson strongly believed that Aryans were fundamentally a state-making people. Wilson's views on the value of studying the history of non-Aryan institutions seems to be closer to Adams than Freeman's Aryan-centric methodology, emphasizing the need to approach the study of history and politics inductively and comparatively without restriction:

> For purposes of widest comparison in tracing the development of government it would of course be desirable to include in a study of early society not only those Aryan and Semitic races which have played the chief parts in the history of the European world, but also every primitive tribe, whether Hottentot or Iroquois, Finn or Turk.[30]

Wilson's advocacy of a broadly comparative view of the study of institutional development signals his affinities with Adams' views as a scholar and his teacher's qualified endorsement of Freeman's Aryan-centric methodology. Further down, however, Wilson reveals assumptions of racial hierarchy that more closely resemble Freeman's—and ultimately Adams' normative vision and belief in Euro-Aryan, Teutonic supremacy in politics:

> In order to trace the lineage of the European and American governments which have constituted the order of social life for those stronger and nobler races which have made the most notable progress in civilization, it is essential to know the political history of the Greeks, the Latins, the Teutons, and the Celts principally, if not only, and the original political habits and ideas of the Aryan and Semitic races alone.[31]

As did Freeman, Wilson fuses the normative and the scholarly, conjoining a belief in the superiority of Aryan races with a call for boundless scientific rigor to examine the world's peoples and political institutions regardless of their level of sophistication, if only to further underscore Euro-Aryan superiority. To paraphrase Parker's assessment of Freeman's racialist and Euro-Aryan views against the backdrop of late 19th century nationalism, Wilson could be characterized as a racial liberal, though a rather tortured form of liberalism.

On the one hand, Wilson was a liberal nationalist and universalist who advocated the principle of nationality and the right to self-determination for certain peoples and their descendants. Wilson's enthusiasm for the nationalist aspirations of subordinated Euro-Aryan descent groups did not extend to the supposedly lesser races. Subordinated nationalities who were descendants of a once-proud Aryan and to a lesser extent, Semitic, lineage merited a nation-state. Subordinated nationalities descended from inferior races, on the other hand, did not.

As president of the United States, Wilson's racist and racialist world views found outlets in both domestic and foreign policy. Like many Teutonist and Euro-Aryan thinkers, Wilson's racism had national and transnational dimensions, within the framework of a single nation-state as well as the nation-state system as a whole. Based on the chain of associations that linked nation, state, and people in homologous order, a racial hierarchy within a single nation-state could be assessed on the basis of the actual composition of the population within the territory. Higher order races would, naturally, assume the role of leadership in such nation-states, whether as tutors or absolute masters, depending on the degree of degradation and lack of political sophistication of the lower racial orders within.

Wilson's ideas about racial hierarchies constituted and evidenced in politics found distinct expression in the League of Nations, his attempt to construct—in concert with leaders of the world's powers of the early 20th century—a comity of nations based on commonly shared norms and codes of conduct. Much early scholarship on Wilson's attempt to build an enduring transnational consultancy and organization treats him as a visionary, ahead of his time, undermined by opposition within his own Democratic political party and cabinet. More recent scholarship of the details of the League of Nations, however, reveals an organization that was largely designed to maintain Western imperial dominance in the system of nation-states and the distribution of territories, dominions, and protectorates formerly ruled by Imperial Germany and the Ottoman Empire, administered by the victorious Allied powers in the aftermath of World War I.[32]

Conclusion

Despite Freeman's absence from all accounts of the field, his role in the development of a discipline specifically for the examination of political institutions, texts and language (what contemporary political scientists would refer to as political culture) is important for four reasons. First, a more historicist approach to understanding comparative politics provides a means to reemphasize the historical and methodological linkages between comparative politics and other fields within the social sciences and humanities that emphasize comparison. Second, Freeman's contributions help bridge the gap between the forms of comparative political analysis most often attributed to thinkers such as Aristotle and Socrates for the ancients, Montesquieu and Rousseau for the moderns, and the formalization of a movement and field of comparative politics in the period following World War II. Third, Freeman's distinction between what he considered the unprecedented challenges of modern political communities and the political communities of ancient Greece and Rome more closely resemble the normative and strategic concerns of students of comparative politics in the 1950s and into the contemporary period. Specifically, Freeman's anxiety about the presence of diverse peoples in a single polity helps translate a worry of 19th and 20th century domestic and foreign policy into a research problem with its own epistemological puzzle. Fourth, Freeman's efforts as a teacher, scholar, and popularizer of the comparative study of political institutions helps us link specific ideas of race (of Freeman and his cohort) to political institutions, not only in his ultimately specious methodological claims, but in many governments and political institutions in modern Western politics. The dynamic relationship between history, ideas, and political institutions has been a major preoccupation within Western political science and sociology.

Freeman's racialist views then, should not be viewed in isolation, but as part of a wider array of racialist and racist ideologies institutionally embedded in scholarly initiatives in several academic departments of research institutions in the United States, Germany, and England. Up to now, the spectre of racial difference lurking behind the field of comparative politics has gone unnoticed, even as race and racial hierarchy as a theme in other fields of political science, and most other disciplines in the social sciences and humanities, has been acknowledged and explored to varying degrees by its practitioners.[33] His recommendations for the study of comparative politics, along with his general observations about the relationship between race and polity, provide an opportunity to trace a largely ignored theme in comparative politics. In Freeman's view of politics both modern and ancient, the idea of race was central to political life; to the formation of a polis, commonwealth, and institutions; and ultimately, to the conjuncture of nation and state. The power of race lay ultimately not in its biological provenance, but in commonly held beliefs and assumptions shared by groups of people who conjoin to form political communities.

Freeman's preoccupations can be contrasted with the subsequent generations of contemporary comparative politics studies that, for the most part, have relegated the study of racial and to a lesser extent, ethno-national, hierarchy to area and ethnic studies—in other words the periphery of comparative politics' substantive and methodological interests. In conjoining bigotry with science, Freeman's view complicates the relationship between fact and value, with an explicit valorization of Euro-Aryanism that ultimately undermines his scientific pretensions. Although subsequent generations of political scientists with interest in comparative politics are largely unfamiliar with this particular pioneer, the nexus of race and polity, so central to Freeman's conception of a discipline of comparative politics, has been a central feature of Western politics in the 20th century.

Nonetheless, his efforts to create a science of comparative politics would not pass muster amongst a jury consisting of contemporary political scientists—and for good reason. Students of comparative politics, particularly those interested in the themes addressed in this chapter, can effectively read Freeman against himself, to examine the faulty logic and leaky concepts utilized to rationalize the exclusion of certain populations from participation in a polity based on superficial differences that are perceived as irreconcilable. Unfounded assertions, such as the existence of a Euro-Aryan race, correlations between language and population (racial origins), and an inherent capacity for certain races or ethnicities to create modern political institutions undermine Freeman's emphasis on scientific rigor. The porosity and ambiguity of his concepts would render any attempt to apply his method to actual civilizations and nation-states an exercise in futility.

Ultimately, his scientific and racialist ambitions have their respective dead-ends. Yet Freeman's normative claims, particularly his most bigoted, reveal anxieties and dispositions about the prospect of what we would now call multicultural or plural societies that have been expressed by state- and nonstate-based political actors in the contemporary world.

Freeman's doubts about the ability of societies of the Americas to accommodate so many diverse people in their polities also harbor an implicit critique of the nation-state and its ability to house a diversity of political systems. Freeman's dissection of the United State and other societies with diverse populations is essentially a form of *disaggregation*, asserting, in effect, that nation-states are no more than composite forms of multiple populations. These peoples, strewn together by the dictates of empire, labor, migration, and coercion, had distinct capacities and opportunities for creating and sustaining political institutions. For the racialists, differences in the capacity of groups to produce modern politics were first evident in their presumed origins, which would foretell their actions, a form of political predestination. Times of crisis would unleash chaos if members of politically or racially inferior groups assumed institutional power, namely, the state and its governing apparatus. Freeman and his fellow travelers in the Teutonic school of nation-state building were primordialists before the primordialists. By the end of his life and career, Freeman's changed outlook could be characterized as social constructivist racist with positivist ambitions.

A lesson we learn from racial theorists such as Freeman is that the nation-state, as a conceptual container, presents its own epistemological puzzle. It may contain distinct components that are not coterminous, whether by abstract definition or in purely political terms, with the definition of the national population provided by a state, whether by constitutional procla-mation or in its national symbology. As Evans-Pritchard pointed out in his critique of Freeman's "racial origins" thesis of the nation-state, the over-whelming majority of populations categorized as national and subject to the rule of law of a single state are actually composed of peoples with distin-guishing religious, ethno-national, and presumed racial forms of identifica-tion. If a national population is not composed of one group, but several with distinguishing characteristics, there is a possibility that certain populations within a national community might have a distinct set of political motiva-tions, whether the desire is to assimilate into the larger and plural national community, to dominate other subnational populations in their midst, seces-sion, or plural competition. These four scenarios represent actual political responses to population differences within a society and polity and are not unique to Freeman's Euro-Aryan imaginary.

Though not positivist in the sense in which the term is used today, Free-man believed that comparative political science required a specific set of methodological tools and concepts. His preoccupation with racialism and racial hierarchy has no known successors in contemporary comparative politics. As I will detail in the subsequent chapter, however, the appropria-tion of the culture concept in political science and the formation of a move-ment or tendency known as political culture were premised on the assump-tion that cultural variation produced political and administrative variation. Although the culture concept would supplant the race concept in political science by the late 1950s, the presumed correlation between individual or collective identification, on the one hand, and institutional capacity and complexity, on the other, remained as a core operative assumption among students of political culture.

A small upsurge in scholarship on Freeman contains an attempt at his re-habilitation by distinguishing his arch-racist views from his innovations in the study of comparative politics. This rehabilitation is based upon the rationale of Freeman's rejection of scientific racism. Morrisroe, for example, claims that Freeman's *Comparative Politics* requires a revision of consideration of

"Freeman as an arch-racist and confident proponent of Aryan superiority" given his critique of Greek, Roman, and ultimately British imperialism as a blight on Aryan civilization.[34] Curiously, Morrisroe does not problematize the category of the Aryan which, as suggested earlier, is Freeman's first interpretive error—and a grave one. Nor does she distinguish, as Freeman himself does, the Aryan from the Euro-Aryan; the latter category of "civilization" Freeman locates in Teutonic Europe.

Even if we were to accept, as Morrisroe suggests we do, Freeman's retreat from racism based on an equation of racism with biological reasoning, there is an ample literature on racial reasoning that evidences forms of racialist thinking in politics that did not—and does not—rely on biological or phenotypical definitions, instead emphasizing civilizational, cultural, and national distinction. What makes such reasoning, even on the aforementioned grounds, "racial" reasoning is its invariable insistence that certain populations, like oil and water, cannot mix, and as a result, cannot be unified under a national state. Each race to its own territory, language, culture, and state. Isn't this the dream of the Donald Trumps, the Marine Le Pens, and the Boris Johnsons of 21st century politics?

For 21st century students of politics and political science, Freeman's normative concerns are discomforting for some, inconvenient for others, and inconsequential for the rest. His methodological innovations have long been surpassed by several generations of methodologists. Nevertheless, a question remains whether the comparative research themes he proposed warrant further exploration, not only as valuable research topics, but as a way to provide a more thorough account of comparative politics as both movement and field.

2

Race Development, Political Development

Having provided an interpretive account of E.A. Freeman's contributions to the comparative analysis of political institutions in the previous chapter, we can now link his unacknowledged efforts to the considerably more recognized pioneers in the study of comparative politics in the 1950s. While there is a considerable gap in Freeman's time period, ideological disposition, and professionalization and those of Gabriel Almond, Sydney Verba, Lucian Pye, and other members of the comparative politics movement in the 1950s, they have one aspiration in common: to develop research methods appropriate for the examination of rapidly evolving political phenomena. For all of Freeman's snide comments about great apes, murdered Negroes, and hanged Irishmen, his observations about race, society, and polity are in some sense prescient. The ongoing struggles in the United States and elsewhere for a more democratic polity and society without ethno-national, religious, or cultural restrictions remains an aspiration, not an assumption.

By the end of Freeman's life and career, his shift in thinking about the race idea and its relation to politics reflected a broader scientific shift away from race as some form of biological inheritance to an idea of race as a social fact. Yet Freeman, like all good racialists, took the race concept one step further, from its origins as a socially mobilizing principle to a principle for politics.

At the start of the 20th century, several prominent students of political science were aware of the disjuncture between the race concept's scientific limitations and its sociopolitical resonance. Like creationism, or Ptolemy's theory of the earth's relation to the galaxy, the race idea became the early 20th century example of a scientifically discredited assumption that nevertheless retained popular appeal and mobilizing power. As we have come to discover over the course of the 20th century, discredited ideas often have extended shelf life in the mall of the popular imagination, long after their death sentence in the social, physical, and natural sciences. Politics, ideology, and institutions kept the race idea alive. This recognition leads us to a more fundamental distinction between problem solving in the social and natural sciences; political and social problems recur across time and space, the existence of solutions notwithstanding.

Charles Merriam, a towering intellectual presence in the political science department at the University of Chicago in the first two decades of the 20th century, took notice of the scholarly and political ferment around race and nation. Merriam's "Recent Tendencies in Political Thought," the first chapter in *A History of Political Theories: Essays on Contemporary Developments in Political Theory*, provides an overview of "the most significant social tendencies of the time and a sweeping view of the broad types of ideas developed"[1] over the course of the late 19th century and early 20th century. Of this period, Merriam identifies "the development of industrialism and urbanism, the new contacts of diverse races or nationalities, and the rise of feminism, as the outstanding social forces."[2] Related to these forces were movements including suffragism, syndicalism, and socialism in response to capitalist industrial development and class formations, and movements for minority rights and self-determination.

Merriam highlighted the methodological innovations of the period as scholars attempted to discern specific patterns or tendencies among an ever growing number of political phenomena. Merriam considered these innovations, however, more satisfying in their capacity to pose questions rather than provide comprehensive answers. Among the methods and approaches considered was the comparative method and its potential for allowing scholars to discern a global range of patterns and fundamental truths about politics. Merriam cites James Bryce, whose *Modern Democracies* focused on the emergence and machinations of modern political institutions, as the most outstanding representative of historians and writers concerned with the genesis of political institutions and their history.[3] Freeman was not among those listed.

Merriam was skeptical, however, of the capacity of any comparative politics methodologies to generate universal theorems of politics from the vast and disparate range of political phenomena. For all their methodological innovation, Merriam concluded that the global search by methodologists "for specimens of institutions past and present, analyzed and classified material" resulted in little "success in the development of general principles of politics. In fact, many of them expressly repudiated the possibility of discovering any general principles or ideas in the realm of the political."[4] In this sense, Merriam was one of the earliest observers of the intra-disciplinary tension between students of politics who insist on generalizability and those who maintain that all political knowledge is contextual and historically specific. Here also, we observe the lacunae that advocates of "middle range theory" sought to fill in subsequent eras of the field.

Another trend identified by Merriam was developments in anthropology, ethnology, and archaeology that not only influenced political thought or political theories of the period, but how political theory or theories developed. He noted that anthropology was not an impartial realm for the examination of the "characteristics of various races of man" and "was often overlaid with race prejudice, or with national influence or propaganda of an absurdly transparent type."[5] In Merriam's view, these partial or tainted anthropological and ethnological inquiries into politics were significant for the period because they helped at least locate the motivating source or origin of political thought or political theory regarding the origins of the state, an ordering concept for political scientists.

Was the state an ideal, and as such, an abstraction, or was it the manifestation of the will of a party, class, presumed race, or ethnicity? Merriam formulated the question thus: "Should class, race or land become the basis of the state?"[6] In doing so he succinctly captured the link between an idea of race development, the development of a so-called people (which could be nationalist or internationalist), and institutional (state) development, in both the study and practice of actual politics. There is methodological import in Merriam's question about the sources and motivations for state formation. To fully comprehend the genesis of state formation, the state could not be studied in isolation from the societal forces, dynamic circumstances, and political actors that brought the state into being. To study state formation and the politics emanating from it, one had to understand the cultural and normative factors that helped motivate the state's architects and builders.

Merriam identified the ideological currents coursing through various nationalist and regional movements at the dawn of the 20th century. Emergent nationalist movements, ranging from the nonhistorical nations of the fallen

Hapsburg Empire, Pan-Slavic, Pan European, and Pan-Africanist movements, along with irredentist movements to recapture "lost" or diminished territories of some putatively ancient people, all exhibited the presumption of necessary symmetry between a state, a territory, and a people. The acquisition of state power provided a political opportunity—among other opportunities—for nationalist actors to mobilize masses on the basis of perceived racial, ethno-national, religious, or class-based affinities, and develop laws and norms that set criteria for inclusion and exclusion from the political community. Merriam referred to this process as political rationalization.

Social Science and a World of Comparisons

Fallen empires, global war, direct and indirect rule, proxy conflicts, and emergent nation-states dotted the landscape of global politics after World War II, just as those phenomena had done after World War I. Yet there were key differences between the two epochs. Many nationalist movements in Central and Eastern Europe were led by elites who were members of extant linguistic and cultural communities—nationals without states. National identification among an often diverse array of linguistic and cultural communities in Africa and parts of Asia, however, occurred only after state consolidation, when the idea of the nation could be circulated post facto. The era of nationalist mobilization after World War II was clearly tied to decolonization and the diminution of empires (French, British) and the political opportunity created for nationalists by imperial retreat. At the beginning of the 20th century, nationalism was a preoccupation of Marxists, a small cohort of scholars, and advocates of nationalism who themselves were, or were about to be, dispossessed of their homelands. By the second half of the 20th century, nationalism, especially what Lenin referred to as the smaller nationalisms of the nonimperialist type, was a significant preoccupation among governments and political actors the world over.

With the shadow of Nazi Germany, Falangist Spain, and Mussolini's Italy hovering above post–World War II politics in Europe, many social scientists not only sought to understand the causes and sources of fascism, xenophobia, and state racism, but began to question some of the anthropological assumptions of previous generations of scholarship that often provided little more than apologias for colonial domination. However backward and exotic the new nation-states appeared to many Western observers, the Third World governments bore all the formal characteristics of their Western counterparts—statehood and sovereignty, citizens and leaders—who at minimum required formal recognition in a world of nation-states and transnational institutions, the United Nations among them. In brief, the new nation-states and political actors of the developing areas, later known as the Third World, became recognized agents in global politics.

Western governmental responses to the anticolonial movements after World War II ranged from fears of a global "race war," based on the belief that the darker nations would exact their revenge upon Western nation-states,[7] grudging acceptance of a new geo-political template, suspicion of the capacity of the darker peoples of the world to preside over a modern state, and in limited instances, selective approval and encouragement. For its part, the Soviet Union, led first by Lenin and subsequently by Stalin and Khrushchev, continued its strategic relationship to "small" nationalisms in the Third World fighting against Western imperialism.

It is precisely for these reasons that the new nation-states posed interpretive challenges for the post-war generation of comparativists in the social sciences. For earlier generations of imperialists—whether of the scholarly, realpolitik, or coffee shop variety—sovereignty and statehood for the darker nations was inconceivable without Western tutelage in politics and command in the economic sphere. For Freeman and Woodrow Wilson, national independence for the Irish or Hungarians was conceivable and worthy of support, in part due to their "family resemblance" to Euro-Aryans, country cousins with a certain charm, if not the nobility of their more advanced brethren. Black and brown nationalists, however, whether in India, the Belgian Congo, Guyana, or Indochina, bore no such family resemblance, only aspirations to statehood that at best could only mimic modern politics and at worst produce, to paraphrase Martin Delany, burlesques of government.[8]

Thus, social scientists interested in actually studying the new nationalisms and postcolonial societies were faced with an epistemic crisis: how could Western social scientists name and classify political actors and institutions that did not resemble their own? Conversely, would it be possible to objectively analyze political actors and institutions with the concepts and categories of a Western social science steeped in Eurocentrism and imperialist justification? This interpretive challenge amounted to no less than being able to understand the new, fledgling polities and societies on their own terms without lapsing into a flaccid relativism, or without resorting to the language and assumptions of an Edward Augustus Freeman, Herbert Baxter Adams or Woodrow Wilson, which consigned the darker nations to long term, if not eternal, backwardness. Much like the humanists of the late 19th century who were confronted with the limitations of their own categories (whether, for example, to call the writings of an Ibo or a Native American proper literature), social scientists had to first jettison the ideological and normative baggage built into their discipline before they could actually produce new knowledge about politics in unfamiliar parts of the world.

Each discipline had their respective tool kits: the ensemble of concepts, methods, and internal debates that not only defined them in their singularity, but also in relation to other social science disciplines. Clifford Geertz, in his inimitable way, characterized the uniqueness of an era: "The main meeting ground of . . . the social sciences has been the study of the so-called Third World. . . . In this enigmatical setting, anthropology, sociology, political science, history, economics, psychology . . . have found themselves in the unfamiliar position of dealing severally with essentially the same body of data."[9]

For social scientists interested in explaining or predicting phenomena in the world, events of world historical significance not only provided this opportunity, but also the chance to demonstrate why their discipline possessed explanatory superiority compared to other disciplines. At this juncture, as in all earlier claims for a science of politics, political scientists were not only mindful of conceptual and methodological developments in other disciplines (including but not limited to the social sciences), but freely appropriated and deployed whatever they considered useful. Then, as now, the field of comparative politics was not "pure" but informed by a diverse array of concepts and literatures outside itself: anthropology, history, psychology, mathematics and economics, sociology, psychology, classics and comparative literature, and communications theory, among others.

This context enables us to trace comparative politics' evolution from a practice of largely self-taught, idiosyncratic historians to an emergent discipline with its own canon (replete with classics from other disciplines), and then to an increasingly probabilistic and positivist approach to the study of politics. The last moment or iteration of comparative politics, in contrast with earlier periods, is much more auto-referential, with far less cross-pollination with the more interpretive, historical, and qualitative fields of the social sciences. Consequently, comparative politics is further from area studies and the discipline of anthropology than it has ever been, with several negative consequences.

Area Studies: Disciplining the Social Sciences

In the era of decolonization and emergent nation-states, area studies became increasingly important as sites for interdisciplinary exchanges between scholars of divergent disciplines and from far flung parts of the world. Furthermore, the studies were a resource for nurturing and retrieving valuable sources of intelligence for the purpose of statecraft: espionage and counterterrorism, as well as confirmation of land ownership, lines of descent, and leadership claims of autochthonous actors in Asia, Africa, and Latin America. Several generations of scholars have probed the relationship between knowledge production, colonialism, and statecraft, especially in providing material support for scholarly examination of the people, languages, cultures, and social and political movements of the so-called Third World.[10]

Political scientists figured prominently in this cohort of area studies scholars. Some even collaborated with governments that deployed their knowledge in ignoble deeds. Nevertheless, area studies provided an opportunity for scholars to compare notes across disciplinary, cultural, and regional divides. It became a site for disciplinary cross-pollination and a means for scholars to better appreciate the methodological tool kits of their sibling disciplines. African societies became laboratories for some of the most prominent students of comparative politics to test the validity of their hypotheses about wide ranging topics, including political development and modernization, corruption and kinship, and politicized ethnicity. At stake for both the comparativist and the regional studies specialist (often one and the same person) was whether their more generalizable hypotheses culled from disciplinary developments and trends accurately captured the essential political dynamics in their field sites.[11]

The era provided ample opportunities to employ novel concepts, theories, and methodologies to new and unfamiliar primary materials. The novels, essays, plays, poetry, and autobiographies, as well as political thought of the post-World War II era's intellectuals in Asia, Africa, the Caribbean, and Latin America offered a window into societies experiencing rapid change. Jomo Kenyatta's account of the Mau Mau in Kenya, Frantz Fanon's granular descriptions of the daily struggles—including those of the Maghreb and their struggles with French colonialism, the 26th of July movement's overthrow of Batista in Cuba, Ho Chi Minh and Mao Tse Tung's pronouncements to mobilize their respective masses against Western imperialism—provided opportunities for many Western scholars and audiences to compare the experiences of these nationalists and internationalists alongside their counterparts in other times and places.[12] Their contributions to political thought, or what could be called thinking in politics (Merriam's political rationalization), provided additional source materials. Most of the examples in this chapter are from political science and area studies scholarship on African politics, with some disparate examples from area studies scholarship in South Asian studies.[13]

For many Western social scientists interested in understanding political phenomena seemingly at the furthest remove from West-centric understandings of formal politics (a politics of state), Africa represented the largest theater of the unfamiliar: mayors and chiefs, market women, peasants and entrepreneurs, kings and presidents, healers and Western trained doctors often operated in parallel and overlapping spheres of power and influence. Not only was it largely assumed that the convergences and juxtapositions of African politics were new and unprecedented (with tribal and ethnic politics replaying long-standing disputes since time immemorial), but that a lot of the political actors, institutions, pageantry, and conflicts to be found in the African theatre could not be found elsewhere, especially in the US or Europe.

By contrast, area and regional studies specialists often had a more nuanced and finely etched understanding of how the politics of the so-called developing areas were actually an ensemble of local, national, regional, and international actors and institutions in dynamic interaction. The presence of Western multinational corporations and industries on the African continent, coupled with the proxy conflicts of the Cold War, also meant that African politics during the era of decolonization and independence was in part the politics of European imperialism and postimperialism. African politics after World War II could not be otherwise. Labor and union organizing, political parties, and elections all bore the mark of long-standing interactions, across the political spectrum, of Western presence.[14]

African political systems were not purely indigenous but composed of colonial administrators, traders, religious institutions, and autochthonous political actors who themselves often received baccalaureate and postgraduate education in Britain, the United States, France, and other European Union countries.[15] The key point here is that the African, Asian, and Latin American political systems analyzed by students of comparative politics offered primary evidence of the continued entanglements and legacies of Western rule—direct and indirect—in addition to providing firsthand assessments of the strengths and limitations of autochthonous African political institutions and leadership.

Area studies specialists, because of their training in the history of a particular region, were often crucial to the development of local knowledge, which became official knowledge of a people, institution, or region, to be cited in discussions among internal leadership, but also in disputes with

Western powers and multinational corporations. Several area studies specialists became participant observers in the struggles for African national independence. Basil Davidson chronicled his experiences as comrade-in-arms with the likes of Samora Michel and Amilcar Cabral, but also sought to comprehend the more conceptual and epistemological implications of African politics for the study of modern nationalism, politics, and power in political communities more generally.

In several of his books, Davidson compares a wide array of institutions, political actors, symbols, and cultural forms in African politics to similar and dissimilar politics in the European context, across space and time.[16] For Davidson, chieftaincy, colonial authority, and nationalist political parties (among other sites of politics) could be analyzed in isolation, comparatively, and against the backdrop of European colonialism.

Davidson, who was neither a political scientist nor in the strict, formal sense an academic, provided a powerful rejoinder to political and social science treatments of contemporary African politics as well as African political history, especially the notion that African politics was somehow an anomaly, a wildlife reserve for exotic political creatures and habitats. In much of his scholarship on African politics in general and the continent's nation-state system in particular, Basil Davidson undertook cross-spatial comparison to demonstrate aspects of state power, administration, and symbols in Africa to their counterparts in Euro-US political culture. Read below, for example, his comparison of the Golden Stool of the Akan people in what is now known as Ghana:

> One may compare its power and meaning with the power and meaning of the English Crown: not the crown the monarch wears . . . but the Crown which no one has ever seen or ever can see: the initiating symbol of the English nation's unity and welfare, ritually acquired and ineffably empowered by convenience, coercion, and the manifold accretions of history. The Golden Stool, like the English Crown or comparable symbols, embodied a transcendental power beyond its material existence.[17]

Davidson was an interested but highly skeptical observer of the emergent literature and debates among social scientists of the period about political orders in Africa that preceded and were not derivative of colonial rule. The questions and conceptual riddles that preoccupied Davidson, one of African history's keenest observers, were distinct from those posed by anthropologists and political scientists about the existence, forms, and contours of state power in Africa. In his description of political structures in precolonial

Africa, Davidson writes, "The political sociology of Africa, in brief, has been peculiar to itself but peculiar in no other sense. Its seeming eccentricity or inexplicability has existed only in the eyes of those who have not really looked."[18] Here Davidson identifies the problem of perspective, or what in psychoanalytic terms would be called the gaze, in an understanding of political community rooted in the examples of feudal, absolutist, and ultimately republican forms of state power and authority in the West. Davidson understood the epistemological divide separating those with a deeper knowledge of African political systems and those who sought to superimpose models of state and polity derived from elsewhere—invariably modern Europe—upon African history.

And yet Davidson's act of comparison also reveals an interpretive opportunity that can be linked to Charles Merriam's questions about state formation: Who built the Golden Stool? How is it maintained? How is it projected to its constituency? How is it shielded and protected from its enemies and rivals? Considered in this way, the tasks of Akan state builders, functionaries, and representatives of state may not be as complex as that of much larger governments (in Africa and elsewhere), but no less diversified.

Davidson's comparison raises another theme that was integral to the migration of concepts from anthropology into political science; the state was not just an administrative form, effect, and monopoly of sanctioned coercion, but perhaps most fundamentally, a symbolic system. Like Geertz, who wrote of myth and ritual as the source of state power in Bali, Davidson wrote that the Akans' Golden Stool, "however mystically descended, was above all an artifact of practical statesmanship."[19]

Davidson's description of the Golden Stool as an artifact of practical statesmanship is an example of a form of local knowledge which, through comparison, can be understood more abstractly to resemble artifacts of state in Western polities. In contrast to direct rule, which required, first and foremost, pacification, indirect rule required knowledge of key actors and institutions in specific contexts—knowledge about which actors and institutions are most likely to wield power, influence, legitimacy, and authority—to convince or coerce people into doing things that they would not otherwise do, or alternatively, persuade them to commit their land, labor, and other attributes to purposes beyond their individual or communal benefit.

Rather than engage yet again in wars of pacification, British colonial policy increasingly (though not exclusively) relied on indirect rule. As noted by Hobsbawm and Ranger in *The Invention of Tradition*, indirect rule required local knowledge sufficient to enable colonial administrators, often with

British industrialists, subcontractors, and entrepreneurs in tow, to identify and distinguish leaders from led, chiefs who could be bribed and those who could not, and marginalized or deposed local political actors in search of new political opportunities to usurp local authority and legitimacy.[20] In India, the Raj was an invention of British colonialism, which came to wield its own power and influence in Indian colonial society. In Africa, chiefs and local authorities were often shrewd negotiators, using indirect rule to both accumulate local power and delimit the extent of British local authority. Yet the objective of indirect rule was the same as direct rule: limit political opposition to colonial policies to extract the most material and human resources with minimal expenditures and maximum profits for the British Empire and national economy. Indirect rule provided a layer of political intermediaries—colonial and indigenous leadership—that offered varying degrees of political autonomy and self-governance at the local level.

It is impossible to consider the ethnic chauvinisms of the new states of Africa after 1945 shorn of colonialism, whether as ongoing fact or legacy. Ethnic conflicts were often exacerbated by Western powers. The list is quite long, but an abbreviated one should suffice: the French in Indochina and Rwanda; the British in Guyana flaming tensions between East Indians and Afro-Guyanese and between colonial whites and autochthonous peoples in Kenya; the so-called ethnic tensions of Katanga Province in the Belgian Congo; and conflicts between Arabs and Pieds Noir in Algeria. These and many other examples suggest that despite Geertz's own qualification of the use of the term, "primordialism" could just as easily be defined as a political ploy to mobilize mass competition and resentment, with ethnicity, phenotype, presumed race, religion, or language as the preferred instrument of Western powers and, consequently, by political actors in Africa who were well aware of the power of ethnic claims in the new political environment of nationalism and decolonization.

Fellow Travelers: Political Science and Political Anthropology

Anthropological categories, followed closely by sociological ones, had the most significant impact upon students of comparative politics involved in the politics of the developing areas movement. As the discipline most explicitly implicated in the study of human diversity, anthropological research was frequently cited by philosophers, sociologists, and economists as the evidentiary basis for judgments about the capacities of various peoples to make love, war, states, design, economies, commerce, agriculture, and other human endeavors.

Anthropology made significant strides as a discipline by the 1950s, considering its origins as a bridesmaid of sorts to the marriage of racism and imperialism. By the early 20th century, anthropologists had largely abandoned confidence in scholarship supporting polygenesis and the race concept as valid descriptors of human evolution and variation. Anthropology's combination of the ethnological and conceptual innovation made it better equipped to provide denser portraits of forms of political community in Asia, Africa, Latin America, and the Caribbean. The reason for this was largely methodological.

Both Marxism and liberal rationalist economic calculation were largely bereft of the conceptual tools needed to decipher power dynamics at a micro level. Concepts of race, ethnicity, and culture were the most obvious, but segmented societies, primordialism, thick description, among others, also became part of the comparative politics lexicon, anthropology's progeny in political science. Part of the interpretive challenge for political science was in the acknowledgement that the political actors and institutions easily recognizable in Western politics would likely appear in different garb (literally and figuratively) in Java, Accra, Bali, and Kenya.

Students of comparative politics such as Rudolph and Rudolph recognized this limitation in political science and social science concepts more generally during their first forays into field work in India's Madras state.[21] Context and history were of primary importance in any attempt to gain understanding of how communities were organized; family arrangements and dynamics, societal roles, status, and subject positions vary greatly from one society to another, and even within one national society from one region to another. All kinds of relationships, whether between individuals, individuals and institutions, or formal and informal institutions, involved matters of authority, legitimacy, conflict, and invariably, power. In societies where precolonial, colonial, and postcolonial forms of political power existed simultaneously, at times complementing and at other times competing with one another, it made sense for political scientists to be able to identify multiple sources of political power, especially those that did not outwardly resemble the modern state. Thus, for many students of comparative politics beginning from the late 1950s until the 1980s, anthropology seemed to offer a deeper probing of the multifaceted forms of power and symbolic interaction that helped structure political communities and their rationalization for inclusion and exclusion.

In a 1963 lecture at the London School of Economics, E.E. Evans-Pritchard, considered the founder of political anthropology, said that "comparison is, of course, one of the essential procedures of all sciences and one of the elementary processes of human thought."[22] Pritchard would also cite Aristotle, along with Machiavelli, Montesquieu, and Condorcet among the most significant thinkers to draw comparisons between states, constitutions, and systems of government, and in reference to one scholar in particular, "sift the general from the particular."[23] The creation of a subfield of political anthropology within the field of social anthropology was prompted by two distinct impetuses. First was the field's recognition of the need to further conceptualize how politics distinguishes humans from all other forms of animal life. Second was that political anthropology provided a means to counter criticisms leveled by political scientists that anthropologists had a too diffuse and consequently imprecise understanding of the political sphere.[24]

Comparative politics and political anthropology shared several formal and substantive themes. Common to political anthropology and comparative politics was a belief in the diversity of political life across the world. Though political anthropology preceded comparative politics as a formally recognized subfield within anthropology, both movements were initiated by scholars who perceived the need for additional conceptual vocabulary and methods to explain phenomena and circumstances that were seemingly unprecedented. Where political anthropologists diverged from students of comparative politics was in the latter's belief in the ability to isolate a specific sphere of politics in non-Western polities, in the same way that students of politics in Europe or North America could identify a parliament, congress, or legislature, and officers like a prime minister, cabinet member, or president. If there was a division between anthropologists and political scientists about the study of political phenomena, it was in the recognition by anthropologists that political phenomena could often be found in dynamics and arenas of daily life not nominally identified as political, namely, in arenas not immediately associated with state power. Well into the 1960s, Western political science was almost exclusively focused on elections and campaigns; individual, ethnic, regional, and class-based voters; political candidates; and elected officials.

Political anthropology became the subfield within anthropology most concerned with demarcations of the political. Political scientists and anthropologists alike criticized structural functionalists for what was then considered a static view of political and cultural processes.[25] The functionalist Radcliffe-Brown, in his preface to the edited volume by Fortes and

Evans-Pritchard titled *African Political Systems* (a classic in the field of social anthropology), cautioned, "If we are to study political institutions in abstraction from other features of social systems we need to make sure that our definition of 'political' is such as to mark off a class of phenomena which can profitably be made the subject of separate theoretical treatment."[26] Radcliffe-Brown's statement is at once an effort to clarify for the reader the raison d'être for the subfield of political anthropology, but also a subtle reminder that political phenomena and political institutions are not one and the same.

As Balandier writes in his 1970 book *Political Anthropology*, political anthropology was a rather belated specialization in anthropology, partially in response to criticisms leveled at anthropologists by political scientists that anthropological research had a rather diffuse view of politics.[27] As a consequence, anthropological research on politics was often insufficiently defined. If politics and the political were everywhere, how would researchers distinguish politics of societal consequence and politics that reflected domestic or interpersonal squabbles? By focusing on state- and nonstate-based forms, Balandier asserts that political anthropology helped refine the "definition and a clearer knowledge of the political field," providing evidence, through ethnography, that *all* human societies produce politics and that they are *all* subject to the vicissitudes of history."[28] For both the political anthropologist and the political scientist, variation in human governance gave evidence of cultural distinction—difference. All human societies produce politics, but not all human societies produce politics in the same way. The challenge for specialists of comparative politics in both disciplines went beyond identifying a field or space of politics and the political in disparate societies. A no less important challenge was to identify what factors or variables contributed to distinctions in forms of politics and political institutions.

Structural-functionalism provided an opportunity for the student of comparative politics to deploy interpretive tools that identified political phenomena without any first order correspondence to Western political institutions. Thus, a chief, shaman, or an elder could be the political equivalent of a head of state (or perhaps an alderman) without electoral bona fides, embracing the possibility that a political phenomenon could be identified by its fundamental purpose and objective, not its institutional façade.

Unlike many political scientists of the era, Balandier and other practitioners within the new subfield of political anthropology believed that attention to centralized governmental administration provided only a partial view of governance in Third World societies. *African Political Systems*, published on the eve of nationalist and protonationalist mobilization on the

African continent, implicitly argued for the importance of anthropological knowledge in understanding the new nation-states once administered and ultimately ruled by the British: "The policy of Indirect Rule is now generally accepted in British Africa. We would suggest that it can only prove advantageous in the long run if the principles of African political systems . . . are understood."[29] The "general acceptance" of indirect rule in British Africa came after long periods of pacification and negotiation, protracted wars involving colonial armies and administrators, and indigenous resistance. In a changed global political climate where most regions and nation-states of the world were involved in World War II, strategies of rule that involved high doses of coercion would not have garnered much public support, nor enabled the Allied powers of World War II to claim moral supremacy over either the Soviets or the vanquished racial state of Nazi Germany.

Evans-Pritchard's "The Comparative Method in Social Anthropology" addressed several key debates in his discipline that were—and are—resonant in political science concerning the value of cross-spatial comparison and large N research.[30] For anthropology, he concluded that more statistical forms of a comparative method, with their objective of developing generalizable principles about vastly divergent societies and cultures, cannot "exercise the required control over ethnographical sources for so many and heterogeneous cultures and societies, and this has become . . . more difficult as ethnographical material has increased and is increasing."[31] His skepticism about the widening of hypotheses to encompass and explain a larger number of societies, cultures, and phenomena hinged upon his belief that "apart from the question of what restricted validity such hypotheses may have shown to have, the wider their range, the more universal they aim at being the more tenuous their abstractions become."[32] For Evans-Pritchard, ethnography provided greater depth and validation for testing theories and concepts. The value added from good ethnography exceeded the virtues of large N comparison.

The Politics of the Developing Nations

As with most scholarly and even artistic movements, the development of new "schools" of thought or technique is rooted in an emphasis on some previously neglected or unknown object, practice, or method. The source of neglect is invariably attributed to (a) an underestimation of a subject or technique's intrinsic value or worth, (b) a parochial bias, or (c) incompetence. In the case of comparative politics, the proliferation of nation-states and critical realignment of global geopolitics after World War II provided an opportunity for a "movement" in the field of comparative politics largely based upon justifications of a and b. Seeking to deploy new concepts and methodologies first developed in other disciplines—particularly psychology and anthropology—the politics of developing areas signaled the development of new research methods and concepts for the new nation-states of Asia, Africa, Latin America, and the Caribbean.

The unveiling of the "Politics of the Developing Areas" movement bears two hallmarks of modern social and political thought. Participants in the comparative politics movement largely believed they were engaged in an unprecedented endeavor: the development of research methods, theory, and concepts that would enable students of comparative politics to shed the prejudices and biases that plagued earlier examinations of non-Western political institutions. And in the most recent past—World War II—biases resulted in the fomenting of conflicts that produced "race wars" in various forms: genocide, mass expulsion, and internment. The "new" student of comparative politics sought to analyze the polities, economies, and societies of the new nation-states rather than assume that these new nation-states would be, at best, poor imitations of statecraft. That the very vocabulary of the movement—terms like "developed" and "developing," "modern" and "modernizing"—grew out of a desire to supplant value-laden terms like "backward," "premodern," and "primitive" (deployed by Marxists, liberals, and conservative observers alike) provides an indication of the degree to which participants sought to discard older ways of thinking about political institutions and phenomena, especially those in the former colonies.

It is important to underscore, in light of the sustained critique of "The Politics of the Developing Areas" project organized by Gabriel Almond and the Committee on Comparative Politics convened by the SSRC in 1955, how Almond understood his political and intellectual objectives: de-Westernize the study of political institutions and government in comparative perspective and develop methods of comparison that freely utilized techniques, concepts, and theorem from other social science disciplines, particularly sociology and anthropology, for the study of political institutions. Almond represents his task as follows:

> It wasn't clear from the outset what the scope of the Committee on Comparative Politics was going to be. Should it include the Third World? . . . At that time, comparative government substantially was European government. It seemed to make sense to have a Committee on Comparative

Politics that would deal with more than the Western and the developed areas. But how to do that? How to relate to the prejudices existing in the profession, and at the same time, set up a committee that could take some initiatives.[33]

Though Almond does not elaborate on the "prejudices existing in the profession," from this interview it is plausible to suggest that "the more senior and conservative faculty in the profession" had articulated sufficient condescension—if not antipathy—towards non-Western modes of governance and perhaps non-Western peoples, which led him to conclude that more conservative and senior faculty in the profession could not constitute the core of his new initiative. Further down, in his discussion specifically of the politics of the developing areas, Almond concluded:

> It's easy to exaggerate the naiveté of the people who were doing that work. We knew that it was going to be a very first approximation, but it was better than nothing. It was looked upon as a demonstration . . . you might say it was an effort to push the field ahead theoretically by showing what it's possible to do.[34]

Students of the newly established field of comparative politics believed that structural functionalism, the school of anthropology, and the methodological tools developed by Evans-Pritchard would enable political scientists to isolate modes of deliberation and adjudication, institutions, and law (written or unwritten) from the rituals and forms in which actors and institutions of politics were embedded. The political, in other words, could be isolated and distinguished in their cultural context from other behavioral and institutional forms. Freedom of speech and assembly and individualism were activities and institutions that if cultivated would propel the new nations in the era of decolonization toward the template of Western politics and away from politics premised upon ethno-national identification and kinship, on the one hand, and colonial modes of authority on the other.

Culture, the learned patterns of behavior, seemingly supplanted racial and regional determinism in the assessment of non-Western political and economic advancement. Here, the student of comparative politics interested in the role of culture in non-Western political development borrowed from the political anthropologist a more relativist, circumspect understanding of cultural differentiation. Almond declared that the new student of comparative politics would "have to break through the barriers of culture and language and show that what may seem strange at first sight is strange by virtue of its costume or its name, but not by virtue of its function."[35] Science provided the means to transcend the parochialisms of the analyst when faced with the unfamiliar. Functionalism, in Almond's view, was an antidote to the parochialism of norms and judgments about the diverse forms and appearances of political practices, actors, and institutions.

For Almond, all political systems, regardless of their location and ideological orientation, shared four characteristics: structure, functionality, multifunctionality of political structures, and a mix of various forms.[36] The more Hegelian distinction between societies founded in formal states and those without them was jettisoned: "The classic distinction between primitive societies which are states and those which are not should be reformulated as a distinction between those in which the political structure is quite differentiated and clearly visible and those in which it is less visible and intermittent. We are dealing with a continuum and not a dichotomous distinction."[37] Form and function could be separated from content and symbolism. By the end of the introduction, Almond employed Enlightenment-laced rhetoric ("a stronger and steadier illumination"[38]) to make the following claim: "Casting our problems in terms of formal theory will direct us to the kind and degree of precision which are possible in the discipline, and will enable us to take our place in the order of the sciences with the dignity which is reserved only for those who follow a calling without limit and condition."[39]

For all of the deployment of new research methods (not only quantitative but ethnographic) on research sites, however, the new regime of comparative politics treated the configuration of nation-states—both new and old—as the most appropriate template for examining the politics of the developing areas, even as power struggles between autochthonous and nation-state leadership, between once powerful local actors, national governments, multinational corporations, and nongovernmental organizations, persisted.

The concepts of political culture and civic culture in both the American and comparative politics subfields implicitly and explicitly generated their own biases and assumptions about development and modernization that contained more than traces of the racialist and racist assumptions of a previous era. Although the culture concept supplanted the race concept, culture often appeared in static form in comparative analyses of developing and nondeveloping nations.

The term "race" was largely jettisoned for both symbolic and substantive reasons, although as the anthropologist George Stocking writes in *Race, Culture and Evolution*, the culture concept "provided a functionally equivalent substitute for the older idea of 'race temperament.'"[40] "It explained all the same phenomena, but it did so in strictly nonbiological terms and indeed its full efficacy as an explanatory concept depended on the rejection of the inheritance of acquired characteristics."[41] Human variation, evidenced in politics, could be attributed to spatial and cultural rather than racial terms. Culture, however, could serve as a form of imprisonment much in the way that the race concept did, relegating entire populations to a set of behaviors and institutional practices that would consign them to eternal mediocrity—or worse. As with Woodrow Wilson in an earlier era, the scholarly efforts to understand different political cultures on their own terms did not conflict with the belief that Western politics was *the* modular form of politics the rest of the world should aspire to.

Modern politics was attainable by people throughout the world, not just so-called Euro-Aryans and their descendants. A rationalist political culture, not genes nor heritage, was the key to political modernity. Explicit racialism and racism in political analysis was not only discouraged but considered unscientific. Yet the very concept of modernity operative in the "Politics of the Developing Areas" scholarships projected implicit and explicit assumptions about Western political institutions as ideal types, which obscured or ignored how many non-Western political actors (or even political actors within Western polities) actually encountered Western modes of governance in highly unequal, often authoritarian forms, impediments rather than benefactors of democratic politics.

Thus, the race concept's obsolescence did not render ethnocentrism obsolete. Almond understood, for example, the ethnocentric hubris of earlier generations of Western scholars who not only believed that non-Western nation-states should follow the lead of the West, but that the inevitable march of science and progress were valid assumptions. Almond wrote, "No transgression has greater capacity to strike fear in the hearts of contemporary social scientists. The nineteenth and early twentieth century notion of progress and the view that progress was embodied in western civilization and particularly in its Anglo-American variant remains in our memories as the great moral error of western political theory . . . our moral error was compounded by scientific error."[42] Another way of framing Almond's insight is that faulty normative assumptions begat faulty science. Their conceptual containers privileged some concepts and minimized others. For example, Western-influenced coups, a source of political instability, received less attention than ethnicity, authoritarianism, corruption, and kinship in African, Latin American, or Asian politics.

While the politics of the developing areas project helped challenge assumptions and prejudices about political institutions and actors of the Global South, the project also helped reinforce assumptions about the West's positive role in African, Asian, and Latin American political development. As several commentators responding to the "politics of the developing areas" scholarship of the 1960s and 1970s pointed out, the underlying teleological assumptions of much of the scholarship privileged Western modalities of politics, notwithstanding the efforts to understand politics outside of the West on its own terms: "The political scientist who wishes to study political modernization in the non-Western areas will have to master the model of the modern, which in turn can only be derived from the most careful empirical and formal analysis of the functions of the modern Western polities."[43]

Further research into Gabriel Almond's and the SSRC's archives could provide an answer to whether the resemblance between Almond's and Freeman's declarations is merely coincidental, their affinity driven by the passion for the certitude of science over the vagaries of prejudice. Consider, however, Almond's call to science and enlightenment noted above, alongside E.A. Freeman's just below:

We must cast away all distinctions of 'ancient' and 'modern', of 'dead' and 'living', and must boldly grapple with the great fact of the unity of history. As man is the same in all ages, the history of man is one in all ages.[44]

The scientific student of language, the student of primitive culture, will refuse any limits to their pursuits which cut them off from any portion of the earth's surface, from any moment of man's history since he first walked upon it.[45]

Like Freeman, Almond believed that comparative politics would provide limitless possibilities for methodological innovation. Despite the clear variance at the point of racialism, however, Freeman, Almond, and cohort movement members believed it was possible for students of comparative politics to transcend their nationality, religion, and origin to produce a value-free approach to the study of comparative politics. Yet to create such a science of comparative method, these students would ultimately have to transcend themselves: the cluster of norms, categories, concepts, inclinations, and proclivities that helped constitute their worldview. Like the discipline of anthropology, comparative politics' object of analysis was the non-Western world, which served to reinforce the belief that political life in the non-Western world was distinct enough from First World politics to make comparisons valid by way of contrast. By ignoring the entanglements between politics in the developed and developing worlds, they neglected to consider the possibility that their studies of non-Western politics were in part an examination of Western politics, and that for comparativists of Europe, the legacy of Western colonialism and imperialism could be evidenced not only in Africa, Asia, or Latin America and the Caribbean, but in the domestic politics of those very same Western nation-states known as modern and developed.

The template of nation-states and regions upon which the politics of the developing areas was mapped corresponded largely to the reconfigured world map of the nation-state system. This template, however, as I will explore below, was an often insufficient accounting of the world of nation-states that was at once overlaid and undergirded by multiple, sometimes conflicting allegiances and solidarities: class, the Cold War, nonalignment, and ethnic groups that straddled nation state borders. Any representation of the nation-state system that relied exclusively on formal territorial boundaries, declarations of sovereignty, and territorial contiguity was at best one-dimensional and, ultimately, misleading.

Ample literature examines the limitations of modernization theory as an accurate explanation of the incorporation and evolution of new nation-states within the nation-state system. I am more interested, however, in underscoring how dominant Western nation-states delimited and often frustrated attempts by former colonies to develop fully democratic and participatory political institutions, by encouraging, and in several instances supporting, racial and ethno-national conflict. These policies, as I will elaborate below, were often the extension of policies within these nation-states to manage internal, state sponsored divisions within polity and society.

Like comparative studies in anthropology and literature, Western students of comparative politics in the mid-1950s and 1960s tended to assume that the study of comparative politics involved the examination of politics of non-Western societies. The politics of developing nations could be identified not only by their formal distinctions but by their geographical location, discrete and separate from the politics of developed nations. Comparative politics thus emphasized spatial distinction, with the nation-state as the unit of analysis. Spatial distinctions could then be correlated with distinctions in ethnicity, religion, and nationality; in a word, culture. Cultural distinction informed distinctions in political culture and institutions. Freeman's nexus of race and polity was replaced by the nexus of culture and polity. As with political anthropology, the subfield of comparative politics was the realm in which cultural difference—the other—and its relation to politics could be examined. Within comparative politics, methods and concepts from anthropology would eventually give way to methods incorporated from psychology, sociology, and economics. But Freeman's basic assumptions and chain of inferences would reappear in the subsequent generation of comparative politics scholarship. Spatial distinction could be correlated with cultural, and ultimately, distinctions between forms and qualities of politics, political actors, and institutions.

Conclusion: The Ethnos and Ethos of Democracy

This chapter links a formal disciplinary narrative of the field of comparative politics to the broader currents and crosscurrents of innovation in comparative politics methodologies both prior to and during the 1950s. In this sense, we can revisit the question of cumulative knowledge that has been posed by several key practitioners within the field.[46] The development of comparative politics as a distinct field opened up new institutional possibilities within the discipline to conduct social science research and to secure funding from governmental and nongovernmental institutions to study political actors and institutions cross-spatially and cross-temporally.

The mid–20th century students of comparative politics believed a more positivist approach to the study of comparative politics would rid their field of its idiosyncrasies, prejudices, and bigotry, in short, moving from value-laden to value-neutral. Henceforth, a science of comparative politics could be further differentiated from the more idiosyncratic students of comparative politics in the late 19th century and early 20th century. In Freeman's pseudo-scientific methodology, value masqueraded as fact. While the positivists within the comparative politics movement avoided the outright racist and xenophobic attitudes of earlier eras of scholarship, a collective bias toward Europe, Western, and Anglo-American forms of political community not only remained, but was encouraged as the ideal against which the rest of the world would be analyzed and even judged.

The prospect of cultural bias, was not new, but still rooted in the conceptual presuppositions of an earlier period. The conceptual containers brought into the field by the postwar generation of political scientists largely compartmentalized the instances of statecraft and economic policy (usually described as "foreign" policy or "international relations") that negatively impacted the politics of the developing areas and in many cases, the human and material resources of the new nation-states as well. Conceptual containers such as "democracy" or "development" expressed as operative categories were more often than not ideal types that hardly resembled the forms of democracy and development experienced by the bulk of Western populations in countries such as the United States, France, and Britain during the 1960s and 1970s.

The politics of the developing areas project contained prominent strands of Cold War neocolonial reasoning. Often implicitly, but at times explicitly, many scholars associated with the comparative politics movement expressed the hope that ultimately the new nation-states of Africa, Asia, Latin America, and the Caribbean would resemble the nation-states of the so-called modern West: rational, orderly, shorn of particularist (tribal and primordial) leanings. Participants in the politics of the developing areas undertook an unenviable and ultimately paradoxical intellectual task—to create research methods and critical perspectives that were less Eurocentric while relying heavily upon an intellectual tradition that valorized the political heritage and legacies of Europe and the United States. Viewing the issue in this manner, we are reminded of Marx's dictum:

> No social order ever disappears before all the productive forces for which there is room in it have been developed; and new, higher relations of production never appear before the material conditions of their existence have matured in the womb of the old society.[47]

The task undertaken by Almond and the other members of his cohort to advance the scientific study of politics across time and space were not unlike the challenges faced by his predecessors—Freeman, Wilson, and Merriam (who was a teacher of Almond's at the University of Chicago) among them. Each sought to expand the methodological horizons in the study of politics and believed in some form of scientific inquiry as the means to do so. On a continuum, Almond is closer to Freeman, certainly *not* in terms of racist beliefs, but in the belief that political science could eventually achieve the analytic precision and parsimonious symmetry of the hard sciences. An increase in scientific rigor would be inversely related to the diminution of local knowledge, area studies, languages, and cultural sensitivity. For Almond, the increasing breadth and accuracy of probabilistic theory would imply "the obsolescence of the present-day divisions of the study of politics into American, European, Asiatic, Middle Eastern, African, and Latin American 'area studies.' "[48]

One of the remaining tasks for contemporary students of comparative politics is to undertake an initiative similar to a development in social and cultural anthropology in the 1990s: *de-othering* comparative politics by analyzing Western and non-Western polities alongside one another, as well as undertaking intraspatial comparison of polities in the Global North. Like political anthropology, comparative politics will be better able to identify the political (along with economic and cultural) entanglements of polities across regional and geopolitical divides. Many laws and policies first devised by imperial nation-states to administer colonial populations in foreign lands were transformed into domestic policies designed to administer to racially subordinated populations at home, in the metropole.

The dynamic relationship and interaction between Western and non-Western polities has mirrored the economic entanglements of "developed" and "developing" countries much in the way that profits from colonialism and racial slavery bolstered individual, industrial, and national wealth. The developing world could not be examined in isolation any more than countries of the developed world. Through the examination of the politics of actual nation-states, rather than ideal types, a more complicated internal portrait emerges. As will be demonstrated in the subsequent chapter, the multiple sources of political power, and distinct, often conflicting modalities of political rule in Western politics can be evidenced in their histories of management of minoritized and racialized populations.

Less examined aspects of the dynamic relationship between the governments of the United States, France, and Britain, on the one hand, and their colonies and governed settlements on the other are the cross-flows of bureaucratic information, administrative experience, and techniques deployed to assist in the management of minoritized populations. Nation-states and colonies alike contained internally and externally differentiated populations (race, ethnicity, nationality, gender, and religion) that required state administration and management. Both colony and nation-state harbored populations who were either forcibly imported (slaves) or conscripted (indigenous labor) to provide poorly paid or unpaid labor. These populations posed difficulties for administration when they sought to exercise freedoms from the dictates of exploitive racial and labor regimes.

The *realpolitik* of the West's entanglements with new nation-states bore little resemblance to the ideal types implicitly and explicitly referred to as the basis for comparison with non-Western political actors and forms. Racial and ethno-national regimes, to be explored in the subsequent chapter, were no anomaly of a rogue Nazi state but a common practice of Western polities, which included, of course, the Allied Powers. The exemplars of liberal democracy and republicanism, the United States, Britain, and France, harbored their respective ethnos of democracy within their ethos of democracy.

Considered more broadly, the racial and ethno-national regimes inherent not only in colonialism, but in the politics of the metropole, were not anomalous to political modernity and modern nation-states, but one of political modernity's constitutive institutional components. Although new technologies of warfare, communication, resource extraction, and administration in the 19th and 20th centuries transformed how colonialism and imperialism were conducted, the imperatives and objectives of 20th century imperial powers bore a striking resemblance to the objectives and imperatives of older, earlier empires, whether city-states or nation-states: to extract human and material resources from one part of the world at the expense of peoples in other parts of the world. This, too, was part of the story of Western political modernity, though not necessarily part of the story that the pioneers of a new comparative politics, in mid–20th century, wanted to tell.

3

Society and Polity, Difference and Inequality

In this chapter we return to a central claim of Edward Augustus Freeman noted in chapter 1, namely that "the United States—and in their measure, other parts of the American continent and islands—have to grapple with a problem such as no other people ever had to grapple with before. Other communities, from the beginning of political society, have been either avowedly or practically founded on distinctions of race."[1] This chapter will assess the veracity of Freeman's assertion from two distinct yet interrelated vantage points. First, Freeman's claim that race has been a central criterion for membership in a political community leads us back to classical Athens, where ideas of democracy first took shape and where its norms and institutions were first performed. As noted in the introduction, Athens figures prominently in the origin stories of political science, and comparative politics in particular, as the birthplace of both democracy and the study of distinct political cultures, regimes, and institutions. The aim here, also noted in the introduction, is to distinguish between the idea of democracy and democracy as a specific set of political practices. Second, the United States, from Freeman's perspective, is an exceptional political society not because of its experiment with democracy, but because of the creation of a type of democracy which allowed, in principle at least, members of presumably distinct racial groups to be members of the same political community, to represent, and be represented by, the same government.

Freeman's claim is difficult to prove or disprove, in large part because race is, to paraphrase Stuart Hall, the great floating signifier, invariably infused with religious, national, material, ethnic, gendered, and other associations, forcing a recognition that the scholarly examination of racial matters, particularly in relation to matters of political community, requires the examination of a range of concepts and phenomena outside the boundaries of the race concept itself.

With this prologue, we can approach Freeman's question from yet another angle, however, and make it relevant for cross-temporal comparison. Was political society in classical Athens based upon presumptions of racial homogeneity? Have all other political societies since classical Athens been premised avowedly or practically, on racial criteria? The findings offered in this chapter suggest that answers to these questions are not straightforward. The multiple meanings and applications of the race concept over time (nation, ethnicity, people residing or originating from a specific territory) would frustrate any attempt to draw a continuous line from classical Athens after the Persian Wars to the contemporary nation-state system based upon a transhistorical (ahistorical) definition of racial difference. My explication is on safer ground with the following claim: ideas of human difference and variation, whether based on presumed racial, ethno-national, religious, or gendered distinction, have been correlated with access to political rights by governments in eras of city-states and nation-states.

By comparing and contrasting the political institutionalization of difference in classical Athens, the Americas, and several key democratic polities in the West, we can come to a closer approximation of the role of difference in the relationship between democracy and political inequality. Chapters 4 and 5 will examine France, Britain, and the United States, through a combination of primary materials and secondary literature, to demonstrate how the majority of democratic polities in the Americas and Europe have elaborated differentiating citizenship regimes designed to exclude certain categories of people from formal membership in a political community while incorporating others. Common to all of the polities under consideration is the idea of irreducible, irreconcilable differences among populations, differences that require selective access to citizenship and political rights.

The political institutionalization of presumed human difference has not occurred in a vacuum. Several exogenous and endogenous factors predominate in the development of delimiting and exclusionary citizenship regimes: war and mass migration, demographic shifts in a society, and the presence of populations deemed politically unreliable or unworthy can be found in a number of polities with histories of population diversity.

Racial and ethno-national hierarchies, once deployed in politics, have served as instruments of political inequality and exclusion in the majority of democratic polities. The focus of this chapter is not whether race exists per se in any or all of the polities under examination. Instead, this chapter will consider what relevance do the interactions between difference, slavery, and democracy in classical Athens have for how we understand the practice of democracy in the contemporary world. Recognition of the entanglements of democracy and inequality in classical Athens helps provide a fuller account of Athens as the prototype not just for democracy, but for the undergirding of democracy with highly unequal labor regimes and political inequality in contemporary societies and polities.

Classical Athens: Democracy, Inequality, and Disciplining Political Science

Specialists within various disciplines and fields ranging from classics, political theory, philosophy, ancient history, and rhetoric have largely concerned themselves with the Athenian polis and the democracy it spawned. We know democracy, however, was not a self-sustaining enterprise. The enslaved, through coerced labor, provided the material sustenance for citizens to participate in political deliberation. Although Athenian women and metics (Aristotle was among the latter category) could participate in certain public rituals, they did not, unlike their Athenian male contemporaries, have voting privileges. The delimiting of citizenship status and rights to certain groups of people does not negate the uniqueness of the Athenian democratic experiment, particularly when considered against other forms of political life that did not—and do not—allow public deliberation at all. It does, however, complicate our reception of democracy's relation to political and economic equality; democracy, then and now, did not render everyone within a society equal, or even citizens.

Contemporary specialists of classical Athens have probed more deeply than previous generations the relationship between the Greek polis, its citizens, and the broader array of people and institutions of the ancient city-state. One of the great advantages of recent scholarship is its provision of a more nuanced portrait of how democracy and citizenship in the Greek polis were influenced by the realities of immigration, labor needs, empire, and of course, slave labor. The portrait of the polis that emerges from recent scholarship is situated in a more dynamic material, social, and legal-juridical context.

We gain a better understanding of the antinomies of Athenian democracy by exploring the relation between a regime premised on political equality and the range of unequal economic and social practices considered critical to democracy's maintenance. The seemingly straightforward genealogy that reduces democracy to its formal and performative elements ignores how coercion, empire, and forced labor have been deeply intertwined in democratic experiments in the Greek city-states and in contemporary societies. Further examination is required, then, for the ideals and proclamations about democracy, citizenship, and the polis, but also a look at the exclusions that made the practice of democracy possible.

Specialists of Athenian democracy identify the period between the 5th and 4th century BCE as the era of classical Athens, a pivotal period in the development of Athenian democracy after intermittent periods of rule by noble families, tyrants, and oligarchs. The creation of a constitution, citizen-based courts, and juries and the valuation of citizenship independently of wealth and conversely, poverty, mark the era of Solon's 6th-century rule, which nurtured the preconditions for a more radical democratic period to follow. There is a substantial literature on this period and its complexities, which readers can explore in the references.

One of the complexities of the institution of slavery during the classical era is the distinction between public and private slaves: public slaves, or *demosioi*, owned by the demos; *douloi*, owned by individual citizens; and *demiourgoi*, public servants. Those in the third category were often publicly acknowledged specialists of a particular craft, and often itinerant, meaning that they traveled frequently to perform their specialized duties.[2] Although public slaves were not citizens, it was not uncommon during the classical period to encounter slaves with very specialized roles in the politics, society, and economy. For example, records show public slaves serving as currency authenticators, scribes involved in translation, as well as bodyguards. Several scholars of slavery during the period of Athenian democracy suggest that such slaves represented the first public servants of state—without actually being invested with citizenship and, more precisely, being a member of the servile class of people living and working in Athens. Ismard suggests that part of the reason public slaves became entrusted with the responsibilities of the administration of critical functions of civil and social life was to separate such functions from actual politics, namely deliberation, law creation, and adjudication. Such a distinction between the role and function of a public servant (which ultimately meant servant to the citizenry) and a citizen engaged in matters of actual rule lessened the prospect that citizens with specialized administrative knowledge could have political advantages not available to citizens who were less knowledgeable in the ways and means of civic life. This distinction, however, also bore the assumption that Athenian citizens were knowledgeable enough to distinguish between administration and deliberation of civic life and therefore less likely to be manipulated and misled by citizens with more specialized knowledge of Athenian administration and institutions of state power.

Such distinctions in the type and status of the enslaved in classical Athens requires caution in drawing comparisons between the enslaved in classical Athens and the institutions of New World slavery after European conquest, colonization, and settlement in the 17th century. Some of the enslaved in classical Athens contributed to the practice of democracy, even though they were not citizens. It could be stated that these types of slaves were the embodiment of the different meaning and deployment of the term *demos* in Athenian life between the 6th and 4th centuries. Public slaves in particular were part of the demos, insofar as demos was understood to mean the population of Athens and not understood as the citizenry, or an administrative unit.[3]

In Athenian democracy as well as in French, British, and US democracies, the premise of slavery was not considered antithetical to the practice of democracy. The existence of an enslaved population to attend to the material needs of citizens (and in most instances, generate profit) was deemed central to democracy's functioning. The more central question was not the institution of slavery and the practice of enslavement, but who was deemed suitable or unsuitable for enslavement and labor through coercion in a society with a democratic polity. Distinctions between a people and a population, society, and polity are important markers for distinguishing between members of a political community, nonmembers (those excluded from any form of political participation), and those who contribute to the functioning of political society without formal membership in political society, namely, the state. During the classical period, Athenian laws were revised to limit the prospect of impoverished Athenian citizens becoming enslaved, losing portions of their lands, harvests, or worse, their citizenship status to wealthy creditors. Thus, threats to the status of citizens could be generated from within Athens (through debt or some violation of Athenian law) or externally induced (the prospect of invasion and conquest).

As classical scholars have noted, the concept of freedom only became an important sociopolitical affirmation of political rights and sovereignty after the Greco-Persian Wars of the 5th century BCE. Prior to these wars, the concept and practice of freedom was largely associated with its then opposite, tyranny. Tyranny and oligarchy, concepts describing phenomena in which individuals amass significant power and wealth, threatened to undermine the practice of democracy. Kurt Raaflaub concludes that the concept of freedom was imbued with political implications when it grew increasingly evident that freedom as a social fact, a form of negative liberty (I am not a slave), had political implications.[4] The prospect of Athenian subjugation and rule by a foreign power, the denial of Athenian "rights" to self-determination as a polis of self-possessed individuals, led to an unprecedented emphasis on freedom as a political concept tied to the practice of democracy.

In his conceptual history of freedom in ancient Greece, Raaflaub stresses how the concept of freedom did not exist in isolation, but evolved in relation to other concepts and exigencies of the period. He poses a series of questions relevant to his investigation that are also relevant for this chapter; how the concept and practice of freedom—and by extension, liberty and democracy—is informed by other concepts and practices:

> When trying to determine the possible significance of freedom within a given societal framework, we thus need to take various aspects into account. What kind of freedom, and how much? For what classes in society was it of primary importance, for which secondary, and why? Was freedom uniformly and permanently important, or was it significant only under certain conditions or in certain situations (for example, prompted by specific problems)?[5]

Distinctions between civil and political life in classical Athens, however, also complicate efforts to compare the role and function of the enslaved in Athens with latter day chattel slavery in the New World. The formal legal restrictions upon slaves (publicly and privately held), metics, and ultimately women in political life suggest that prescribed slave roles were perhaps more varied in the Athenian realm than in the New World, where administration of matters of state and economy were largely restricted to slave owners, particularly elites in positions of power and authority in the polity or economy. Athenian political life required distinct modes of administration and rule for the citizen and noncitizen, but nonetheless interlocking modes of administration and rule. Different forms of political and economic life required different governmental modalities. Enslavement required coercion and prohibitions against enfranchisement. Democracy required relationships among equals, and between government and the governed. Finally, relationships between equals and unequals, in other words, across these groups, also generated discussion, commentary, and formal and informal institutions. Noncitizens and citizens required administration and management to foster participation in their respective political and social roles, and ultimately, to regulate and impose limits upon their interaction.

Understanding democracy's reliance on regimes of exclusion is relevant for an examination of the contemporary world, not just for studying an ancient political life long past.[6] For comparative politics in particular, a recognition of the constitutive tensions between slavery, poorly remunerated labor, and political order might help illuminate political phenomena largely ignored within the field. What I am concerned with most specifically in this chapter is, to paraphrase James Baldwin, *the price of the ticket*, the manner in which preordered hierarchies of difference have helped determine and structure the conditions of membership and participation in a democratic polity. Racial hierarchy, from the birth of the nation-state system to its present-day composition, has influenced state formation and expansion, immigration and citizenship law, interstate relations, as well as conquest and withdrawal of government intervention into national and colonial societies. One of the main charges of this chapter is to situate racial hierarchy in a line of politically salient distinctions institutionalized by Western nation-states from the 18th century onwards, as a means to highlight racial hierarchy as modern political rationalization of the relationship between democracy and inequality—a filter to distinguish societal members from polity members.

Very little scholarship within comparative politics considers the relationship between egalitarian and inegalitarian institutional practices that existed at the core of the Athenian polis, and at the core of most societies categorized as democratic in both the contemporary world and in the canon of comparative politics. Instead, what are often evoked and invoked are the ideas of particular thinkers rather than a foregrounding of institutions and practices that served to instantiate and maintain those democratic practices form the core (if not the sole) attention of students of comparative politics.

There is also a dearth of scholarship on the impact of slave regimes within nominally democratic societies upon that society's democratic institutions. Instead, comparative politics, on the whole, has turned to ancient, normative theory rather than its context and historical institutions for cross-temporal assessments of how democracies evolve and why they matter.[7] This chapter draws upon literature in political theory, history, American, and comparative politics to further probe the nexus of slavery and democracy and to encourage a research agenda with slavery and democracy as deeply intertwined themes.

By paying closer attention to how democracies thrive amid a cluster of unequal economic and political practices, we could actually revisit a classic concept in political science and comparative politics—polyarchy—which in unforeseen and unintended ways can be used as a conceptual container for what are considered racial regimes (developed in the subsequent chapter). Racial regimes are one example of polyarchic politics and societies at work, in how governments develop criteria and associations to distinguish between citizens and those who are supposed to serve them.

Among the relevant questions, then and now, unique to an ancient city-state and a contemporary nation-state with aspirations toward democracy are: (a) what contributions, if any, can noncitizens provide to a society and perhaps the polity itself? Slaves who fight on behalf of a republic are just one example; (b) are there paths to citizenship for noncitizens whose contributions to society or polity place them at least on par with, or exceeding the contributions of, the average citizen? (c) by what criteria and forms of enforcement should various categories of noncitizens be excluded from the polis?

Part of the challenge in tracing a genealogy of comparative politics back to philosophical debates in classical Athens is deciding which aspects of political life in the cluster of city-states are most important and relevant. By the late 19th century, many prominent political scientists and sociologists identified Aristotle as the progenitor of a scholarly discipline based upon systematic comparison of political institutions, actors, and cultures.[8] These scholars emphasized Aristotle's comparative assessment of different forms of political community, and his conclusion that mixed government—timocracy—was the most preferable form of political society. Aristotle's conclusions were not based on ideal types, but on his knowledge of actual polities and societies preceding and contemporaneous to his. In Aristotle's view, then, a society that was fully democratic, namely, with all of its members having the status of citizens, was no more practicable or ideal than societies that were exclusively or predominantly unequal.

Athenian citizenship, however, was not based upon some transcendental definition, but myth and selective application and omission of law in response to changing political circumstances. It is an articulation of *jus sanguinis* law, of a particular kind. Pericles' Citizenship Law of 451 required dual Athenian parentage for citizen status.[9] Myth had its role, in the form of descent-based citizenship criteria, based upon an origin narrative that proclaimed King Erichthonius actually descended from the earth. The origin tale and its retelling as a tale of autochthony made blood a principal criterion for civic membership. Subsequent Athenian citizenship law and criteria for polity membership were thus based on the seemingly natural, irreducible differences between the territorial citizens and immigrant noncitizens, even though no one, not even Athenian citizens, were *really* descendants of the earth. The actual paternity of the large majority of Athenian citizens could be traced to parents who, more often than not, were themselves Athenian citizens. As noted by Kasimis, "Athens granted citizen status only to those who could persuasively claim an uninterrupted and uncorrupted blood tie to their native founder. Laws governing marriage, citizenship and inheritance concretized the ideology's emphasis on descent: on the basis of blood, they disenfranchised metics and their offspring. Only the children of freeborn natives were eligible for democratic citizenship."[10]

Although racial categories such as those in currency in the modern era were not operative in the ancient world, jus sanguinis citizenship law, combined with an origin myth, effectively made citizenship coterminous with descent, not rights and responsibilities, and thus established what Susan Lape refers to as an ethnic-national or racial prejudice.[11] Lape and McCoskey concur that racial categorization and preferences were not manifest in a preoccupation with skin color or phenotypic features, but through the articulated preference in law, daily interactions, and in public culture for Athenians amid the plurality of subjects in ancient Athens.[12] Utilizing contemporary critical racial theory to make their conceptual claims, race and racism as such are not reliant and thus not reducible to skin color, but meanings associated with presumed difference and otherness which, under certain circumstances, are rendered salient in politics.

Students of Athenian democracy are not in agreement regarding a "race in Athens" thesis. Yet the use of myth that fused ancestry, gender, and territory with civic membership shares at least one similarity with the modern use of race and ethnicity: in both the ancient and modern examples, state makers and managers create a story that conjoins political membership with territory and origins; the attempt, via law and politics, is to *naturalize* citizenship through an emphasis on bloodlines and origins rather than rights and responsibilities—the performance of citizenship itself. Athens provides one of the earliest recorded instances of a government prescribing laws for political membership based on distinctions allegedly inherent in nature, but in fact are based in mythology, ideology, and changed political and demographic conditions (the influx of unwanted foreigners).

This naturalized distinction is precisely what we encounter in E.A. Freeman's determination to link a presumably fixed racial identity to a political community; the former as artifice, the latter as art, or fact.[13] Gendered, racial, and ethno-national criteria for political membership and exclusion in modern politics have served a similar purpose, based on the assumption that certain peoples and populations are naturally inclined toward or against politics. For example, Joan Scott writes of debates in revolutionary France about the purportedly natural and essential role of gender as a mode of political distinction, namely a means to differentiate women and exclude them from participation in politics: "By a kind of circular logic a presumed essence of men and women became the justification for laws and policies when, in fact, this 'essence' (historically and contextually variable) was only the effect of those laws and policies."[14]

The political rationalization of inequality is distinguished by a configuration of laws and norms, formal and informal mechanisms designed to partially or wholly limit certain groups from political participation. The constitutive tension between democracy and political inequality is wrought by the distinction between society and polity, which continues to resonate within nation-states with democratic polities. By paying closer attention to the interaction between the rationalization of political inequality, polity, and society, we gain a better understanding of how a democratic polis and polity influences, and is influenced by, highly unequal citizenship and labor regimes, and the ethno-national and racial hierarchies that, in the modern nation-state system, largely accompany these regimes. What makes democratic polities unique is not the absence of political inequality, but the dynamic interaction between democratic and antidemocratic politics in the same polity—the systematic accrual of political privileges among certain groups at the expense of other less privileged groups.

Race, Politics, and the Social Question

Here, then, we can begin a more complicated consideration of the Athenian polis and its implications for the world of modern politics. The nation-states of Europe and the Americas that were founded upon democratic principles, or at least aspired to democratic principles, shared several commonalities with their Athenian predecessor: the coupling of a democratic polity with highly unequal labor and citizenship regimes. These two features were not in conflict with each other, but had intertwined political and material objectives: maximize profits for elites while minimizing the circulation of economic profits and political privileges among those populations deemed unsuitable for civic participation.[15]

The rise of capitalism and industrialization in Europe and subsequently, the United States, generated new forms and sources of wealth, but also new forms of poverty: a class of impoverished and unemployed who were the casualties of capitalism and not the previous feudal and agricultural orders. Malthus, Ricardo, Marx, but also Charles Dickens, Proudhon and Emile Zola wrote about these casualties in ways that highlighted the limits of republicanism, the Industrial Revolution, and the rise of the bourgeoisie in addressing the needs of the poor. The predicament of the poor under conditions of capitalism came to be known as "the social question."[16]

Writing in *On Revolution*, Hannah Arendt devotes a chapter to "the social question" and hones in on the relationship between slavery, the social question, and revolution.[17] The term itself has its own lexical history in both political (French) and economic (British industrial) revolutions. Her examples range from the ancients to the American and French revolutions. Among the commonalities Arendt highlights between ancient Greece and Rome (her usage) and two of the major democratic revolutions of modern politics, the US and French revolutions, is the nexus of slavery and freedom, slave labor, and democratic practice. Her writings provide an interpretive means to examine the relationship between the institution of slavery, the practice of democratic politics, revolution, and social inequality in comparative perspective.

In *The Promise of Politics*, Arendt suggests that politics is freedom, the ability to participate in the polis.[18] This freedom, however, was made possible by what Arendt refers to as prepolitical liberation, a form of negative liberty in which "man could not be subject as a slave to someone else's domination, or as a worker to the necessity of earning his daily bread."[19] Arendt considers this form of liberation (what I am calling negative liberty) prepolitical because it is based upon freedom from coercion: the domination of slaves by members of the polis. Further down, Arendt distinguishes slavery in the Greek polis from capitalist exploitation (presumably wage labor) insofar as the objective of capitalist exploitation was profit and wealth, while the objective of Greek enslavement was the freedom to participate in politics.[20]

Notwithstanding differences between the material objectives of elites in 18th century France and the United States, on the one hand, and the political objectives of ancient Greece and Rome on the other, Arendt highlights how, as in ancient Greece, the architects of the political revolutions of France and the United States largely overlooked the "social question." In her chapter on the social question, Arendt rhetorically wonders whether "the goodness of the poor white man's country did not depend to a considerable degree upon black labor and black misery . . . the institution of slavery carries an obscurity even blacker than the obscurity of poverty; the slave, not the poor man, was "wholly overlooked."[21] The practice of freedom, even for poor whites, was premised upon the enslavement of blacks and on the prohibitions against indigenous participation in the US polity. At this point in her argument, Arendt seems to consider slavery as part of the social question, since citizenship was directly related to slavery.

Comparing the US and French revolutions, Arendt concludes, "Slavery was no more part of the social question for Europeans than it was for Americans so that the social question, whether genuinely absent or only hidden in darkness, was nonexistent for all practical purposes." Invariably, the French and American revolutions "spelled freedom only for the few and was hardly felt by the many who remained loaded down by misery."[22] Arendt is clearly without irony here and misses an opportunity to explore the relationship between the racial question and the social question. Blackness and darkness were key tropes in a chain of associations that equated enslaved Africans with political and other forms of inferiority, a darkness of mind and spirit to complement their phenotypic darkness. Blackness, in its human embodiment, was associated with darkness and property. The racial question was inescapably embedded in the social question, not epiphenomenal to it.

Moreover, since most dimensions of human interaction are in some way social, the "social question" as a generic description of poverty as a social phenomenon produced under capitalism requires unpacking. In the case of the French and US revolutions, the poor included peasants, indentured servants, dispossessed agricultural workers, and slaves, even though this last category of people was not part of either the French or US's foundational pact binding citizens to the state.

Arendt's elision of the racial question provides an interpretive opportunity to peel away the layers of the social question and reveal its multiplicity in both the US and France; the racial question set limits on both the French and US revolutions, as did the question of woman's suffrage. Mulattos in both the United States and Saint-Domingue complicated the bipolar schemes of racial management operative in France, the United States, and in many instances, their colonies.

On the one hand, the social question is an acknowledgement of the existence of inequality, and the possibility that elites—revolutionary or otherwise—have the material means, through economic redistribution or wage increases and social benefits, to diminish or eradicate inequality. Unfortunately, the social question has too often been framed in economistic terms. If the sources of inequality were, and are, varied, the range of pre-scriptions would also vary: women's suffrage and civil rights movements in post-revolutionary societies provide examples of a variety of political exclusions with social consequences that are not immediately derived from material life. Revolutions across the 19th and 20th centuries which prom-ised to end certain forms of inequality often ignored or countenanced other forms of inequality.[23] Nationalist and anticolonial revolutions across Asia, Latin America, and Africa of the 1960s and 1970s often left unresolved prob-lems of inequality affecting women and ethno-national and religious mi-norities, mostly problems that could not be resolved through exclusively economic means.

Undergirding the social question is the premise that governments and elites in a given society actually have the means to eradicate or limit in-equality. As such, solutions to problems of inequality have distinctly politi-cal origins. The question of difference—whether articulated as culture, class, religion, gender, nationality, ethnicity, or race—is embedded in these social questions: Who will supply the labor needed in society, and under what terms? How do we explain the existence of inequality? Is it the result of God's will, feeble-mindedness, or a lack of civilization and culture among cer-tain groups? Or is inequality largely explained through brute expressions of power and coercion?

Arendt's emphasis on the social question helps highlight the fact that political elites, even the most revolutionary among them, have often tabled issues of concern for the poor and marginalized of the societies in which their revolutionary ideals have been hatched, and in some cases successfully outfitted. The deferral of the social question was and is a matter of politics. In the next section I will provide examples of the substantive and strategic exclusion of issues pertaining to slavery, freedom, and the rights of women and minorities in the New World, demonstrating that the conjuncture of democracy and exclusion remain an enduring legacy of ancient Athens.

Creole Pioneers, Popular Egalitarians, and the Social-Racial Question

Perhaps the most significant distinction between experiments in democracy among the city-states of the ancient world, on the one hand, and modern nation-states, on the other, is the impact of republicanism, or, even more radically, what I shall call popular egalitarian movements, which advocated for mass political enfranchisement. In the perspective of many national elites in Latin America, the expansion of suffrage was equated not with the deepening of democracy, but the devaluation of their own political, economic, and social privilege.[24] As with the revolution in France, republican movements in the Americas did not resolve the social question, the racial question, and more fundamentally, the land question, which disadvantaged the popular classes.

Benedict Anderson's *Imagined Communities*, a synthetic treatment of nationalism as a cultural and material artifact of print capitalism, reintroduces the concept of creole pioneers to a nonspecialist audience to characterize the political and economic activities of colonial elites in the Americas who were influenced by the republican ideologies of the French and US revolutions while at the same time ensuring their continued dominance.[25] Rather than merely extending republican ideals of direct, participatory democracy to the unenfranchised masses, these elites devised ingenious laws emphasizing literacy, property ownership, and other criteria as barriers to popular suffrage and polity participation. By contrast, popular egalitarian movements such as rebellions among the enslaved and indigenous, along with peasant uprisings, sought to abolish slaveholding regimes, serfdom, and tribute. Part of the political challenge of creole pioneers was to convince the enslaved and their descendants, along with indigenous populations and byproducts of miscegenation, that national independence was in the interest of both elites and masses. In many instances, such as Colombia, Cuba, and the United States, the enslaved and indigenous participated in nationalist movements in the hope that their participation would bring about emancipation and suffrage.

Three key features characterize creole pioneers. First-generation descendants of Europeans, they considered it their providence to create independent nation-states with laws and mores of the nation-states and societies of Western Europe, principally, Spain, Portugal, Britain, and France. Yet they were not in Europe and as a result of their newly honed political affiliations and aspirations, no longer Europeans in a political sense. Their primary political affiliations lay with the societies and institutions they sought to create in the New World. Moreover, they were faced with the following political challenges: forge new societies premised upon the model of European nation-states with populations who were neither European nor necessarily interested in contributing to social, political, and economic systems that largely served to marginalize them in new ways. The role of slaves, peasants, poor women, and indigenous populations in independence movements across a geographical span ranging from the longitude of the United States to the latitude of Argentina exemplify the challenges faced by *criollo* elites to transform colonial outposts into new societies and nation-states. Finally, they were, with the exception of the United States and Canada, demographic minorities and thereby outnumbered. Creole nationalists shared at least one objective with their earlier Athenian counterparts—they proclaimed a democratic republic for a selected few, generating both economic profit and political freedom from slave, serf, and peasant labor while limiting (when not prohibiting) popular political participation of the very people they enlisted or conscripted for national independence. This will become evident below in the consideration of Simon Bolivar in his management of political crisis in racial politics in Gran Colombia.

Consequently, criollos set limits upon the extension of the franchise in societies such as Cuba, Haiti, Argentina, Brazil, and Gran Colombia. In this sense, these pioneers adapted the constitutive tension that first emerged in the Greek polis to the New World and later, in the United States and France. They desired enfranchisement and sovereignty for themselves upon seemingly virginal territory, and they furiously debated whether indigenous and African-descended populations, who also inhabited the territory, should and could be made citizens.

The majority of American nation-states from Canada to Chile abolished slavery *after* obtaining formal independence (See Appendix). Even in instances where popular support from marginalized populations (the enslaved, freedpersons, the indigenous, and the poor) was pivotal in the success of a revolutionary nationalist movement, freedom for slaves and their dependents was not simultaneous with national independence. Once independent, most American nation-states devised federal laws to limit (when not prohibiting completely) formerly enslaved populations and their descendants (Colombia, the United States, Paraguay, Uruguay, Argentina, and Brazil among them) from participating in civil and political society as citizens with suffrage and property rights, two significant attributes in the political cultures of liberal nation-states after the 18th century.

Slave emancipation in the Americas, along with the granting of suffrage, combined elements of negative and positive liberty. With suffrage, former slaves became empowered (if only in theory) to determine the terms of both their labor and their politics. In this sense, their newfound freedom would seem to close the distance between themselves and their former owners. Could the same polis that enacted egalitarian laws to level relations between elite and mass also enact laws or policies designed to maintain and perpetuate distinctions between citizen and noncitizen, which in turn provided the polity with the means to exclude marginalized populations from political participation? Racial regimes provided the means to institutionalize and ratio-nalize hierarchies premised upon phenotypic distinctions, which themselves were based upon interpretive schemes of differentiation that had no natural or scientific basis. Institutions, laws, and edicts provided the scaffolding for normalization and routinization of racial hierarchies, moving them from the realm of idiosyncratic, individual prejudices to standardization of difference.

Republican nationalisms in particular posed self-inflicted dangers of uncharted democratization. How could black and brown subjects, who re-mained associated with slavery, menial, or at best artisanal labor, become the social equivalent of citizens who were, more often than not, white and male? The leveling of distinction harbored the potential that criollo male elites, progenitors, and benefactors of suffrage could be dislodged or displaced from their position of newly won political *and* social privilege. If everyone was equal, who would rule? Who would labor? Criollos were not prepared to undermine the very means by which they accrued economic and political power—cultural prestige.

It is important to understand the political and economic ramifications of this prospect, not only for former slaves and their descendants, but for former slave owners and those privileged by whiteness. A transformed po-litical status for former slaves meant a transformed political status for the aristocracy. The problem of identifying and justifying aristocracy harkens back to Aristotle, but also to other times and places where inheritance was an important criterion for distinguishing between nobles and humbly born. Thus, polities diverse as ancient Athens, the revolutionary United States, France, and all of the nation-states of the Americas were confronted with the following scenarios upon the founding of their republics.

Scenario one entailed the denial of suffrage and voluntary association for slave, wage, and indentured labor. The second scenario involved a partial incorporation of enslaved and poorly remunerated labor into political soci-ety, whether through religion, sport, education, or military service. A third scenario included the full incorporation of subjects formerly excluded from the polity—in the majority of cases slaves, women, and foreigners—with all the rights once reserved exclusively for citizens.

The first scenario could only be enacted and maintained with a high de-gree of coercion and the corresponding institutional support to both sustain spatial segregation and deny voluntary association. The third scenario was never actualized. Neither Athens nor the slaveholding democratic polities to follow allowed foreigners and noncitizens as a class or group the possibil-ity of full participation in a polity. Most examples fall somewhere between scenarios 1 and 2, the result of contestation and negotiation between non-citizen subjects and a governmental institution.

Creoles, often together with colonial loyalists, created novel criteria for political exclusion to ensure that former slaves did not wield the same political rights as their former owners. Institutionalized inequality was re-made by rule of law to adapt to new political prospects and dangers, namely the democratization of society to enable former slaves access to the polity, thereby making (along with women and foreigners) members of polity and society one and the same.

Several cases from the Americas, including the United States, reveal the constitutive tension between society and polity, between labor and racial regimes designed to provide profits for superordinates and political subjection for subordinates. These tensions were not merely "colonial" questions isolated from political and economic machinations in the imperial nation-states. The political, economic, and ideological conflicts of imperial powers—France, the United States, and Britain among them—were informed by colonial prosperity and crises. Conversely, not only a colony's political economy, but its norms, protocol, social relations, and religious affiliations, were informed but not determined by debates and changes in attitudes and beliefs in the metropole.

The revolutions, rebellions, and social conflicts in fledging colonies and later nation-states in the 19th century Americas are significant not only in themselves, but because they augured the contours of conflicts during the third wave of anticolonial nationalism after World War II: insurgent colonies seeking independence and utilizing the language and concepts of rights, freedom, antiracialist democracy. Emancipatory discourses ranging from the Levellers, Jacobins, American revolutionary colonists, and religious gospel provided some of the means to extend democratic and republican ideals into more popular spheres. Taken together, along with what I have referred to earlier as popular egalitarian discourses, slaves and their descendants, peasants, so-called half-castes, and the indigenous had an additional language to proclaim their equality. Democracy was not the exclusive province of white elites, but a currency that could be shared with all peoples. As was the case with the Haitian Revolution, it would be these marginalized groups, not the elites of colonial society, who would take the ideals of the French Revolution to their most radical conclusion; *any* member of society, even a slave, could become a member of the polity.

The racial and social question, discussed in relation to Arendt above, became a principal concern for colonial officials and the economic actors, ranging from planters, traders, and entrepreneurs, who relied upon slave labor for their livelihood. Though varying in form and combination with other criteria, color and presumed racial distinction became a means to separate the citizen from the non- and partial citizen, to at once affirm political, phenotypic, and spatial segregation in New World societies.

In their examination of racial politics in Cuba, Puerto Rico, and the Dominican Republic, Mark Sawyer, Yesilernis Peña, and Jim Sidanius introduce the concept of "inclusionary discrimination" to characterize the formal and informal institutions that have served to delimit the ability of Afro-descendants in Latin America and parts of the Caribbean to participate in the economy, society, and polity as fully enfranchised citizens.[26] Latin American racial regimes, though exclusionary, often were more irregular and less systematic in their application of segregationist laws, in part due to less highly centralized state power and authority exercised throughout a national territory. Nicaragua, Colombia, and Brazil are three examples of societies with regions that could not be effectively regulated by an administrative center and consequently had multiple ethno-national and racial orders within its national territory, where boundaries between groups varied depending upon location. Citizenship laws based in whole or in part upon descent, literacy, and property requirements nevertheless served to limit political access of Afro-descendants in the upper reaches of society, polity, and economy of Latin America. They were, in effect, as in earlier, colonial times, relegated to the realm of labor, not the realm of rule.[27]

Haiti

The French Revolution, with its robust republican ethos, resonated in various parts of the world by the end of the 18th century, but no more forcefully and practically than in the New World. Colonial outposts throughout the Americas were affected by the revolution's ideals—and its antinomies. Jacobinism, along with other nationalist and revolutionary ideologies of the 18th and 19th centuries, critiqued aristocracy for its discouragement of meritocracy and social ascension on the basis of talent and achievement, not birth. Yet even the Jacobins of the French Revolution imposed limits upon the degree to which the new citizens of the republic could participate in the polity.

The Haitian Revolution, which began as a slave rebellion in 1791, brought both the antinomies and ideals of the French Revolution to the forefront of debates in the colonies as well as the new nation-states of the Americas.[28]

Slave rebellion in Saint-Domingue, France's most profitable colony before the French Revolution, generated intense discussion and ultimately fear among New World slaveholders about the moral, economic, and political costs of slavery. The apparent contradictions between French bourgeois claims of the rights of man and citizen, on the one hand, and their reliance upon profits garnered from human trafficking and coerced labor on the other, resonated throughout the Americas and the Western imperial nation-states that presided over these colonies. The prospect and eventual reality of an independent black republic led to changes in domestic policy in the United States and colonial policies regarding the institution of slavery and related trafficking and monitoring of slave populations.[29]

In his account of the Haitian Revolution, C.L.R. James wrote that slavery served to remind the Jacobins and their progressive and missionary allies of the colonial question—the spectre of the colony in their deliberations regarding republican freedoms. Yet with the exception of an organization devoted to the abolition of slavery, the Friends of the Negro, "everybody conspired to forget the slaves."[30] Referring to debates in the French Assembly at the moment when conflicts between left and right prompted the Thermidor reaction (the Terror) and the brutal countermeasures to follow, James concluded that "the colonial question again and again split the bourgeoisie, made it ashamed of itself, destroyed its morale and weakened its capacity to deal with the great home problems which faced it."[31]

The Jacobin right strategized to forestall discussion of slavery, particularly at the moment when colonists in Haiti, Martinique, and Guadeloupe warned of the prospect of race war in the Francophone Caribbean if slavery was abolished and mulattos gained full political rights. Abolition advocates ranged from those who distinguished, in keeping with the forms of rights under consideration in France at the time of the Revolution, civil rights from political rights, to advocates like Sieyes and Condorcet who believed in full civil and political equality for freedpersons and slaves. Proslavery advocates often referred to divine right, racial laws, or simply an assertion of their privilege as justification for the continued servitude of their black subjects.[32]

Regardless of their positions on the question of slavery, abolition, or political rights for freedpersons, the rebellion and subsequent revolution on Saint-Domingue brought practical political and economic exigencies to the fore: the colony was far too profitable to simply relinquish. But what kind of compromise could enable poor whites to retain their status vis the enslaved and mulattos, allow slaves greater freedoms (if not full civil and political rights), and retain the monopoly of force of the maritime bourgeoisie and big whites to ensure their continued extraction of profit—all at once? Given the intensity of the conflicts in Saint-Domingue, could a compromise be reached among these contending positions? This juncture in the Haitian Revolution foretold the challenges of administration and management at a similar period in the Algerian Revolution, when the French government sought to repress the national aspirations of their colony while proclaiming democratic relations with it. One participant in these discussions in France during the period of the Terror succinctly captured the problems not only of France, but of democracies more generally:

> Without speaking here of the danger and folly of slavery in democratic states, I could cite the history of all the peoples who have had slaves and depict the torments of the government whether it tries to keep them in a yoke that often quakes with their struggles and tries to diminish . . . their too great population; or whether it tries to restrain the cruelty of the masters. I could cite the laws that rapidly succeed one another, the regulations that follow upon regulations.[33]

This passage, taken from his speech celebrating the abolition of slavery just two months earlier, was written by Pierre Gaspard Chaumette, a leading journalist and member of the Paris city government during the revolution between 1790 until his date with the guillotine during the Terror in April 1794. It succinctly encapsulates the problems of law, population management, and administration incumbent upon governments that administer democratic and enslaved institutions simultaneously. Saint-Domingue, but also Demerara (see below), Harper's Ferry in Virginia, the Morant Bay Rebellion, and many other slave rebellions in the New World resonate with Chaumette's description of the consequences of a dualist regime that ultimately becomes untenable.

The colonists of Saint-Domingue, however, wanted nothing less than a maintenance of the dualist regime. They understood that any change in the racial order of the region would upend the colonial political economy and thus the basis of French colonial power, authority, and wealth. Whites in Saint-Domingue viewed black and mulatto political participation in colonial society as a threat to their very existence as a dominant racial, economic, and political force. Within Saint-Domingue, tensions between blacks, mulattos, and big and small whites during the period of the revolution further underscores how racial regimes became operative throughout the French empire: territorial France and its *départements* and colonies. If, as the Jacobins claimed, the Declaration of the Rights of Man was a truly universal document, then shouldn't those rights proclaimed therein apply to slaves—and other people—as well? This point was raised by, among others, Danton, and was opposed by, among others, Robespierre. There was a political explanation for the tabling of this very particular "social question," the question of slavery: if the Jacobins amended the Universal Declaration of the Rights of Man and Citizen to include slaves, then it would be impossible to convince those recently empowered by citizenship that either God, nature, or pure coercion justified their subjugation and unremunerated toil. The source of wealth for a good portion of the French monarchy and the French maritime bourgeoisie would disappear. Consequently, the political rights eloquently proclaimed in the final document pertained to those already endowed with citizenship, whether residing in metropolitan or colonial France, and not the unenfranchised.

Moreover, the mulattos of Saint-Domingue posed particular problems for whites big and small within the colony. Unlike mulattos in many parts of the Caribbean, mulattos were a formidable political and economic force in Saint-Domingue. The more prosperous among them were also slave owners. Mulatto leaders argued that as a group they met age, property, and gender qualifications for active citizenship, which put the planter class in Saint-Domingue on the defensive. Though not against slavery, Robespierre advocated for mulatto rights. Since mulattos were born free and met much if not all criteria for citizenship under Jacobin requirements, Robespierre could support unqualified rights for mulattos without contradiction.

Recent scholarship on Saint-Domingue and the Haitian Revolution has provided insight into additional tensions not only between mulattos, whites, and blacks, but among the category referred to as free people of color (*gens de couleur*), which included African-born women and men who somehow acquired freedom, as well as children who were offspring of unions between slave owners and enslaved women. The barriers created by whites within colonial society to restrict full economic and political participation of the enslaved, free blacks, and free people of color affirmed what critics of enslavement and colonialism referred to as the "aristocracy of the skin." Laurent Dubois provides primary evidence of colonial laws devised to prevent free people of color "from practicing law and medicine, from holding local administrative positions, even from buying luxury clothes and furniture."[34]

The political aspirations of the mulattos of Saint-Domingue generated the most anxiety among the *petit blancs* of the colony, because wealthy or well off mulattos had already become an economic force there. The repression of their political interests was accompanied by brutal repression of mulatto attempts at political and, ultimately, military mobilization. In a chapter appropriately titled "Parliament and Property," C.L.R. James provides a foreboding historical context to the eve of the revolution, as tensions between slaves, slave owners, small whites, and the maritime bourgeoisie reached the point of irreducible conflict: "It was the quarrel between bourgeoisie and monarchy that brought the Paris masses on the political stage. It was the quarrel between whites and mulattos that woke the sleeping slaves."[35] The brutal repression and denial of citizenship by small whites in the colony of mulatto aspirations for political rights represented an attempt to maintain a racial regime that ensured white dominance and black, mulatto, and freed-person subordination during a period of intense political crisis and change, when the conditions of possibility seemed to suggest, at least in Paris, that active citizenship could be extended beyond the bourgeoisie to all members of society, not just members of the polity.

In France itself, Jacobin proponents of both emancipation and citizenship were few. Tessie Liu, in her forthcoming manuscript on the impact of the Haitian Revolution in France, describes the complicated reasoning of Robespierre, Danton, and lesser known Jacobins Victor Malouet, Narcisse Baudry des Lozieres, and Joseph Barre de Saint Vincent—all children of the Enlightenment—who supported Napoleon's attempt to reintroduce slavery in French territory after its abolition in 1794.

Despite enormous exogenous constraints and internal conflicts of color, caste, class, and agriculture, the newly formed Haitian state sought to unify disparate groups of people (mulattos, the Polish mercenaries who deserted the French Imperial Army, slaves) under the category of black peoples. For example, the Imperial Haitian Constitution of 1805 forbade whites from owning property in Haiti, a response to fears of French reoccupation through land ownership rather than military conquest. Foreign blacks were given special status under civil laws and were to be treated as Haitian citizens. Article 14 of the constitution required all Haitians, regardless of color, to be referred to as black.[36] The constitutionally mandated citizenship granted to African descended populations was an acknowledgement of this unprecedented imagined community, based largely in recognition of the widespread condition of apolity of African-descended subjects the world over. Moreover, the constitution also authorized military operations against any and all nation-states and peoples who held African-derived people captives and profited from their labor. Making good on this constitutional prerogative, Boyer, the fourth emperor of Haiti, invaded the adjoining Spanish colony (now the Dominican Republic) and successfully—albeit temporarily—freed slaves there. Additionally, the constitution declared any African-descended person a potential citizen of Haiti, and thus articulated an automatic law of the return.[37] Thus, "home" for Haitians and by extension, blacks, was constituted in the act of sovereignty and the attendant claim of territorial dominion rather than place of origin; there was nothing "natural" about this virtual space for politics created by mostly African-born slaves and their descendants in a territory formerly held and administered by the French empire.

When viewed against the landscape of invasions by standing armies of any era, which have largely been predicated upon territorial border disputes, geo-political advantage, precious resources, as well as ethnic and religious differences, the invasion of another territory for the primary purpose of freeing slaves has been a rare occurrence. In this sense, the Imperial Haitian Constitution contained elements of what Kant described as an ethical state—an ethical code of conduct in both domestic and foreign policy—as a prerequisite for perpetual peace.[38]

For its efforts, the sovereign republic of Haiti was ostracized by Western powers. Not a single Western nation-state recognized Haiti's formal sovereignty after gaining independence in 1804. To put Haiti's nationalist and abolitionist efforts into perspective, Britain was the first imperial power to formally abolish the slave trade in its colonies in 1831, over twenty-five years after the declaration of Haitian sovereignty. France did not recognize Haiti formally until 1838, and only after imposing in 1825 the condition that Haiti pay an indemnity for the losses France incurred during the war. Haiti agreed to pay the indemnity, which further impoverished the financially weak state. Britain, Denmark, the Netherlands and Sweden commenced diplomatic relations with Haiti soon after France's conditional recognition in 1825.[39] The Vatican would not recognize Haiti as an independent republic until 1860.

The Vatican's refusal to institute an independent diocese in Haiti, one of the requisites of Vatican recognition, denied Haiti a system of formal education at a crucial moment in the new nation-state's development.[40] The United States did not formally recognize Haiti until 1862, though both governmental and private business interests had engaged in trade throughout the period of isolation. Haiti's predicament, in this respect, foreshadowed the conundrum of Cuban-US relations in the latter half of the 20th century, as the political logic of the major hegemon in the region greatly hindered the economic, political, and cultural access a small Caribbean nation-state and its peoples had with the rest of the world.

Haiti's sanctioning and isolation by Western states inaugurated the pattern of political marginalization of black political actors and states in the international political economy of the post-Westphalian era. Haiti's political behavior, however, would also serve as the archetype for future black political mobilization on a global scale, whether in Africa, the Caribbean or points elsewhere, in the succeeding century. As Trouillot notes, each Haitian state leader after 1802—Louverture, Dessalines, Christophe, Pétion, and Boyer, all concurred that "slavery as an institution was to be forever abolished from Haiti."[41]

The embargos, sanctions, and retaliation against the republic of Haiti indicates the degree to which Western powers were quite hostile to the idea and practice of a black nation-state with the right of sovereignty and recognition in the international system of nation-states. Haiti was viewed as a threat to the geo-politics of Western colonialisms and the fabulous profits and status privilege generated within them. A people who had overcome the institution of racial slavery and colonialism to create an independent nation-state and society could have been viewed as the heirs to the French and US revolutions. Instead, Haiti became the scourge of the nation-state system.

Guyana

Another significant slave revolt, though less successful than its Haitian counterpart, was the 1823 Demerara slave revolt in what was then known as British Guiana (now Guyana). The Demerara revolt did not overthrow a slave regime or the colonial apparatus that coveted it. At its height, however, between 10,000 and 12,000 slaves "rose up in the name of their 'rights', imprisoned and killed slave owners' families and employees, destroyed plantations and property."[42] Local colonial authorities and planters blamed missionaries and the Haitian Revolution, among several other factors, as causes of the revolt, rather than the institution of slavery itself.

In the ensuing struggle, 200 slaves were killed and many others imprisoned. As in the case of the Haitian Revolution, the slave owners' efforts to quell rebellion was simultaneously an effort to maintain a racial order at a moment of political crisis, when more radically egalitarian notions of political community informed and transformed notions and ideas of rights among the enslaved.

The crisis in the British colony was precipitated by the contradictions between formal declarations of reform and liberalism by the British government, on the one hand, and the economic imperatives and priorities of a plantation economy. Imperial reforms of conduct codes regarding the treatment of slaves and ultimately, the formal abolition of slavery in British colonies, collided with the increasingly desperate and determined efforts of the planter class and colonial elites to maintain the institution of slavery and the social, cultural, and political privileges associated with that institution. Evangelical missionaries in Guyana and in other parts of the English speaking Caribbean exacerbated colonial tensions by presenting a version of Christianity that was incompatible with slavery and servitude, and in keeping with the leveling of social distinctions to be found in more radical discourses in Britain. As noted by Emília Viotti da Costa, the tensions found in Demerara in the months leading up to the actual revolt were resonant in plantation societies throughout the New World:

> Like slaveowners everywhere, they were caught in a process that seemed to condemn slavery and the system of values and sanctions associated with it to oblivion. To them, the missionaries represented new, powerful, and threatening historical trends that were undermining their ways of living. For it was not only slavery that was coming into question, it was the colonists' sense of status, their notions of discipline and punishment, their ways of conceiving relations between masters and slaves, blacks and whites, rich and poor, colony and mother country. It was not only their right to property that was being challenged, it was also the monopolies and privileges they had always enjoyed in the mother country.[43]

Arbitrary color classification—often referred to as race—was inextricably linked to status, power, wealth, privilege, origin, and spatial location (colony versus metropole). As in Saint-Domingue, when rebellion, revolt, and revolution threatened to upend the status quo, a higher order of coercion was necessary to reassert planter and white supremacy.

The Demerara revolt is significant for two reasons. First, the British government, the arbiter of Guyana's colonial regime and administration, continued to intervene in Guyanese politics and society at several points in Guyana's colonial and postcolonial history as an independent nation-state. The British government, relied heavily on the racial order designed during the colonial period to foment distrust and enmities between Afro-Guyanese, who were descendants of slaves, and Indo-Guyanese, descendants of indentured laborers brought to Guyana by the British after abolition.

The political continuities between British disruption of Guyanese politics in the period before and after abolition will be explored more fully in chapter 4.

The second point of significance is the manner in which the subsequent colonial government trials to determine the guilt or innocence of many slaves and missionaries in the planning and execution of the revolt further revealed not only the schism between British reformists and colonists, but the practical legal and juridical problems that arose as a direct consequence of colonial Guyana's racial regime. Immediately after the rebellion was quelled, many slaves (women and children among them) were summarily executed on plantations. Slaves who were identified as rebellion participants or were simply in proximity to rebellious slaves were placed on trial. Slaves were tried and convicted in colonial court for crimes ranging from staring at a slave owner or colonial official in a menacing manner to being a leader or principal conspirator in the revolt's planning.

Procedural difficulties emerged during the trials, however; they were the result of the encounter between slave and citizen in a colonial court where colonial-imperial and metropolitan-liberal juridical claims clashed. In most slave societies of the New World, slaves were rarely allowed to testify in court. Slave testimony in trials involving whites was prohibited until the 18th century.[44] Yet cases ranging from proof of manumission, paternity, and sale and purchase of slaves often revealed that despite the formalities of population segregation, slave and master often interacted with one another in the most intimate of ways. Freed blacks often encountered similar difficulties when involved in transactional disputes with whites (such as payment for services rendered), since they were often not allowed to testify in court against whites. Impartiality and justice, then, was subordinated to the racial order.

The post-rebellion trials were remarkable not only for Guyana but for British colonies in general because of the colonial government's decision to allow slaves to serve as witnesses under oath.[45] In theory, this meant that slave and master had equal status as witnesses in court. In practice, however, the discursive deployment of symbols associated with the differential status of slaves, whites, and slave owners was made apparent in court procedure, which served to highlight the lowly status of slaves and the exalted status of whites. With the exception of the one white missionary—John Smith—who was executed for his radical evangelicalism, slaves, not whites, were on trial. Only one slave prisoner and an acknowledged leader of the rebellion, Jack Gladstone, was provided counsel. In one of the many historical ironies embedded in these trials, slave Jack Gladstone was owned by John Gladstone, father of a future British prime minister and the owner of the plantation *Success*, where the rebellion began.

Under the pretext of formal equality before the law, the discursive framing of defendants, plaintiffs, and witnesses revealed the inequities and disparities in the social sphere that were coded by race, class, gender, and colonial status. Emília Viotti da Costa, in her study of the revolt and subsequent trial proceedings, reviewed testimony and descriptions of witnesses presented before the court. Descriptions of witnesses, plaintiffs, and defendants reinscribed individuals within an existing social order, not within the purportedly status-neutral environment of the colonial courtroom:

> The slaves were usually identified only by their first name and the name of the plantation to which they belonged. Their color was also often mentioned—a reflection of the complex system of social stratification and of the colonist's preoccupation with differences among blacks, mulattos, and whites. . . . Some slaves, probably Africans, had two names: one African and one English. . . . No woman was given a surname. . . . Slave crafts or jobs were never mentioned, although some were drivers, others were artisans, boatmen, servants, and field workers, serving a great variety of functions in complex hierarchies. Whites, by contrast, were always identified by their names and their profession or standing. This was true whether they were managers, overseers, plantation owners, merchants, or professionals.[46]

In the aftermath of the ultimately unsuccessful slave rebellion, the nominal effort to systematize court proceedings with slaves and citizens as plaintiffs and defendants under rule of law designed only for citizens provides some insight into the legal implications of the entanglements involving slaves, their masters, their descendants, and in some instances offspring in post-abolition court proceedings.[47] These and other proceedings reveal the fault lines of static systems of racial hierarchy and governance when people, free and unfree, live according to their desires and principles rather than law. The racial regimes of colonial, imperial, and national orders pervaded court proceedings involving whites and blacks, as well as many other shades on the color-racial continuum, in places as disparate as Australia, New Zealand, Brazil, South Africa, the Netherlands, France, Britain, and the United States.

Racial Regimes in South America

The political predicaments for creoles resulting from the prospect and actuality of freed slaves can be evidenced throughout the Americas. Creole elites in former Spanish colonies, in addition to the former Portuguese colony of Brazil, faced similar challenges on their charted path to national independence, a path that combined full suffrage and political participation for white creoles and delimited suffrage for the poor, women, indigenous, and ultimately freed slaves. A richly detailed literature exists on the measures undertaken by creole elites to ensure their continued political dominance, access to cheap labor, and cultural privileges associated with whiteness, and the corresponding travails of slaves and freedpersons after independence in Latin America and the Caribbean (see Appendix).[48]

One significant example is included here from Spanish America to underscore the extent to which racial slavery and emancipation became a significant social and political challenge for white elites who sought to both institutionalize and secure their political and social privilege at the crucial moment of nation-state foundation. The dynamic interactions among slave owners, royalists, slaves, freedpersons, indigenous, their immediate descendants, and their "mixed" offspring helped produce, when codified in law, the definitions and categorization of both citizen and noncitizen. Simon Bolivar, one of the most prominent advocates of Pan-Americanism in Latin America and perhaps the most significant state builder in the region during the 19th century, unified what came to be known as Gran Colombia in a successful war for independence from Spain. The French, US, and Haitian revolutions deeply impacted Bolivar, perhaps more so than any other nationalist of the Americas, because the fate of his nationalist and Pan-Americanist projects were directly impacted by the Haitian Revolution.

After two separate attempts to achieve independence from Spain were thwarted by royalist troops and lack of local support, Bolivar sought refuge in Jamaica and Haiti. Jamaica was a British colony and a source for great wealth for the British Empire, its capitalists and colonial elites, as well as a locale for British politicians and plantation owners to experiment with economic and social policy. Haiti provided a safe haven for Bolivar after Spain briefly reclaimed Gran Colombia in 1816. Alexandre Pétion, the Haitian monarch, provided Bolivar with sanctuary, money, weapons, and ammunition with one condition: liberty for all slaves within the territories of Gran Colombia.

Bolivar partially fulfilled his promise upon his return to Venezuela and therein revealed his distinctly creole political calculus, a combination of liberalism, monarchy, and racial rule. After Gran Colombia achieved independence from Spain in 1821, Bolivar and his followers drafted a constitution that combined French republican principles, British parliamentary democracy, and monarchial prerogatives to enable Bolivar to rule indefinitely and creole elites to inherit political offices. As part of the new constitution, all children born to slave mothers after 1821 were declared free.

As in Brazil's *ventre livre* law of 1831, the 1821 manumission law of Gran Colombia did not actually outlaw slavery, but provided formal freedom to the unborn while keeping their mothers, as well as fathers and nonwhite relatives, in conditions of bondage or passive citizenship. Historian Aline Helg notes that the Colombian constitution, like other Latin American constitutions crafted after successful independence movements in the 1820s, "stressed its protections of Colombians' 'liberty, security, property and equality.'"[49] Property was at once an inclusionary and exclusionary criterion for active citizenship, since propertyless males were thereby disqualified from active citizenship. The majority of slaves and freedpersons could neither read nor write Spanish. Thus, Colombian constitutional criteria for citizenship effectively limited suffrage and active citizenship to creole elites and Euro-descended members of Venezuelan society, excluding blacks and zambos (so-called half-castes, mixtures of indigenous and African peoples). Finally, "property" included slaves.

The United States

There is simply too much scholarship on racial politics and inequality in the United States to consider in one portion of a chapter, or an entire book for that matter. Instead, this brief consideration of the United States has as its focus several largely neglected aspects in the development of racial regimes in the United States. Comparative analyses of racial politics and inequality that include the US as a case study often examine fully developed national laws and policies that are determined to be racially preferential or prejudicial to one or more groups and thus can be viewed as racial or racist policies. Instead, what will be emphasized here is how in the United States racial regimes developed in relation to policy formation and legal precedent, which at first take were unrelated to racial and ethno-national differentiation: international relations, surveillance and movement, and immigration policies, in addition to the maintenance of the racial and ethno-national hierarchy within the domestic territory of the United States.

Common to the evolution and development of racial and ethno-national regimes in the majority of cases assessed above and in subsequent chapters is the development of legal precedent and informal institutions designed to maintain a racial or ethno-national order in moments of political indecision and crisis. Changes in the interactions between citizens, noncitizens and partial citizens force a state to adapt formal and informal regulations to either repress or authorize changes in the nature of citizen- noncitizen interactions.

An analysis of federal and state law, policy, and juridical decisions in the United States in the period spanning the late 18th century and the mid–19th century provides an opportunity to locate the United States within the larger cluster of cases analyzed here and in subsequent chapters. During this period, the French and Haitian revolutions prompted changes in US federal and state laws to heighten surveillance of republican-minded radicals with seditious ideas, and at the other end of the spectrum, to more closely monitor the trafficking of slaves brought to the United States from the Caribbean, the region where the Haitian revolution took place.

The United States government responded to the French Revolution with the creation of the Alien and Sedition Acts of 1798. The acts sought, among other things, to stem the flow of European political radicals into the country. Regarding the Haitian Revolution, the US government was not only concerned with the spread of ideologies via elite discourse, but with the circulation of rebellious ideas among slave populations. Winthrop Jordan writes how white observers noted that US slaves grew more insolent with news of the Saint-Domingue revolt.[50] Whites, especially in the Eastern seaboard states, were wary of the presence of West Indian slaves who accompanied their masters from Saint-Domingue and the possible synergies between the imported and established slave populations. The iconographic depiction of the contented black slave was replaced with the icon of the "Negro as potential rebel," to use Jordan's words.[51] State, local, and federal governments began to pay close attention to the types of slaves brought into the country.[52] The South in particular fed upon the rumors of rampant mayhem in Haiti as an example of what would happen if slaves were given their freedom.

The response of slave owners throughout the New World to the fall of Saint-Domingue to a group of rebellious slaves bears some similarity to the response of French Prime Minister Jacques Chirac after the World Trade Center attacks of Sept. 11 in New York City, "We are all New Yorkers." Similarly, the rebellion at Saint-Domingue made all New World slave societies French. The exodus of French colonials and their slaves from the colony of Saint-Domingue began in 1793, two years after the revolt. Jordan chronicles how US citizens and local governments, through philanthropy and governmental assistance, provided safe haven for some colonial refugees of Saint-Domingue[53] (many Saint-Domingue colonials fled to Cuba before moving elsewhere). The major powers and industries that profited from the slave trade and plantation economies empathized with the calamity that bourgeois and maritime France experienced, which could happen to any world power with colonial political economies and subject populations.

The prospect of slave revolt led many state and municipal governments in the US to adopt laws that tracked and monitored slave populations and their internal movement, as well as the influx of slaves imported from the Caribbean. South Carolina prohibited importation of all slaves in 1792 and prohibited slaves from Hispaniola (the island Haiti shares with the Dominican Republic) from entering the state in 1803, as did Georgia.[54] In Virginia, slave owners and importers had to take an oath that they had not imported any slaves from the West Indies or Africa. North Carolina imposed a similar statute in 1795.[55]

Many southerners believed that the Haitian Revolution was caused by an uncontrolled slave population; thus, prohibiting the slave trade was a direct result of the revolution and a concern for safety.[56] Not surprisingly, West Indian slaves were considered more dangerous than African slaves, and US slaveholders began to pay greater attention to ethnic distinctions among slave populations than they had done before, and as had been done in the Caribbean where slave revolts, resistance, and rebellion were more frequent. Laws were devised to curtail and monitor movements of black populations in many states and to prevent the arrival of French West Indian blacks. The increased attention to diversity within slave populations was an implicit acknowledgement of their internal ethno-national and regional variation. With increased fears of black revolt, freed blacks were in an even more precarious position. They were often re-enslaved for minor infractions of state law, or if they moved from one state to another.[57] Runaway slaves were often captured in free states and brought back to the site of their enslavement.

Virginia was the only southern state that did not adopt restrictive laws against the entry of West Indian slaves.[58] A random, but nonetheless instructive, analysis of state legislation of slave and freeperson movement in the states of Philadelphia, Delaware, Mississippi, and Illinois demonstrates that all four states passed legislation prohibiting black migration into and within their territorial domain in the 18th and 19th centuries. Out of 686 statutes passed between 1788 and 1798 in Pennsylvania, four statutes pertained to free blacks, mulattos and slaves. Two statutes, passed in 1788 and 1789 respectively, relate to the eventual abolition of slavery in the state and the formation of the "Pennsylvania Society for Promoting the Abolition of Slavery."[59] Of the four statutes, only the 1795 statute pertains to slave movement, specifically, slaves of colonial refugees from Saint-Domingue. The statute, in tortuous language, makes a noted distinction between slaveholding and nonslaveholding refugees, and provided monetary relief of up to $2,500 for the latter.[60]

Delaware provides an interesting example because of its geographical location at the axis between free and slave states, North and South. Between

1803 and 1813, seven acts directly related to free blacks, mulattos, and slaves were passed. Four of seven acts regulated internal movement, emigration, or intermarriage of any member of the aforementioned population with whites. In the case of Mississippi, a slave state, eleven acts were passed between 1820 and 1830 concerning slave, mulatto, and black freepersons. The provisions of the adopted statutes include prohibition against the employment of a Negro in a printing office and the entry of slaves who have been convicted of a criminal offense. Even Illinois, a free state and the land of Lincoln, passed laws prohibiting and regulating slave and free movement and migration. Of 22 acts passed between 1809 and 1818, only two concerned free blacks, mulattos, and slaves. One of these two, however, dealt expressly with the entry of free blacks and mulattos.

In the cases of Mississippi, Illinois, and Delaware, all three passed statutes that required a kind of "racial registry" whereby freepersons and mulattos had to register and, in some instances, pay a fee to reside and remain within the state. What all of this suggests is that a system of intrastate identification, registration, and surveillance was devised during the 19th century to monitor black and colored presences in both free and slave states. These racial registries have their sole parallel in immigration provisions and restrictions in state and federal law.

Inevitably, the retention of slavery necessitated clarification of other federal laws and policies designed to distinguish people from commerce, the movement of actual or potential citizens, and slaves. Both state and federal law evolved to distinguish the transport of slaves from the emigration of freeborn persons. The ninth section of the first article of the US Constitution concerning Congress' ability to monitor immigration and slavery led to Supreme Court cases in which individuals and states challenged federal capacity to tax foreign immigrants entering the United States, and to determine whether Article 9 applied to slaves, immigrants, or both. Though these cases did establish the precedent of congressional ability to impose taxes upon slaves and immigrants after 1808, the larger distinctions between importation of slaves and migration of immigrants were unavoidable. For this reason, laws and policies with respect to immigration evolved, in part, out of the acknowledgement of their presence within the nation and the need to distinguish black and slave status from free whites. In so doing, the United States government not only developed immigration policies for the entire population, but further underscored the distinctive marginality of the black population excluded from the category of citizen. At the same time, subsequent waves of immigration from Europe and Latin

America would generate crises of racial and ethno-national classification—how should these new immigrants be classified according to existing criteria? How close or how far away are they from our ideal citizen?

The decisions of the United States Supreme Court with respect to the so-called Passenger Cases, *Smith v. Turner* and *Norris v. the City of Boston* (1849), led to the emergence of federal immigration law.[61] At issue in these cases was the federal government's exclusive ability to impose taxes upon incoming immigrants, as well as a state's ability to levy duty charges upon slave traders who brought slaves into the country. In the decision, the Supreme Court declared that states, as a policing authority, could monitor the entry of paupers, convicts, and slaves. Slaves fell under the category of commerce, while paupers and convicts (whites) were considered public safety hazards. The entry of white men into a state, however, was distinct from the entry of paupers, slaves, and convicts because free white men were not restricted from citizenship.

What is significant about this ruling, in addition to its structuration of a formal immigration policy, is its classification of slavery, vagabonds, and paupers under the auspices of police authority and, hence, criminality, non-citizens whose entry "might trouble the internal tranquility and security of the state."[62] Thus slaves, vagabonds, and paupers would fall under criminal codes, while citizens and foreigners would be first classified under civil codes.[63] While the court's opinion acknowledged the right of individual states to devise laws to monitor public behavior, the power to tax the entry of foreigners resided with the federal government.

The decision regarding the Passenger Cases is significant for at least four reasons: its distinction between the criminal and the noncriminal, the distinction between slave and free persons, and the criminalization of undesirable populations that were free and unfree, white and nonwhite. The distinction between importation and migration acknowledged a wider distinction between voluntary and involuntary movement of persons across nation-state boundaries. The development of immigration and commerce law with respect to these populations became the federal government's way of maintaining the distinctions between them in jurisprudential and material terms.

A far better known case is the much-examined Dred Scott decision of the Supreme Court. In the majority decision, Justice Roger B. Taney explained his rationale: Europeans were considered citizens by individual states before the formation of the United States, and subsequently in the crafting of the constitution. African-born or descended peoples, however, were slaves more often than not and consequently had no rights to citizenship in the

US Constitution or in federal courts. Thus, Dred Scott did not even have the right to bring a case on his behalf before a federal court:

> The question is simply this: Can a negro, whose ancestors were imported into this country, and sold as slaves, become a member of the political community formed and brought into existence by the Constitution of the United States, and as such become entitled to all the rights, and privileges, and immunities, guaranteed by that instrument to the citizen?[64]

Taney's question frames the distinction between society and polity in the context of US politics and, as a result, the Supreme Court decision to remind his audience—jurists and nonjurists alike—of the stakes involved in the distinction. Two ingenious, albeit perverse, rhetorical maneuvers underlie Taney's argument. First, Taney utilized a very Jacksonian understanding of the relationship between state's rights and federal law to argue for the supremacy of state law in adjudicating matters of race. Secondly, Taney argued that England, as a European nation, prohibited the political participation of a "degraded race" in its colonies, and concluded that the United States should be similarly consistent in its racial perspectives. The perverse nature of this argument is its rhetorical alliance in racial terms with the very imperial power it successfully freed itself from on the grounds of political repression. So much for American exceptionalism.

The broader national terrain against which Taney portrayed the relationship between US African Americans and the body politic is important for another reason. Rather than treat the US North and South as having distinct race relations premises, Taney focused on the commonalities of herrenvolk rule as a racializing comparativist with echoes of Freeman. The constitutive tension of society and polity became manifest in the Dred Scott decision and in the broader efforts of federal, local, and state governments in the US to not only curb the aspirations of free blacks but to limit prospects for black revolt, especially among the slave population.

Indices of Difference: The Conduit Between Democracy and Inequality

Could it be that even under the most practicable conditions for the elaboration of democratic and republican ideals, a subordinated laboring majority population with limited or nonexistent political rights was necessary for the functioning of democracy for the few? And if so, by what criteria of political judgment would citizens be determined? Would birth, origins, or responsibilities determine or strongly impact the definition of the citizen? Charles Merriam, an important political scientist on the cusp of the 19th and 20th centuries, suggested that racial hierarchy became a means to extend, maintain, and broaden a belief and practice of aristocracy, through the idea of a racial nobility and racial paupers. Merriam identifies the need for "credentials of the aristoi" across the ages, from Aristotle, the National Socialist Party of Germany and the US South:

> Aristotle lamented that there was no sure distinguishing mark to serve as the infallible index of the slave nature, although he thought that in general this might be observed in the cringing manner of the inferior. Slaveholders of the South found the missing link, they said, in the color of the Negro. In more modern times the Germans have found the mark of superiority in the alleged characteristics of the Aryan.[65]

In fact, Aristotle's recognition of the absence of a sure distinguishing mark of enslavement upon a person or group evidences the philosopher's suspicion of slavery as a natural condition, and his belief that slave nature is actually plastic (*phisus*) molded by institutional and social forces, not by nature (*natura*).[66] As Jill Frank highlights in her explication of Aristotle's understanding of human nature in *Politics 1*, Aristotle rejects any naturalist justification for enslavement based on heritage, body types, or coercion, instead justifying slavery by way of varying human capacity for critical reason, leadership, and docility. In other words, the more docile and cowed among us are more disposed to accept the conditions of enslavement.[67]

Nevertheless, Merriam is clearly impatient with what he called the "indices of difference" as accurate indicators of a predetermined aristocracy; wealth, heredity, arms, or birth may all be cited to support a theory of aristocracy, but none actually provides an explanation for why and how aristocracies are produced.[68] As a conceptual innovation, indices of difference introduces a means to begin theorizing and identifying empirical evidence of how the idea of race, among other ideas, becomes part of the language and keywords of politics, providing an interpretive means to both categorize and hierarchize populations through institutional and bureaucratic means and ultimately, in dynamics of power. Whether it is Aristotle's interpretation of the cringing gesture, blackness in the United States, or so-called Aryan features in Nazi Germany, the mark of inferiority, constituted in social and material relations, was an instrument used to distinguish those who would labor for others and those would labor for themselves or not at all. Race and color in more recent times had become, to paraphrase Charles Merriam, indices of difference. This particular indicator became politically salient not through biological and ecclesiastic rationalizations for inequality, but in machinations of political institutions and the social dynamics structured by them.

Certainly, racial and ethno-national hierarchy are not the only ways in which a student of comparative politics can track the evolution and emergence of institutional development and variation. But racial and ethno-national hierarchy in modern politics provides many opportunities to examine institutional development, complexity, and differentiation. Here we have reached the point in the development of my argument where racial hierarchy and its institutionalization in racial regimes can be considered alongside a once prominent concept in the study of American political development and comparative politics: polyarchy.

Polyarchy, Oligarchy, and the Social Question

One of the most influential conceptual developments for the study of comparative politics based on classical Athenian precepts was the concept of polyarchy formulated by Robert Dahl.[69] In this formulation, Dahl considers democracy an ideal type never fully realized. Even the most democratic regimes and societies have inegalitarian, nondemocratic features. For Dahl, polyarchies represent one pole in a four-point model with the other endpoints (in counterclockwise order) consisting of hegemonies, inclusive hegemonies, competitive oligarchies, and at the highest order on the right, polyarchies. Dahl defines polyarchy as "relatively (but incompletely) democratized regimes . . . regimes that have been substantially popularized and liberalized, that is, highly inclusive and extensively open to public contestation."[70]

A large literature covers the concept of polyarchy and its applications in the study of both US and comparative politics. Readers would be best served consulting the significant primary and secondary literature on the concept and its empirical applications, especially the work of William Robinson.[71] It is important to remember that Dahl's definition of polyarchy relies heavily on the degree of electoral competition and voter participation, with less emphasis on nonelectoral democratic forms. The specific concern here is with circumstances under which political actors determine the necessity of internally differentiated political administration, the circumstances which, as a feature of societal management and administration, first brought about polyarchic regimes.

Dahl provides a number of examples that help frame the polyarchic limits of the democratic order. One of his most prominent examples is US African Americans after Reconstruction and their relationship to the polity:

"If the freed Negroes had been allowed to participate in the system of public contestation in the South, they could not have been subjected to systematic expression by coercion and terror. . . . It was only by excluding them forcibly from the polyarchy that the system of coercion and terror could be maintained in the South. And precisely the extent that black people were excluded, polyarchy in the United States was not fully inclusive. It was, in fact, less inclusive than most other polyarchies after the First World War, for following the general adoption of universal suffrage no other country with a polyarchal regime . . . contained an excluded group of comparable size.[72]

For Dahl, the US was an exception to all other polyarchic regimes, save Switzerland and Argentina, because of its exclusion of a large minority population—blacks—from participation in the polity. At the same time, Dahl considered the US consistent with other polyarchic regimes in the placing of limits upon formal political participation of foreigners. Thus, racial hierarchy, expressed in formal politics and institutions, becomes a means to outline the parameters of polyarchy in the United States.

Whether one is persuaded by polyarchy's analytic reach and empirical grasp or its normative claims, the passages above lay bare political dynamics peculiar to the relationship between social and political inequality, not only in the United States, but in the history of polyarchies more broadly. Dahl draws revealing comparisons between Ancient Athens and the United States during the most tumultuous period in national black freedom struggles for equal rights in the latter case: "Athenian and American democracy each furnish us with an example of a competitive system that was inclusive with respect to one part of the population but hegemonic with respect to another (slaves, and in the United States, also ex-slaves)."[73]

Dahl writes of the circumstances of regime formation and maintenance in the United States and Athens in dualistic terms, wherein coercion, particularly in the US case, was the cost of the racial order willingly borne by both white elites and the mass public. Additionally, we must consider the fact that the regimes of violence imposed upon slave and ex-slave populations, in the case of the United States, were not separate and apart from the general workings of local, state, and federal government. The intertwined nature of federal, state, and local government within racial regimes was laid bare during periods of intense violence in the US South during the era of the civil rights movement, when governmental authorities and agents assigned to protect civil rights activists from angry mobs and organized paramilitary organizations like the Ku Klux Klan were also members of these same organizations. Their allegiances in many instances were, at best, conflicted.[74]

Within Dahl's dualist political order, members of excluded groups (and their allies) contest the conditions of their subordination while dominant group members, through formal and informal institutions, maintain dynamics and conditions of their domination. The polyarchic conditions of political inclusion and greater electoral competition are affected by extralegal coercion. And the "hegemonic"[75] sphere (in Dahl's terminology) of high coercion and political repression has to be situated against the backdrop of nominally democratic institutions and claims-making by dominant group members.

The US civil rights movement, and the successive riots in France and Britain beginning in the 1990s, provide enough empirical evidence to demonstrate that the divide between hegemonic and polyarchic in Dahl's conceptualization is more analytic than real. Dahl's dual system is actually one system of political rule that allows for inclusionary and exclusionary political regimes operating simultaneously.

This leads to two critical points for the purpose of exploration of the spectre of race in comparative politics. First, lurking behind the institutional variation described in Dahl's account of polyarchy is institutionalized population variation. Institutions emerge out of a perceived necessity for order and regularity in many spheres of human commerce and interaction. Population distinction and variation have necessitated institutional variation in the administration and management of populations associated almost exclusively with labor and segregation, on the one hand, and assimilation and formal politics on the other.

Second, although Dahl treats both Athenian and US democracy as exceptional polyarchic regimes with highly coercive dimensions reserved for their respective enslaved populations, the fact is that the dominant Western nation-states beginning in the 17th century (Portugal, Spain, France, Britain, Belgium, the Netherlands, and the United States) each have had some version of inclusive polyarchies and highly restrictive political criteria to delimit access of slave and colonial labor to spheres of political contestation and power. A way of understanding the functional relationship between polyarchy and racial regimes within Dahl's framework is to assume that racially or ethno-nationally superordinates have the best prospects for behaving politically in ways that most closely approximate a democratic ideal.

Similarly, the repression of subordinated group aspirations for political equality not only delimits political participation of excluded groups, but ultimately affects full polyarchic articulation in politics, since the polyarchical participants must expend material, institutional, and human resources to exclude racially and ethno-nationally marginalized groups.[76] In brief, racial hierarchy requires management, ranging from subtle dissuasion to blunt coercion. Understood in the scenario framing offered at the outset of this chapter, Dahl's explication of the US polyarchy-democracy conundrum in relation to racial hierarchy represents the borders between scenarios two and three. Not only US African Americans, but several ethnic immigrant groups, and women more generally, have through collective action and political protest contested the limitations of real life versions of scenario one, which led to changes in law, institutions and norms in the period roughly spanning the 1920s and 1960s (women's suffrage to the Voting Rights Act). Their efforts and the subsequent concessions and amendments of national governments made scenario two a political and social reality by the early 1970s. Scenario three, the least empirically manifest analytic, is the democratic ideal most fully prevalent in society and polity. Scenario three is often invoked by defenders of US democracy and exceptionalism as well as by critics of US democracy who have desired political inclusion. In scholarly and political terms then, scenario three represents the limits or aspirations of not only US democracy, but the democratic polities throughout the world in which elites have economically and politically profited from slave labor, gender bias, and colonialism.

Why be So Hard on Democracy?

One of the many helpful questions raised in constructive criticism of an earlier version of this chapter concerned the relationship between democracy and political inequality. As with economic inequality, democracy is hardly the only culprit in the widespread failure of societies and economies throughout the world to address the widening gap not only between rich and poor, but between the middle classes, the poor, and the most destitute. "Why lay the blame on democracy, when autocratic, totalitarian, and other forms of political rule have tolerated multiple forms of inequality for much longer period in human history than democracy has?" This is a fair question.[77] Democracy is certainly not the sole culprit, and certainly not the originator of economic and political inequality in modernity. As the examples explored in this chapter and chapter 5 demonstrate, fledgling and hegemonic nation-states accommodated and in many instances encouraged economic and political inequality evidenced in the institution of slavery as well as other forms of poorly remunerated labor. These forms of inequality certainly predate modern republicanism and democratic forms. Moreover, in the case of classical Athens, refinements of citizenship criteria undertaken during the rule of Solon and Cleisthenes were introduced to root out the sale, barter and transfer of citizenship rights from either one citizen to another (in the case of poor citizens seeking to pay off debts to wealthy citizens) or between a citizen and foreigner. Classical Athenian citizenship was neither currency nor individually held; it was a public good. Furthermore, since citizenship presupposed freedom as well as, after the Persian Wars, autochthonous membership, foreigners and slaves were excluded from citizenship and thus membership in the political community of lowercase democrats.

Thus, if the Athenian citizenship regime became more rather than less restrictive during the classical period, shouldn't democratic polities protect themselves against predation and devaluation? It would be politically naïve for a democratic polity, or any polity for that matter, to assume that it could exist in perpetuity without protections against external and internal threats. Furthermore, since institutions of slavery in the Mediterranean as well as many other parts of the world existed before and after the era of classical Athenian democracy, how can democracy be blamed for forms of inequality—the institution of slavery among them—that predate it? If democratic institutions operate nondemocratically and thus by extension, idiosyncratically, is that the fault of democratic institutions as institutions, or the people and ideologies that happen to inhabit these institutions at a given time?

Consider the issue of policing in a more contemporary context, specifically the discriminatory policing that results in disproportionate uses of lethal force in many democratic societies. Policing provides an opportunity to distinguish between political ideologies, political institutions, and political cultures in nominally democratic contexts. Few advocates of a "law and order" approach to policing minority populations would deny the importance of regulation, procedure, and training of police officers in their interactions with any members of a society. Even fewer advocate making policing less transparent and more despotic and authoritarian (though to be sure there are such proponents on the far right). Obversely, most proponents of policing with more "community-centered" approaches advocate greater transparency and community involvement and oversight of police functions and institutions. In this sense, most views on policing in contemporary, plural, and democratic societies assume, or at least aspire to, institutions of policing that broadly reflect the democratic norms the society and polity are supposed to be based upon. Institutions that operate according to racist and xenophobic precepts must ultimately operate in an idiosyncratic, anti-democratic, and highly subjective manner.

The stated goal in most deliberations about arbitrary policing of minority and immigrant groups in societies such as France, Britain, and the United States is the lessening of highly unequal forms of policing experienced by members of these populations, not the disappearance of democratically informed police departments altogether. In sum, the challenge in several societies and polities is to manage or extricate antidemocratic ideologies and actors from nominally democratic institutions. Whether or not policing functions in any society can be democratic, or relatively democratic, is a separate question.

Institutional discrimination, however, gives institutional form to racist (as well as sexist and gendered) ideologies strongly enough in some cases (Ferguson, Missouri, or the banlieues of France, for example) that it becomes difficult to distinguish police officers from the institutions they serve, much in the way that police officers in many tragic instances have come to associate certain groups, certain bodies, with criminality.

Here is where the ethnos versus ethos distinction in relation to democratic political orders is apparent and where modern discourses of democracy diverge from ancient or classical ones. First, what distinguishes the modern practice of democracy from both earlier iterations of democracy and other forms of political rule is its very language and presumption of a horizontal equality between differentially situated members of society. The proliferation of republican ideologies in the 18th century help augur popular understandings of democracy as "people power," pitting the citizenry against governmental authority. By contrast, theocracy and monarchy, drenched in the rhetoric of divine right and inheritance, respectively, do not, by definition, rely on language promoting equality of persons. Thus, discourses of democracy can, have been, and are deployed to decry the unequal treatment of citizens and noncitizens by institutions administered by a democratic polity, institutions whose source of power is based in coercion. Certain democratic theorists would argue that public deliberation of policing in this way is itself an example of democratic practice not permissible in other types of political societies.

Yet we can analyze, even laud democratic experiments in Athens and elsewhere while also recognizing democracy's coexistence, even encouragement, of highly unequal regimes. For example, the existence of the institution of slavery in a society with a democratic polity requires some form of rationalization on the part of democrats. Enslavement is either inconsequential or consequential to the ability of democrats to deliberate and participate in the polity. There was no contradiction, in classical Athens, between the practice of slavery and the practice of freedom, as long as there were no Athenians among the category of the enslaved. Considered at once abstractly but also in terms of its own internal dynamics, citizenship had both criteria and barriers to membership. Both were based upon ideas about gendered, ethno-national, and wealth-based distinctions.

This leads to perhaps one of the few political continuities between classical Athens and modern democratic nation-states—the need to create barriers to political membership. A central question is the following: under what conditions does democracy *require* barriers to membership? How and why do certain barriers to membership become more politically salient than others? Although both democratic and nondemocratic states devise criteria and barriers to membership in political communities, it is democracy where the criteria of membership and exclusion from the political community is undertaken—at least in theory—with the consent of the citizenry.

The key is to understand the conditions and circumstances under which polities create and maintain barriers to membership. As Brubaker highlights in his classic comparative study of citizenship regimes in France and Germany, formal citizenship grants membership in a national political community, not a world of humans.[78] Consequently, citizenship is ultimately a selective and exclusionary cluster of rights and responsibilities. Times of crisis often become justification for heightened and more restrictive citizenship and immigration regimes, during wars for example. Changes in immigration and citizenship law and surveillance in France, Britain, the United States, and Germany in the first decade of the 21st century were motivated by terrorist attacks by mostly nonstate actors in Europe first, then after 9/11 in the United States. Crises also provide opportunities for actors desirous of more exclusionary conditions for political membership to advocate more restrictive immigration and citizenship regimes, even at the expense of inclusionary norms and laws.

Thus, we arrive at a question that can be examined empirically with a range of methodological tools: which barriers to political and civic membership are considered tolerable, and which ones aren't? Barriers to certain forms of civic membership, such as same sex marriage, gays in the military, reproductive and transgender rights, voting rights for racialized and minoritized populations, and immigrant and migrant rights are examples of institutionalized barriers to membership in a democracy or polity that have been significantly lowered in the past 20 years in several countries and regions of the world. These barriers did not just fall, however, due to some telos intrinsic to democratic polities; they fell more often than not, because of the challenges made by those who were excluded.

Conclusion

In the chapter "Looking Forward" of W.E.B. Du Bois' *Black Reconstruction*, the sociologist situates the era of Reconstruction after the Civil War in the United States in a larger discussion about the practice of democracy throughout the world:

> The true significance of slavery in the United States to the whole social development of America lay in the ultimate relation of slaves to democracy. . . . Was the rule of the mass of Americans to be unlimited, and the right to rule extended to all men, regardless of race and color, or if not, what power of dictatorship would rule, and how would property and privilege be protected?[79]

By the paragraph's end, Du Bois refers to democracy as a problem as it "expands and touches all races and nations." Democracy, slavery, color, dictatorship, property, and privilege are the keywords of Du Bois' longer passage, from which we can extrapolate to other times and places, but with his suggestion that we consider democracy as a first-order problem to confront, a barrier in its own right, to equality. The veil of race, to continue in a Du Boisean vein, occluded democracy for some while rendering democracy transparent and readily accessible for others. For Du Bois, access to democracy was not a matter of the capacity of the excluded, in the case of the US, Negro citizens, but of the willingness of whites to allow Negroes access to its practice.

Through the comparative and historical assessment of the development of racial regimes in the Americas offered above, we can now situate the United States within a larger class of nation-states in which elites devised institutions that separated denizens in society from members of its political community. The cases examined above all evidence how slaves toiling for the wealth and sustenance for mostly creole elites did not experience unfettered liberty and freedoms before, during, or after independence. For freedpersons and slaves alike, newly independent governments crafted laws and implemented policies to ensure that freedpersons (whether previously manumitted or freed during the struggle for independence) did not achieve political equality with their former masters. Freedom was often contingent upon participation in the independence struggle. In several cases, slaves fought alongside masters in a failed attempt to extend a colonial order. Freedom then, was often strategic, and not the result of liberal generosity on the part of the nationalist slave owners. New institutional arrangements were constructed to insure continued white elite domination in polity, economy, and society. Haiti was the sole exception to this trend within the Americas, and the newly independent nation-state (albeit monarchy) paid dearly for its independence.

Usurious labor conditions such as debt peonage, serfdom, slavery, and low wages were not merely transferred from the social and economic sphere into the spaces of politics, and not simply moved from one era to another. Rather, political and economic institutions reconstituted barriers to *civitas* in direct relation and response to advances and aspirations toward political membership by marginalized groups. Laws and norms devised to ensure the further marginalization or exclusion of certain groups are not simply lifted from the economic sphere, but are rendered anew. In the cases cited above (among others), the prospect of political opportunities for politically excluded groups generated anxieties among elites, which in turn led to the generation of new laws limiting political participation of marginalized societal members in formal political spheres. These prohibitions ranged from limitations upon travel, nonendogamous marriage, residency, wealth, literacy, and property requirements for suffrage.

For the marginalized, excluded, noncitizens, and semicitizens, their relation to the polity in each of these cases was precarious and highly contingent. Again, Arendt poses a key question to consider across cases in examining the implications of political exclusion, what she characterizes as apolity: "The problem thus arose of how man, if he is to live in a polis, can live outside of politics . . . how is it possible to live without belonging to any polity—that is, the condition of apolity, or what we today would call statelessness."[80]

Arendt's description of the condition of apolity, or statelessness, in ancient Athens reminds us that modern and contemporary paradoxes of statelessness have their origin not in a particular case or example, but in a more fundamental understanding of how states, even city-states, came to create, implement, and maintain the distinctions between territories and peoples. With the backdrop not only of ancient Athens but subsequent catastrophes such as the death camps of World War II or contemporary refugee crises in various parts of the world, the condition of apolity described by Arendt can be separated into two related but distinct conditions. The first concerned the distinction between a society's population and the inhabitants of the demos of that society's polity. The second condition of apolity pertains to those people who could be classified as foreigners, those who are—or were—members of another society and polis, who do not have membership in the polity of the society in which they reside. Racial criteria and hierarchies in modern Western politics can serve as gauges for scholars and policymakers to assess how close, or how far, various populations are from the ideal conditions of a democratic polity. Racial regimes provide scholars with an opportunity to examine polyarchies in all of their forms.

Considered more abstractly, all of the examples offered in this chapter can be understood as illustrations of the following question: "what does it mean to have democracy among a segment of society juxtaposed to the massive exclusion of many (slaves, women, nonpropertied citizens)?"[81] This question, posed by Jeffrey Winters in his comparative study of oligarchy, has implications for examining the development of formal and informal institutions designed to extract labor while limiting politics and profit for some groups, one the one hand, and on the other, extract civic participation, encouraging profit and privilege among them. Winters poses this question after comparing ancient Rome and Greece, the early United States, and apartheid South Africa where Afrikaners "enjoyed a vibrant but exclusionary democracy and economy amongst themselves."[82] Winters' question thus spans the history of democratic experiments, from the Greek polis to 21st century nation-states, where political islands of democracy are overlaid upon vast, highly unequal terrain.

Winters characterizes ancient Athens as "an exclusionary slave democracy heavily dominated by a ruling landed oligarchy," stating just above in the primary text that "oligarchy and procedural democracy, especially in the representative form that had evolved by the early nineteenth century, barely conflict at all. The two kinds of politics are derived from different kinds of power and involve different kinds of political engagement."[83]

The aim of Winters' comparative assessment is an explanation of the endurance of oligarchic regimes in vastly distinct political and economic circumstances, in democratic, authoritarian, and totalitarian orders. A core concept in Winters' explication is the wealth defense regime, designed to insure oligarchic wealth through pacts with state power and governmental authority, industry, and commerce, with a phalanx of legal, juridical, and coercive operatives designed to insure that core oligarchic arrangements remain intact despite changes in political circumstances (such as a regime change or shifts in party affiliation).

The examples drawn above evidence racial and ethno-national regimes designed to defend privileges accrued by members of a dominant group (or groups) by denying or limiting access to political institutions, specific areas of employment, education, as well as privileged spatial locations within society (residential, industrial, and commercial). One distinguishing feature of racial and ethno-national regimes from Winters' wealth defense regimes is that oligarchic power does not require state power or governmental authority to be functional. Moreover, its regimes, even highly unequal ones, persist alongside liberal, democratic polities. Racial and ethno-national regimes, on the other hand, rely heavily upon state power and governmental authority, whether directly, as in the case laws designed to limit citizenship and civic participation in Venezuela, Haiti, and the United States, or indirectly, such as popular movements aimed at repressing political mobilization of marginalized groups, as in the case of free people of color in Haiti, Afro-Guyanese, and East Indians in Guyana, or African Americans in the United States. Racial and ethno-national regimes rely upon collaboration between governmental and state representatives and polity members to enforce and police the hierarchies the regimes are created to impose and maintain.

The political implications of the Haitian Revolution, however, have the most resonance across an array of modern social movements and politics. In social movement parlance, the Haitian Revolution can be considered an "early riser," an anticolonial, abolitionist, and nationalist movement that emerged 150 years before the period of post–World War II decolonization. Its isolation and punishment by Western powers would have been harder (though not impossible) to impose on a global political landscape with well over 100 independence movements in Asia, Africa, Latin America, and the Caribbean within the thirteen year period between 1955 and 1968, the height of decolonization mobilization. Second, the combination of national sovereignty, republicanism (not democracy, initially), and racial equality in the Haitian Revolution was unprecedented in Western politics, social movements, and within the nation-state system more generally. The quest for racial equality in the Haitian Revolution, when conjoined with the question of women's equality in the French Revolution, prefigured two of the most recurrent political challenges within modern politics (in the Global South and Global North) across the 19th and 20th centuries.

Given this political backdrop, it is not coincidental that movements for racial and gendered equality would figure prominently in French, British and US politics. Women's suffrage movements along with anti-apartheid and civil rights activism exemplify the possibility and reality of political participation by actors who were not formally granted the right of full political and civic participation by a state or other governing body. Their struggles, successes, and failures as movements help illuminate a core tension intrinsic to modern democratic politics involving actors who believe that their proximity to democratic institutions and practices entitled them to participate as empowered citizens, not excluded subjects. This tension is what makes contemporary democratic practices distinct from their Athenian ancestor. Proximity to democratic actors, institutions, and practices was no criterion for entry into the Athenian political community for the enslaved or metics. Discourses of universal human rights and the basic equality of all human beings was a political phenomenon of the 18th and 19th century, not 5th century BCE[84]. Thus slavery and racial inequality, no less than Enlightenment and republican ideals, informed the pursuit and ultimately the transformation of democratic practices in Western nation-states and in their colonies by subjects in societies that did not want them to become citizens.

4

Racial and Ethno-National Regimes in Liberal Polities

One of the continuities wending its way from the first instantiation of Athenian democracy to the formation of democratic (and protodemocratic) republics of the 18th and 19th century New World is the presence of mechanisms to exclude or delimit political participation of certain groups or classes of people in society.

Instead of an origin myth in which citizens were required to spring from the earth, many New World nation-states devised citizenship criteria to simultaneously incorporate and delimit citizens based on what Charles Merriam (examined in chapter 3) called "indices of difference." Racial and ethno-national identification—along with gender, literacy, and property requirements—constituted either pathways or barriers to citizenship, depending upon the populations in question and the nation-states in which they lived. Origin myths of another kind, steeped in ideologies of nationalism, religion, and scientific racism, provided the ideological threads for foundational justifications for political exclusion and, ultimately political inequality, in the new nation-states.

Nor were the imperial nation-states of the so-called Old World immune to these delimiting tendencies. In fact, national governments of France and Britain combined elements of domestic and foreign policy to distinguish between colonial and metropolitan political subjects in their colonies and territories, and to restrict immigrant access to metropolitan citizenship.

Limitations placed upon citizenship access were selectively applied to different immigrant groups.

The purpose of this chapter is to demonstrate how France, Britain, and the United States devised racial and ethno-national regimes to delimit political membership within their liberal democratic polities and in so doing, created and maintained political inequality. These regimes imposed highly exclusionary policies including, when deemed necessary, coercion to restrict access to citizenship.

As noted in the previous chapter, common to many Old and New World nation-states is the development of ethno-national criteria for political membership, and implicitly (when not explicitly) political leadership, via requirements that polity members and members of state share a common origin, whether the notion of origin pertains to land, nationality, ethnicity, or what in the 17th century came to be known in the West as "race." The assumption of common origins—or at minimum, membership in a "prepolitical" community which in turn became criteria for membership in a political community (democratic or otherwise)—has been an enduring feature of world politics well into the 21st century. Examples abound of hypernationalist movements that aspire to both homogeneity of national populations, coupled with the expulsion, marginalization, and in some cases, extermination of populations deemed threats to a national community: Israel, Malaysia, Germany, as well as France, the United States, and Britain are among the nation-states with movements with the above stated objectives and tactics in their societies. The fallacy of the race concept, as demonstrated in the human genome project, the debunking of scientific racism by early 20th century forensic and socio-cultural anthropologists, has not lessened the use of race in politics as an organizing concept replete with assumptions, norms, and practices of imagined communities that make electoral choices based on the presumption of irreducible difference. Given this social and political reality, what role does difference play in the functions and processes of democratic polities? How does racial and ethno-national hierarchy, as factors or variables in politics, alter our understanding of democratic polities?

This chapter provides preliminary answers to these questions, by examining the polities and societies of France, Britain, and the United States as democratic polities with robust racial and ethno-national regimes. Their governments have long been considered within the literature of comparative politics as paradigmatic examples of liberal (if not social) democracy, the basis from which to compare and contrast fledgling democracies as well as totalitarian and authoritarian regimes. Yet if we examine these societies only as liberal polities, we ignore their ultimately polyarchic character. Racial and ethno-national regimes, in addition to providing research opportunities for scholars of institutionalism, also provide means to measure polyarchy, the existence of multiple forms of political community and rule in a nominally democratic society.

The combination of political equality and inequality in each society is the result of a constitutive tension at the core of its political and civic life, between populations who were part of the initial citizen-state pact and those populations who were not. Each state, at different points in their history, developed bureaucracies and norms to differentiate among populations within society.

In each case, racial and ethno-national regimes did not first emerge as fully articulated, coherent, and coordinated policies, but developed in response to specific instances where populations who were not originally intended to participate as polity members interacted with citizens. Such instances—prompted by requests for marriage or paternity identification, commerce or trade, or demands by noncitizens to participate in the polity—prompted the need for laws and policies to administer the relationship between citizens and noncitizens.

Immigration and resettlement of formerly colonial populations, in the case of France and Britain, and the agitation for rights among long-subordinated, settled populations in the United States, resulted in many governmental crises in each polity in the period after World War II. Each national government utilized administrative tactics and strategies to manage and in some cases repress populations deemed threats to national security: US African Americans, particularly those engaged in civil rights and left politics; Afro-Caribbean and other black populations in Britain; and Arab populations in France during the era of anticolonial struggle. In each society, domestic unrest—youth movements, feminism, war protests, labor conflicts, civil rights struggles for nonwhite minorities—led to shifts and reformulation of domestic and foreign policy regarding citizenship, the management of immigration flows, and surveillance of protest groups. Changes in state policy and practices regarding immigration, management, and repression of protest, and the differential (and unequal) treatment of minority populations by various segments of the state apparatus, provide evidence of what Etienne Balibar referred to as the "interiorization" of ideas, beliefs, and modes of rule once reserved for the colonies.[1]

The interpretation offered here has three principal consequences for the study of comparative politics. The most obvious is the incorporation of approaches to the study of racial politics into the methods and scholarship of comparative politics. There is a large literature on racial hierarchy and politics in the United States as well as Britain. Increasingly, scholarship on contemporary racism in France in the aftermath of riots in 2005 and 2007 exposed a fault line between France's national creed of republicanism and the governmental and popular attitudes toward Maghrebis and other non-white populations. In all of these cases, evidence of racial stereotypes and attitudes, along with discriminatory practices in social interactions and in the interactions between minority populations and the police, have been richly detailed and analyzed by scholars in both the social sciences and humanities. Rather than focusing on racism and its forms in isolation, I am most interested in how racist attitudes and behaviors inform and are informed by institutional practices. Just as racial and ethno-national regimes influence political development and variation, political development and variation in each nation-state also affects how racial and ethno-national regimes emerged in each context and can help explain the particular form and contours of such regimes in each case.

Second, racial and ethno-national regimes force a reexamination of neat correlations between state policies and regime types. Students of comparative politics tend to associate particular regime types with specific political practices and outcomes. Authoritarian and totalitarian regimes are associated with disproportionate uses of state sanction to manage or eliminate political dissent. Liberal regimes (if not political cultures) emphasize individual rights, freedom of association, and dissent. Social democratic and socialist regimes often emphasize (at minimum, rhetorically) more communitarian aspects of society and polity, deemphasizing individual rights and emphasizing public, collective concerns. Racial and ethno-national regimes, however, complicate correlations drawn between regime type and forms of political rule, since ethno-national and racial regimes can be identified across the ideological spectrum of modern Western politics—the politics of state and nation.

Racial regimes do not neatly correspond with ideological alignments of political parties and the general Western left-right political continuum, though right-wing parties in Western polities have tended to impose more robust and comprehensive racial regimes than left-wing governments. In each of these cases, however, left, liberal, and right wing parties have advocated and implemented policies on immigration, citizenship, and nationality restrictions that made origins part of the criteria for citizenship and naturalization. The presence of racial and ethno-national regimes within most forms of governmental and state institutions may provide further evidence of the enduring human propensity to distinguish one population from another, regardless of forms of government.[2] Neither economic nor institutional analysis, on their own, explains this proclivity across cases. We can both reject Freeman's correlation between race and political community while acknowledging, belatedly, the prevalence of racial regimes in the democratic polities that students of comparative politics study.

Third, the development of racial and ethno-national regimes provides a means to examine the relationship between racial and ethno-national politics and the growth and development of institutions, or in short, political development: the expansion and deepening of state power and authority, the growth and expansion of bureaucracies and related bureaucratic knowledge, and the flow and cross-flows of information between distinct governmental apparatuses. These regimes affect, and are affected by, political developments in other areas of governmental and polity practices.

Although ethno-national and racial regimes vary according to context and circumstance, their development is contingent upon the presence of phenomena identified as a political-administrative problem for state authorities and population management within a territory. In many instances citizenship and immigration regulations develop in response to an actual or perceived influx of populations for whom regulations previously did not exist. When specific populations are deemed a "problem" for governance, calls for immigration and employment controls, increased policing and surveillance, and even criteria for holding elective office were developed in response to the real or imagined increase in populations deemed unassimilable either into society, polity, or both.

In each case, the policies and practices first utilized in colonial societies to manage subordinated colonial populations found their way into domestic policy. Tactics devised and utilized to manage subject populations in a colonial territory, or even within the metropole, became part of the strategies of containment in the domestic sphere in the post–World War II period, evidenced in the following areas of governance: immigration, policing, and counterterrorism policies, and in the monitoring of dissent. Through the adaptation of strategies and tactics once designed for colonial and subject populations outside the contiguous territory of the nation-state for populations within the national territory, domestic policy absorbed features of foreign policy. Racial and ethno-national regimes conjoined features of metropolitan and colonial administration to monitor racialized populations in both metropolitan and colonial settings.

A standing literature in comparative politics examines the effects of colonial rule and Western modes of political administration, legitimacy, and sovereignty upon the politics of developing countries. The obverse—the effects of racial slavery, Western colonization, and imperialism upon the politics of developed societies—has largely been ignored in comparative politics.

The colonial histories of these three nation-states are quite distinct. Britain and France both had far more geographically and numerically extensive colonial outposts. The British Commonwealth and the French départements and protectorates provided the administrative scaffolding and symbols of colonial and imperial relations. Unlike Britain and France, the United States had neither a commonwealth nor department apparatus to mediate their relations with subject populations and nation-states.

The United States government did not have a colonial office as did Britain, which administratively and strategically isolated British colonial policy from domestic and foreign policy. US policies towards its colonies and the regions and nation-states where resource and geo-political stakes for the US government and capital were high, can be found across governmental departments ranging from the State Department, the Central Intelligence Agency, USAID, and Fulbright to the US Chamber of Commerce. Each is involved in devising and implementing policy considered beneficial to US interests, namely interests of state and capital and occasionally, liberal democracy.

Settler populations in colonial territories of Britain, France, and the United States prompted political crises that affected not only colonial orders but national politics within the metropolitan territories. Settler encroachment upon lands inhabited by indigenous populations, expropriation of property (including livestock and agriculture), and laws privileging settlers over local populations contributed to conflicts and rebellion in British as well as French colonies and dependencies. Settler populations in Jamaica, Guyana, Rhodesia (now Zimbabwe), Saint-Domingue, and Algeria at different moments summoned and received military and administrative assistance from metropolitan governments to maintain local racial orders.

The United States, with its much more recent history, did not have as lengthy, extensive, or formalized colonial and dependent relations with territories and subjects in noncontiguous areas. The US government, however, in conjunction with enterprises and industries with investments in the production of coffee, tea, sugar, bananas, and rubber did maintain clientelist and imperial relations with several sovereign governments in the Americas and in other parts of the world.[3] These governments were nominally independent, but largely administered politically and economically by the US government.

As a settler society presiding over a vast territory with multiple conquered indigenous populations, immigration—and immigrants—figured more prominently in US history and politics in the 18th and 19th century than in France and Britain. Slavery and colonialism were significant sources of private and public wealth in each case. Each developed differential citizenship regimes to distinguish between European and non-European immigrants as potential citizens.

The materials and interpretations put forth in this chapter have implications for the field of comparative politics. The period under examination is precisely the epoch in which comparative politics emerged in the United States as a distinct and identifiable field within the discipline of political science, with its own then-evolving canon, modes, and objects of inquiry. The political scientists who helped constitute the Committee on Comparative Politics set the stage for two successive generations of comparative politics training at the graduate level. From this new beginning, students of comparative politics, on the whole, did not engage in intraspatial comparison within those countries known as advanced, industrialized, and liberal democratic, beyond distinctions between federal, municipal, regional, or local governance, principally law and legislation. What they might have found, however, is a family of resemblances between modes of governance, conduct, and political culture associated with the world's developing areas, and modes of governance in the developed world designed to manage and administer noncitizen populations considered "other."

An examination of each case will reveal the existence of regimes emphasizing racial and ethno-national distinction. These regimes are a combination of formal and informal institutions which identify, rationalize, and maintain distinctions among populations within primary sovereign territory. The formal dimensions of differentializing regimes are evidenced in law, procedure, and legislation; modes of governance and control vary by population. Ethno-national and racial regimes help manage and reproduce the spatial, socio-economic, cultural, and political order of disaggregated polities and societies.

Racial Regimes, Formal and Informal Institutions

The concept of a racial regime provides an opportunity to merge distinct scholarly literatures, the first on the nexus of race and state, the second on political institutions. Several scholars whose work is either cited or discussed in previous chapters have made significant contributions to our understanding of the nexus of racial formation and state power in European and Euro–North American polities, demonstrating via empirical evidence how what Omi and Winant refer to as "racial projects" limited access of minoritized populations to citizenship, employment, social, educational, and ultimately, dominant levers in polity and society.[4] Although focused exclusively on the United States, Desmond King and Rogers Smith's "Racial Orders in American Political Development" advances several conceptual innovations that can be applied within a comparative framework to identify and examine what they define as racial institutional orders where "political actors have adopted (and often adapted) racial concepts, commitments, and aims in order to help bind together their coalitions and structure government institutions that express and serve the interests of their architects."[5] King and Smith's formulation of racial orders has several interpretive advantages that could enable comparativists to gain analytic leverage on phenomena previously considered irrelevant for the cross-spatial examination of political institutions. First, King and Smith emphasize that many features of US politics that at first take seem unrelated to racial orders but are upon closer examination greatly influenced by such orders: immigration policy, citizenship criteria, and the development of congressional organizations. At both micro and macro spheres of politics, "racial" institutional orders seek and exercise governing power in ways that predictably shape people's statuses, resources, and opportunities by their placement in "racial" categories.[6]

One key difference between King and Smith's approach and the analysis offered here is their emphasis on "institutional orders" or multiple racial orders competing for political dominance in polity and society as opposed to the state. King and Smith's emphasis on the internal contradictions and contestations regarding *how* and under what terms particular racial orders will be implemented (racially liberal, white separatist, populist) certainly justify the focus on internal contestation and negotiation—in a word, politics. Yet as a mode of domination, institutionalized racial hierarchy also has a distinctly nonpolitical, i.e., coercive, dimension, evidenced in use of force to both organize and repress labor and maintain legal strictures of segregation and immigration. The nondeliberative dimensions of racial orders, in fact, make state-based racial orders possible.

While the term "racial state," as explicated by Burleigh and Wippermann, Goldberg, and Omi and Winant, helps underscore how the coalitions, alliances, negotiation, and contestation of racial orders operate against the backdrop of monopolized coercive apparatuses, the concept does not capture the internal machinations within states over what type of racial or ethno-national regimes to impose.[7] The interpretation offered here seeks to combine elements of both approaches by focusing attention on coercive and political features of racial orders.

In the social sciences disciplines and the discipline of history, regimes are objective-oriented structuring processes that guide actors towards specific outcomes. In the case of laboring regimes, the incentives, rewards, punishment, and coercion have often been imposed in a variety of productive forms (industrial, nonindustrial wage, or indentured and enslaved labor). Taylorist regimes, for example, were utilized in several plantation economies to extract the most productivity from slaves engaged in sugar cane and banana production. Any behavior considered by the architects and supervisors of the regime to be detrimental to its optimal functioning would be prohibited.[8]

Racial regimes are a combination of formal and informal institutions that serve to structure preferences and outcomes in the dynamic interactions between dominant and subordinate groups, based upon presumed racial and ethno-national distinction. Such regimes are not limited to the sphere of economics, specifically mass labor and production, but inform juridical-legal spheres of polity and society. Underpinned by norms, customs, and rule of law, racial regimes perpetuate inequalities in the allocation and distribution of public goods and resources such as education, employment, housing, and social welfare. The bureaucratic and administrative dimensions of racial regimes maintain and reinforce distinctions between groups, which in turn affect opportunities for education, housing, health care, employment, and quality of life overall. With their emphasis on immigration (voluntary and coerced), racial regimes impact domestic and foreign policy. Institutional racism operates within these regimes when institutional actors mobilize biases to justify extra-procedural and ultimately unequal treatment of marginalized and minoritized populations.

Closer examination of the dynamic interactions of states, dominant and subordinate political actors, and institutional settings reveal the tension between society and polity. These dynamics also reveal more abstract lessons useful for students of comparative politics, in the recognition that racial and ethno-national regimes, like the democratic polities in which they are often embedded, are not static institutions. They evolve and transform over time in response to shifting immigration, political, and economic developments.

France, Britain, and the US devised emergency or extraordinary laws to justify suspension of the rule of law in repressing social and political mobilization of marginalized groups; from the arrival of settler populations (preceded by invasion and conquest) which required protection to the maintenance of apartheid and apartheid-like interactions within their colonies. British use of exemplary force in Kenya was based upon tactics utilized in other posts of the British Empire: Ireland, India, South Africa, Malaya, Palestine, China, and Tibet, among other places. The efforts were not only to quell rebellion, but to warn, through the symbol of violence, potential sympathizers and activists of the consequences of contesting British rule. French counterinsurgency tactics deployed in what was then known as Indochina ultimately found their way into metropolitan policing in France. Counterinsurgency policies devised by US intelligence and military personnel were adopted and utilized upon national populations in Chile, Brazil, Guatemala, and El Salvador—by their own national governments. Counterinsurgency tactics, in what could be characterized as "shadow" US foreign policy, were utilized in covert operations against US citizens in the United States during the era of 1960s and 1970s social protest.

Second, political dissent among racialized groups was treated by governmental authorities—and the groups those governments represented—as threats to social order. Criminalization of political dissent by ethno-national and racialized minority groups recurred in all three cases. Evidence of how racial regimes functioned across cases is shown in the British repression of the Mau Mau revolt and the Kikuyu more generally (along with other ethnic groups in the region), France's treatment of North Africans (Algerians in particular) during the protracted war for independence (which was never formally acknowledged by the French government as a war), and criminalization of civil rights and other forms of black, indigenous activism during the 1960s and 1970s in the United States. In all three cases, national governments treated minority claims for sovereignty and autonomy as threats to the unity of the nation-state conjuncture. Thus, conflicts between the treatment by an imperial nation-state (whether through direct or indirect rule) of colonized populations were often considered problems of internal, domestic order rather than matters of international law and human rights. This justification allowed national governments to rationalize the use of force and tactics often associated with interstate war, conflicts involving noncitizens or citizens of other nation-states.[9]

The following abstract scenarios have their empirical referents in each of the cases:

Members of racialized, disempowered groups contest economic and social conditions (housing, employment, education), civil rights (freedom of assembly, voting, dissent), or cultural distinctiveness (religious expression, inhabiting of public space). Their activities entail engaging in demonstration and protest to question their paradox of societal integration and political exclusion. Activities include—but are not limited to—labor and civil rights movements and demand for equal access to housing, education, and employment, and relief from state incursions, including violence, into the daily lives of those less powerful groups.

Governments respond by employing techniques of statecraft to maintain state dominance, including but not limited to negotiation, cooptation, refusal, subversion, surveillance, coercion, and counterinsurgency. In all three cases, local, municipal, regional, and ultimately national governmental bureaucracies grew and expanded in response to the presence of ethnonational and racially marginalized populations and the demands of the larger constituencies for the maintenance of existing social and political arrangements. The dynamic interactions between actors seeking access to the polity and the actors and institutions seeking to deny such access altogether or closely limit the degree of polity penetration, lead to the simultaneous deepening and expansion of racially and ethno-nationally encoded institutions.

Over the past decade, renewed attention has generated valuable insights into various types of institutions, in particular distinguishing between institutions guided by formal rules, law and legislation, and institutions guided by norms rather than formal rules. In distinguishing between formal and informal institutions, scholars such as Helmke and Levitsky develop a useful typology to better comprehend the dynamic relation. Informal institutions often evolve in response to formal institutional dysfunction (weak or corrupt states, for example) or, at the other end of the spectrum, highly centralized modes of governance (authoritarian and totalitarian governments) that discourage creative, innovative responses to societal or governmental problems. Helmke and Levitsky's explication of informal institutions is motivated by a political truism: "Political actors respond to a mix of formal and informal incentives and in some instances, informal incentives trump the formal ones."[10]

Their typology outlines four types of informal institutions, based upon an initial two-part division between institutions that aim to heighten the functionality of formal institutions of governance and those whose objectives diverge and often undermine formal institutional objectives. In the case of state corruption involving kleptocratic regimes, for example, the use of public funds for private gain undermines the ability of a government to utilize tax revenues for collective goods such as roads, public libraries, and infrastructure. Helmke and Levitsky provide analytic nuance to this division by further distinguishing between complementary and divergent informal institutions. This added distinction is based upon "whether following informal rules produces a substantively similar or different result from that expected from a strict and exclusive adherence to formal rules"[11] and the degree of "effectiveness of the relevant formal institutions . . . the extent to which rules and procedures that exist on paper are enforced and complied with in practice."[12] They make clear that their methodological objectives are to move beyond functionalist accounts of institutional processes and effects by "identifying the relevant actors and interests behind informal institutions, specifying the process by which informal institutions are created, and showing how those rules are communicated to other actors in such a manner that they evolve into sets of shared expectations."[13]

First, minority groups in each instance have been clustered in particular areas, the consequence of de jure and de facto forms of spatial segregation. In many examples of extreme racial and ethno-national hierarchy, political actors occupy roles in formal as well as informal institutions designed to maintain a particular racial or ethno-national hierarchy. In the case of Brazil, for example (one of the cases cited by Helmke and Levitsky), many instances are documented in which police officers affiliated with municipal, state, and federal government conducted extra-judicial executions of street children and youth, a disproportionate number of them black and brown Brazilians, as a form of cleansing the streets of *vagabundos*.[14] Nearly 30 years after the documented existence of *esquadraos de morte* (death squads) in Brazil during the waning years of the dictatorship and early years of state democratization, police and paramilitary organizations have routinely targeted *negro* and *pardo* (black and brown) youth in the city and suburbs of Rio de Janeiro and Sao Paulo. The objects of extralegal assassination were not chosen randomly. Unfortunately, the racial dimensions of coercive informal institutions in Brazil remain largely unexplored by students of Brazilian democracy and social movements. Scholars on racism and inequality in Brazil, however, have studied this phenomena and its implications for Brazilian democracy, community policing, and public health.

Utilizing Helmke and Levitsky's concepts, racial and ethno-national regimes could be understood to constitute a hybrid institutional form. Across the three cases, state-sanctioned and extra-judicial acts of coercion against members of minoritized and racialized groups are important components of racial and ethno-national regimes. Spatial factors are important to consider in examining locales (cities, towns, or regions) with long histories of intergroup conflict and state-sanctioned violence against minoritized and racialized populations, especially when those populations have historically been alienated from positions of formal power and authority.

As in the case of the United States, Jim Crow and other modalities of formal segregation were often supplemented with arbitrary extralegal violence to punctuate the racial order. Under these conditions, the informal institutions created to coordinate acts of extralegal violence were consistent with the aims and objectives of the formal state institutions. In many instances the actors were the same, even if the venues and circumstances in which extralegal orders were meted out were distinct. In France, the banlieues of suburban Paris and other regions of France are important coordinates in the racial-spatial order. In Britain, neighborhoods like Brixton in London, Handsworth in Birmingham, Moss Side in Manchester, Toxteth in Liverpool, and Pakistanis in Bradford have also been treated as distinctly minority spaces. In each of the cases, spatial factors are important considerations in at least two distinct ways.

The temporal dimensions of racial and ethno-national regimes are identified in the changes in institutional laws and norms over time. Social movements that have effected institutional and societal change (feminist or womanist, civil rights and antidiscrimination movements) helped bring about changes in law, norms, and procedures of governmental authorities at various levels, including but not limited to police departments. In many instances, however, changes in federal law were often not accompanied by shifts in local institutional cultures, which often resisted the assimilation of newcomers; the Great Migration in the US, the Maghrebi and Sub-Saharan Africans in France, and South Asian, Caribbean, and African immigrants and residents in Britain. Here is where the formal and informal institutions have often diverged, when changes in national law were not unilaterally applied across the country; they were rejected or ignored in parts of the territory where racial and ethno-national regimes are too deeply intertwined with fundamental governmental institutions to dislodge. Institutional racism can thus coexist alongside formal changes in law designed to reflect changes in norms that publicly prohibit discrimination.

The Cases

With these conceptual tools and containers, we can identify and examine racial and ethno-national regimes in France, Britain, and the United States. The British Empire and later Commonwealth, the role of the US government and corporate interests in Cuba and the Philippines, France's administration of ethno-national and racial hierarchies in its départements of the French Antilles, West Africa, and Indochina, provide ample evidence of policies implemented with the objective of distinguishing and separating populations according to ethno-national, racial criteria. These criteria then became the legal basis for rights claims not only in the sphere of formal politics, but in education, marriage and sexual relations, employment, and land tenure and ownership.

One key difference between ethno-national and racial regimes in France and those of the US and Britain is the French Republic's historical prohibitions against ethno-national and racial statistics. Successive British and French governments devised and disseminated propaganda that highlighted the exceptional and democratic character of its political cultures that undergirded, rather than contradicted, their respective histories of colonialism and imperialism. Their conquests and colonization of peoples, just like their versions of parliamentary and republican democracy, were exceptional, imbued with a democratic telos. British and French governments along with their intelligentsia and elites juxtaposed their histories in contrast with the United States. What the three nation-states have in common, however, is what could be characterized as state impression management: the dissemination of propaganda, often in formal public policy, as exceptional nation-states and civilizations in global geo-politics, distinguished by their commitments to democracy and not a racial world order.

Third, national governments in each case relied upon strategies and tactics to manage minority populations, combining bureaucratic controls with coercive practices for dissenting members of minority populations and in instances where settler, expatriate populations called for protections from local indigenous populations. Scholarly examination of the political life of minoritized and marginalized populations have often helped highlight the disjuncture between public law, state ideology, and creed, on the one hand, and political inequality on the other.

The examples below highlight the occasions when the application of liberal law were restricted to polity dynamics involving foundational, Euro-descendent members. French, British and US governments simultaneously developed and deployed differentialist regimes to administer to the specific problems posed by the presence of "unassimilable" minorities and their efforts to gain state and societal recognition. Thus, liberal public law was the ultimate source of political inequality.

Some specialists might object to the framework of this chapter based on a distinction between a colonial state or government and a central government that constituted two distinct governmental authorities designed to administer two distinct territories and populations. Yet the number of examples in the British, US, and French cases wherein governments intervened in the conflicts and dynamics in colonial territory to protect local interests of expatriate communities reveals a degree of coordination and collusion between colonial and central governments. These instances prompt a need for comparativists to reexamine colonialism and its impact upon political development, in both colonial and metropolitan settings. Analytically, such an examination also requires some skepticism regarding the formal distinctions between democracy and foreign policies made by representatives of state, their intelligentsia and elites, that has served as part of a Foucauldian regime of truth.

Britain: Migrated Archives and the State's Reputation

In 2011, the British government acknowledged the existence of previously classified documents culled from the colonial administrations of territories governed by the British Empire. Known as the "migrated archives" controversy, the decision of the High Court to reveal the existence of a secret archive of documents chronicling Britain's role during the era of decolonization was an unprecedented event in the history of British governmental management, not only of its colonial archives but also its colonial legacy. Prompted by the decision of the High Court, the Foreign and Commonwealth Office admitted, after years of denial, of the existence of a secret archive of over two thousand boxes with 8,800 files from 37 former colonies and dependencies. This cache of documents is only part of a larger tranche of documents held by the British government that have not been declassified, some going back to the late 19th century. Previously inaccessible documents made available by the revelation of the migrated archives controversy revealed that while copies of some of these materials were available elsewhere, many significant files were not. The controversy also revealed that different documents had met different fates. While some files had been transferred to Hanslope, London, a high security facility, other material had either been burned or dumped into the sea.

Revealed in many files for the first time is official state documentation of counterinsurgency, espionage, torture, and assassination tactics coordinated and supervised by the British government in many of their former colonial territories and, in some cases, former colonial holdings that became independent nation-states—Kenya and British Guyana. Several scholars in the United States, Britain, Africa, and Asia, along with national governments presiding over populations and territories that were once part of the British Empire, long claimed that the British government had—and hid— documentary evidence of subversion, torture, and repression of national independence movements. In one of the ironies of revisionist historiography, evidence of an official documentary record of British strategies to destabilize several emergent independence governments was discovered in the National Archives of Kenya, a former British colony and a site for one of the most organized and militant responses to British colonial rule, the Mau Mau.

Several scholarly reputations were vindicated by the High Court's decision. David Anderson of Oxford, Caroline Elkins of Harvard University, and Huw Bennett of Kings College London had long asserted the existence of archival evidence of British torture in Kenya, and claimed that a significant cache of materials chronicling British activities in colonial Kenya were missing from the national archives of Kenya.[15] Along with that in Malaya and Guyana, documentation of British decolonization in Kenya has provided the most evidence of atrocities committed by British imperial troops, in coordination with colonial administrators and armed forces plus indigenous loyalists, in response to indigenous mobilization for economic and political sovereignty.

In the case of Kenya, British repression of the Mau Mau revolt, in response to claims by white expatriate settlers of imminent danger, provides ample evidence not only of the actions undertaken by British, colonial, and loyalist forces to enforce, in the words of several scholars, a "gulag": forced labor, resettlement, deprivation of food, livestock and territory, summary executions, and rapes. As Bennett, Elkins, and Anderson conclude in their respective scholarship, these practices were not the result of rogue or isolated military personnel committing atrocities without authorization from superiors. In Kenya and elsewhere in the British Empire, "Widespread mistreatment of the civilian population was legitimated via a complex legal regime. The British created a permissive legal environment conducive to atrocity behavior which none the less contained elements of restraint strong enough to forestall genocidal practices. Law was indeed central to British counter-insurgency, but not in the way normally understood."[16] British policy and covert action regarding the Mau Mau in Kenya can also be contrasted with Britain's lenient policy toward the apartheid state Rhodesia (now Zimbabwe) well into the 1970s.

Central to British imperial strategy during the era of decolonization after World War II was to develop what could be characterized as—to paraphrase

Erving Goffman[17]—impression management regimes, to project a character-ization of the British government's relation to its former colonies as gradu-alist and tutelary with an emphasis on restraint and fairness. What emerges from these revisionist accounts, however, is a British colonial government, in consultation with British metropolitan government, with two interrelated political objectives: structuring the conditions under which formal sover-eignty would be granted, which entailed the repression and neutralization of anticolonial and nationalist opposition during both the colonial and in-dependence period, and the protection of the white expatriate communities who were at once aggressive toward the Kikuyu, Embre, and other indige-nous peoples of Kenya, and fearful of them.

In the specific case of Kenya, it is important to note that these policies were developed and implemented upon the Kikuyu and other populations in response to claims by the white British expatriate community, many of them former colonial officers, bureaucrats, and entrepreneurs, that their way of life was threatened by the presence of disgruntled local populations, the Mau Mau in particular. The Mau Mau deeply resented the encroach-ment upon their territory and the diminution of their lands for both resi-dential and agricultural purposes. The Kikuyu population—not just the Mau Mau—was brought to starvation as a consequence of British colonial policy aimed at quelling the rebellion. The British putatively used colonial admin-istration to "ease" the transition from colonial rule to independence, but actually deployed counterinsurgency strategies designed to neutralize, iso-late, and, when necessary, exterminate opposition to British postcolonial presence and exploitation of their territory. It is important to note that the British government implemented a counterinsurgency strategy upon a pop-ulation in a territory that was already independent and a member of the British Commonwealth.[18]

In addition to the vindication of scholarly reputations, however, there are at least four other implications of the migrated archives controversy. First, blithe proclamations of a more benevolent brand of British impe-rialism upheld by British scholars such as Niall Ferguson can be laid to rest, with evidence of atrocities rivaling, in some particularly gruesome instances, the tactics used by French, German, Belgian, and Dutch impe-rial nation-states during the period of European domination of much of the non-Western world. Second, there is primary evidence that succes-sive British governments, via their colonial apparatus and covert foreign policies, were instrumental in forestalling or limiting the very forms of democratic political culture proclaimed by British statespersons as the legacy of British rule bequeathed to its colonies: participatory democracy, freedom of expression and association, rule of law, transparency, and self-governance.

The era of decolonization and the proliferation of independence movements in the British Commonwealth exposed the gap between Commonwealth rhetoric and the desires of sovereignty on behalf of the colonized peoples in Africa, Asia, the Caribbean, and South America. Third, and most relevant for understanding the implications of the findings for comparative politics, the neat periodization of imperial and postimperial administration offered by several students of comparative colonialisms[19] is rendered less persuasive. On the contrary, the revelations evidenced the maintenance of the ethno-national and racial regimes in the formerly colonial outposts of the British Empire well after formal independence from Britain.

Other files provided information already available and corroborated British destabilization of British Guyana during its period of self-rule leading up to independence. For example, the British central government—with the assistance of US intelligence and personnel—exacerbated conflict between the two major demographic groups in the country, Afro-Guyanese and Indo-Guyanese, which helped undermine the prospect of national unity on the eve of independence.

There are few accounts within comparative politics that address this moment in British imperial history and its implications for how we understand the relationship between democracy and political development. Rather than view the relationship between a fledgling democratic polity and its former colonizer in dyadic and ultimately isolated terms, we would have to understand the relationship between the British government and its former colonies, such as Kenya and Guyana, wherein the political calculus of the Cold War—as well as the racial hierarchy integral to British imperialism—influenced subsequent relations between the British government and the newly independent nation-states of the Commonwealth. In his study of empire, multiethnic polities, and decolonization, Hendrik Spruyt concludes that Britain's policy of decolonization enabled its metropolitan government to reconfigure "its territorial framework without getting embroiled in colonial quagmires, save for incidental clashes such as in Kenya and Malaya."[20] The analysis presented here demonstrates that these and other clashes between the British governmental and insurgent nationalist movements in former colonies were more than incidental and were, in fact, more widespread across other cases.

A skeptic's view of this interpretation might suggest that the British government was merely trying to provide protections and assurances for the expatriate British population in Kenya. Yet British expatriates, those British citizens living outside of Britain, could be found throughout the Commonwealth (with Jamaica and India as disparate examples), as well as in places not part of the Commonwealth. These expatriates, like expatriate communities everywhere, experience the unfamiliarity and anxiety associated with living in a foreign locale. By the 1950s, however, British expatriate communities were scattered about most of the world, even in territories not colonized by the British. Why would the British government authorize counterinsurgency measures in Kenya? Part of the explanation offered by Huw Bennett, Caroline Elkins, Jock McCullogh, and David Anderson is the role of what historian Aline Helg, writing in an entirely different political context, characterized as "icons of fear,"[21] anxieties about white subordination and subjugation at the hand of blacks invoking race war in retaliation for years of exploitation. These fears, expressed in symbols, imagery, and narrative, contained representations of an overwhelming black presence taking full material and political advantage of subjugated whites in many areas of life, but especially political, economic, and sexual domination. Symbols of sexual domination focused almost exclusively on the rape of white women by black men. As in many instances of social conflict described as "racial," gendered dynamics are embedded within so-called racial or racist dynamics. The icons of fear prompted by a gendered racism represented the collective anxieties of the white expatriate community in the aftermath of independence that were largely based upon projections of their own experience with subjugating local indigenous populations and in the rare instances of theft, murder, or rape of whites by Kikuyu and members of other ethnic groups.

Spruyt nevertheless does provide a very useful explanation for why, in certain cases, imperial governments might veto a negotiated settlement of territorial disputes between a newly sovereign nation-state and former colony and the imperial sovereign that formerly presided over their territory: "When key groups (such as business elites, settlers, or the military) take a hard-line stance, and when politicians share their preferences for strategic or ideological reasons, a change in political territory becomes less likely if political institutions provide many veto opportunities."[22] Spruyt's explication is useful not only for the British case examined here, but for the case of France of the 5th republic, which presided over the protracted war with Algeria between 1958 and 1962.

Another implication of the more than incidental strategy of the British, French, and US governments in administering racial and ethno-national regimes during periods of colonial and neocolonial relations is the blurring of the distinction between domestic and foreign policy. This blurring is evidenced in how French and British governments in particular often transferred and applied policies and techniques of colonial rule to manage minoritized domestic populations, and conversely, extended policies of racial and ethno-national hierarchy from the domestic sphere into colonial and satellite societies.[23] This latter form of ethno-national and racial hierarchy was more explicit and prevalent in US foreign policy, particularly in its application of Jim Crow practices in colonial and trading outposts where white governmental administrators and entrepreneurs were forced to interact with black, brown, and indigenous populations in negotiating terms of labor, production, and trade.

In the case of Britain, the migration and disappearance of archival records could not be undertaken without explicit arrangements involving domestic and foreign policy bureaucracies of the same state apparatus. The migrated archives, in effect, made the records of colonial micromanagement and administration part of domestic politics. Colonial administration, records, and rule were, in effect, domesticated. Victims seeking redress for human rights violations administered by the British government outside the metropolitan center could now bring their cases before a British court, generating precedent for subsequent litigation by victims of imperial coercion in other corners of the British Commonwealth.[24]

Context for British Case

Proponents of the British Empire left ample evidence of their commitment to ideologies of Anglo-Saxon racial and civilizational superiority in relation to the rest of the human race, in literature, prose, governmental policies, and in popular cultures from its heyday in the 19th century until its demise after World War II. Lord Chamberlain, Bryce, Disraeli, Kipling, Churchill, and more contemporarily, Margaret Thatcher, referred to the British state's longstanding emphasis on democracy and fair play, even while Britain presided over a disparate and significant array of colonial territories in Asia, Africa, and the New World.

Both World Wars forced British governments to subordinate the rhetoric of Anglo-Saxon racial supremacy since the survival of the British empire required the assistance of the darker races in the British imperial armed forces Representatives for both the British government and its colonial states were aware that they could not, on the one hand, declare the inferiority of their subjects while seeking the support of Indian, West Indian, and African troops on the battlefields. Britain's problems in the Far East, as one student of British foreign policy in the region during this period noted,[25] were symptomatic of the larger balancing act the British government had to conduct in its relations with its darker-skinned colonial subjects; to promote a true commonwealth of equal partners, the British government could not openly promote racial hierarchy and exclusion among its members. The clear exception to this rule, of course, was the Republic of South Africa, with leaders like Jan Smuts and Frantz Botha, aggressive advocates of white racial supremacy, apartheid, and penurious labor regimes for its black subjects.

For example, two years after the Armistice and Treaty of Versailles officially terminated World War I, the British government convened the Imperial Conference of 1921 in London. The conference brought together the prime ministers and representatives of the United Kingdom, the dominions, and India. Japan's increasing belligerence and imperialist aggression against China, Britain, and the United States was the major topic of the conference and signaled the demise of the Anglo-Japanese alliance that held through the Treaty of Versailles. British Prime Minister Lloyd George used the discussion of the paradoxical role of the Japanese in United Kingdom and global geo-politics to underscore the potential dangers of racial conflict within the empire:

> No greater calamity could overtake the world than any further accentuation of the world's divisions upon the lines of race. The British Empire has done signal service to humanity in bridging those divisions in the past. . . . To depart from that policy, to fail in that duty, would not only greatly increase the dangers of international war; it would divide the British Empire against itself. . . . It would be fatal to the Empire.[26]

The irony of Lloyd George's statement noted above is the British Empire's refusal to include a racial equality clause in the Versailles document at the request of the Japanese, Britain's former ally, just two years earlier, an act that angered the Japanese and Indian delegations at Versailles. The refusal on the part of the UK and US to support the antiracialist clause helps partially explain Japan's belligerence toward its former allies in the years leading up to World War II. Given Britain's imperial legacy of racial hierarchy in its own ordering of the commonwealth of nations and its support of the apartheid regimes of South Africa and Rhodesia after World War II, one could wonder which "service to humanity" the British provided on this score. Nonetheless, George's identification of a potential chink in the armor of the empire is an acknowledgement of racial conflict as a potential political problem for the United Kingdom, a problem that required statecraft.

Commentary and speeches by other participants in the 1921 Imperial Conference, particularly the prime ministers of Australia, New Zealand, and Canada, mark two general concerns among participants. First was the US withdrawal from a faltering League of Nations. Second, the prospect of race wars within Europe, and between European nation-states and peoples in other parts of the world, led several governmental representatives to acknowledge the deeply plural character of the British Empire. W.F. Massey, prime minister of New Zealand, commenting on the value of partnership within the British Commonwealth, stated,

> Even a partnership of nations, any more than a nation, cannot stand still. We must either progress or decay . . . there is a far stronger power in the British Empire today than any words that may be placed upon paper . . . the sentiments of the British people. . . . . I am not speaking merely of Anglo-Saxons or Europeans, or any one race. I am speaking of the British people right through the Empire, including the native races.[27]

Platitudes of global peace and racial harmony notwithstanding, the British Empire clearly had its favored nations, those led by what were considered descendants of Anglo-Saxons and, at a minimum, Europeans. Marquess Curzon, secretary of state for foreign affairs for the United Kingdom, a key voice in the discussions and deliberations at the 1921 Imperial Conference, considered the United Kingdom to consist not of one empire, but three, in ascending order of importance: Sub-Saharan Africa, the least significant culturally; Asia, which extended from Egypt to Hong Kong with India as the jewel at the center; and the dominions of South Africa, Australia, Canada, and New Zealand, considered the acme of the British Empire and transnational representation of its civilization.[28]

As noted by Mazower,[29] the British had to maintain the balancing act of advocating a belief in the racial supremacy of the Anglo-Saxon, Teutonic, and Aryan races and their destiny to rule over the lesser races of Africa and Asia (as well as Latin America), while at the same time securing the vital support of those lesser races in the war effort and in generating the wealth that provided the material basis for the imperial and capitalist class of Britain. This balancing act was perhaps best evidenced in the political career of Jan Smuts, prime minister of South Africa, fervent proponent of Anglo-Saxon world supremacy and apartheid rule, and a principal architect in both British imperial policy and in drafting the League of Nations charter.

The combination of denial and recognition of the role of race in Britain's imperial design and geopolitics would find its way into domestic policy, particularly after 1945. The Second World War further underscored Britain's dependence upon its colonial subjects and dominions to assist in the war effort to defeat its former World War I ally Japan, as well as Nazi Germany and Italy. In one sense, Britain's predicament on the eve of World War II was similar to the challenge faced by the Austro-Hapsburg monarchy at war with Russia on the eve of the Austrian revolution. As noted by Ashley Jackson, Britain's great challenge in World War II was to defeat or at least stave off the Axis onslaught while keeping its empire intact. Jackson puts it succinctly: "Britain had a global empire to defend and an economy dependent on global trade."[30] The last strategic fact entailed conscription of colonial troops throughout the empire, safeguarding key strategic positions against hostile forces, and protection of trade and supply routes in the Mediterranean, Asia, the Caribbean, and the African continent.

As noted by Layton-Henry, Small, and Solomos in their different assessments of British statecraft in the post–World War II period, Britain's policy of decolonization was not a function of some liberal, democratic telos inscribed into British governance across the ages, intrinsic to British imperial governance, but the geo-political realities of era. Britain's political leadership recognized the limits of its military capacities both as a standing, conventional army and in its ability to engage in unconventional warfare. Successive British governments sought to avoid race as a factor in the ordering of British society in its metropolitan core—in its immigration policies and relations with commonwealth nation-states. As with France, part of the successive British governments' approach to racial politics was to ignore its existence in foreign and domestic policy, even to the point of denying that these policies contributed to racial tensions in their own countries and in their interactions abroad.

One dimension of British statecraft was the denial-acknowledgement conjuncture evident in the British government's preoccupation with safeguarding white British citizens abroad. The obvious difference between the colonial and metropolitan setting is that whites in colonial outposts constituted a largely settler (and therefore minority) population. The reverse was true in British metropolitan society, where black and Asian British subjects, as well as black and Asian British citizens, constituted the minority populations from which Britain's largely white citizenry needed protection. In both contexts, however, successive British governments formulated and implemented policies designed to limit nonwhite population movement and circulation among white British citizens in both expatriate and metropolitan society. The racial and ethno-national regimes devised by the British government represent the institutional articulation of an underlying anxiety that Britain's colonized subjects, particularly the politically and racially inferior, would exact revenge upon their masters, mentors, and tutors.

For the British government, decolonization presented three specific challenges in the transition from an imperial nation-state to a postcolonial government that administered relations with its former colonies (the Commonwealth). First, the structural damage and loss of life within England during World War II made the maintenance of empire increasingly difficult politically and less profitable economically. The process of decolonization initiated by the British government during the 1940s involved the indigenization of local bureaucratic authority in many of its soon-to-be-former colonies: Africanization of colonial governments in British Africa, and self-rule before independence in several Caribbean nations. Third, the influx of former colonial subjects into "Mother England" prompted changes in immigration law and policy. Changes in immigration policy were crafted in response to popular fears of being overwhelmed by nonwhite Commonwealth subjects, and by the politicians' ability to exploit these fears for political advantage. Well into the 1970s both Labour and Conservative political parties expressed support for specific immigration controls for Africa, Asia, and the Caribbean.

The African, Asian, and Caribbean emigrants who arrived in Britain during this period symbolized the end of a long phase of British dominance, but also the increasingly blurred lines between British subject and citizen, foreigner and native, center and periphery, metropolitan and colonial governance, and foreign and domestic policy. The increased presence and visibility of African, Asian, and Caribbean immigrants and citizens in Britain prompted both public and governmental reactions.

As Small and Solomos write, the reaction to the postwar wave of immigration into Britain was unlike the popular and governmental reactions to previous generations of immigrants. Solomos, Gilroy, Small, and others point out that the increasing presence of Caribbean, Asian, and African emigrants to Britain generated very different types of national anxiety and discussion about the threat posed by immigration to society and a British "way of life,"[31] No other immigration stream into Britain generated a similar reaction among elite and popular political actors in society and government. To further underscore the uniqueness of the British governmental and popular (white) response, sociologist Robert Miles points out that Irish immigration into Britain was much greater in number than Asian, African, and Caribbean immigration combined.[32]

Many excellent studies of institutional and popular racism in British society have been undertaken since formal decolonization. What will be emphasized here is the development of racial regimes in response to the perceived crisis of immigration, evidenced in the efforts by the British national municipal, and regional governments to maintain a racial order by delimiting educational, occupational, and residential opportunities for nonwhite British citizens and subjects seeking to reside in the United Kingdom, or as citizens already living there.

The development of these regimes was not always a coordinated effort between educational, real estate, and employment institutions in partnership with local, regional, and national central government. Rather, they were in a sense cumulative institutional responses to the influx of nonwhites into Britain. Those institutions devised ways of interpreting and administering nonwhite populations—providing evidence of how political institutions determine particular political phenomena as "racial,"—and sought to impose their own version of social and political order.

Thus, the presence of a proportionately small but symbolically significant number of Asian, African, and Caribbean immigrants posed political challenges for British government and society. Conversely, blacks and Asians had few formal political representatives advocating on their behalf in Parliament or other political institutions. In brief, blacks were largely viewed as a problem in British politics, society, and culture, as were Indian, Pakistani, Sri Lankan, and other South Asian populations. This view was reflected in several developments within British government, most notably in the creation of Race Relations Boards, as well as the overhaul of existing immigration regimes.[33] These developments were in direct response to popular and elite anxieties over the post-1945 immigration streams from nonwhite Commonwealth colonies and clamor from both right and left for increased scrutiny of these populations. Consequently, calls for increased scrutiny also affected the nonwhite British communities of African, Asian, and Caribbean descent that had lived in Britain for several generations and, in some instances, centuries.

The 1958 disturbances in Nottingham and Notting Hill (often erroneously referred to as "race riots") were the first significant postwar conflicts involving blacks, the state, and white Britons. The disturbances, which included rioting, violence, and loss of property, were precipitated by white youths who attacked blacks in these neighborhoods. Most public commentary, however, by mainstream journalism and by public officials, attributed the riots to immigration. Many politicians called for increased immigration controls, even repatriation of blacks who immigrated to Britain from other areas of the Commonwealth.

Four years later, the 1962 Commonwealth Immigrants Act specifically targeted non-Canadian, non-Australian, and non–New Zealand immigrants. This act shares some parallels with the McCarran-Walter Act in the United States in the 1950s, which set quota limits on immigration to the United States from countries with large black and brown populations. Subsequent immigration acts in 1968, 1969, and 1971 further curtailed nonwhite immigration and led to increased surveillance of blacks in British society. Commentary and analysis often used "immigrant," "black," and "Asian" interchangeably, even though black and Asian communities have been in Britain since the 17th century, with several generations of citizens among them.[34]

In the aftermath of the Notting Hill and Nottingham disturbances, the British Parliament approved the first in a series of Race Relations Acts, beginning in 1965. The Race Relations Act of 1965 established race relations and antidiscrimination boards in Britain. These boards combined community leadership with governmental officials. The 1976 Race Relations Act, for example, aimed at strengthening existing antidiscrimination policy by acknowledging the existence of institutional racism. The bill did not address, however, discrimination's effects. A subsequent series of Race Relations Acts were created through the 1970s until the shift in British politics brought about by the rise of Margaret Thatcher and the Conservative Party in the late 1970s and 1980s.

One distinguishing aspect of British governmental administration— reflected also in scholarship—was the deliberate framing of the presence of Asian and African residents in Britain as a problem of "race relations" and not symptomatic of either the residual effects of British imperial racism or broader institutional arrangements in British society and political culture. The political implications of race and race relations were also manifested in popular mobilization in political parties and social movements. During this period, both Labour and Conservative parties developed rhetorical and policy agendas designed to appeal to a cross section of British voters.

Black and Asian British citizens overwhelmingly voted Labour, although in recent years the Conservative Party has begun to attract a small percentage of black and Asian voters, a modest increase from virtually no political support from these populations for a Conservative Party agenda. The small increase in support among black and brown British citizens for more restrictive immigration policies is largely attributed to the large increase in white immigrants from the EU, particularly an influx of populations of what used to be known as East Europe: Poland, Romania, and Bulgaria. Increased attention, scrutiny, and debate over the presence and influx of nonwhite Britons also helped generate increased support for far right political parties and organizations.

In 1967, the National Front was founded as an umbrella organization of groups committed to "keeping Britain British" (an equation of "British" with white, Anglo-Saxon citizens) and strongly opposed to continued black and brown immigration. By the 1970s, National Front candidates in local elections drew portions of local electorates toward their anti-immigration and neofascist agenda. As a consequence, both Labour and Conservative parties lost portions of their constituencies to National Front candidates. In response to these political developments, the Labour Party Race Action Group was formed in 1975, involving white and black Labourites, to address charges of racism and insensitivity within the Labour Party itself.

By the mid-1970s, however, a shift in British politics began in the aftermath of the Labour Party victory in the 1974 elections. Several key Conservative Party intellectuals began to develop research institutes (think tanks) and public agendas advocating strategies that came to be known as the New Right. The Adam Smith Institute, the Institute of Economic Affairs, and Center for Policy Studies, three important think tanks for the New Right, were formed following the 1974 defeat. Keith Joseph, later knighted as Sir Keith Joseph, was considered the lead political architect of the New Right and the subsequent institutionalization of their ideas. The New Right agenda attacked Keynesian ideas, promoted privatization, and called for a review if not outright prohibition of nonwhite immigration. Mass media helped fuel the rise in New Right journalism. *The Economist, Daily Telegraph, Spectator,* and *The Times* all supported these ideas. Though not formal outlets of the National Front, their editorial disposition emphasized and championed a significantly reduced social welfare state and suspicion of certain immigrant populations.

Ideologically, New Right pundits and think tanks combined conservatism with liberalism, a belief in individual rights but with an emphasis on tradition and inherent wisdom of the status quo. Market forces were at once meritocratic and democratic. The action of buyers and sellers in the market was more important than government planners. At the time, this tendency was a minority in the Conservative party.

As in the United States during this period, a key distinguishing strategic feature of the Conservative and New Right was the use of "coded language" to appeal to white, especially working and middle class, voters without making explicit references to race. Prime examples of coded language appear in two speeches given by Enoch Powell and Margaret Thatcher, respectively in 1968 and 1977. In 1968 Enoch Powell delivered a speech at the University of Birmingham that subsequently was referred to as the "Rivers of Blood" speech, in which he warned of the dangers of imminent Anglo-Saxon obsolescence if nonwhite immigration into Britain went unchecked.

In a March 1977 interview on national television, Enoch Powell warned of a racial civil war in Britain. The same year, Margaret Thatcher echoed Powell's themes in commentary that articulated the anxieties of her conservative constituency by proclaiming that the arrival of new immigrants amounted to a "swamping" of British culture: "The British character has done so much for democracy, for law, and done so much throughout the world, that if there is any fear that it might be swamped, people are going to react and be rather hostile to those coming in."[35] This speech was a clear example of coded language used by members of Britain's New Right, wherein the word "immigrants" meant nonwhites and the term "swamped" echoed themes articulated in 1968 by Powell, a Thatcher cabinet appointee. Under Thatcher, institutions such as the Commission for Racial Equality became far less active on matters of racial discrimination than in previous governments.

During the first Thatcher government (1979–1983), Sir Keith Joseph was made secretary of state for industry. Joseph made the works of Austrian libertarian economist Friedrich Hayek and the US economist Milton Friedman required reading for senior civil servants. Joseph and other New Right acolytes called for stricter control of the money supply, rather than social policy and welfare expenditure.

Taken together, these ideas became the cornerstone of what has come to be known as Thatcherism, an ideological formation that married liberal principles of a free-market economy to conservative themes of tradition, family, nation, and law and order. Thatcherism resonates with the conservative liberalism of creole nationalists in 19th century Latin America (considered in chapter 3). Its success can be attributed to its ability to "articulate different social and economic interests" within a single political project. Emphasizing a form of what Stuart Hall referred to as authoritarian populism, Thatcher made appeals to "bread and butter" issues of the "common man and woman."[36] Like Reaganism in the United States, Thatcherism helped generate a critical realignment in British politics by transforming common assumptions from British government's welfare state model to a model of government that eschewed post–World War II notions of a social contract between the British state and its citizens.

For nonwhites emigrating to Britain from the Commonwealth, this narrowing of the social contract was more than metaphorical. In practical terms, the abrogation of a social contract could be evidenced in three ways: a reluctance or outright refusal to acknowledge the historical legacy of support nonwhite Commonwealth subjects provided to the British nation-state when it needed it most, during the First and Second World Wars; refusal to acknowledge the need for programs and policies that would help assimilate nonwhites into British society; and the lack of acknowledgement of the difficulties they faced in British society due to discrimination. In many black neighborhoods, for example in Liverpool and London, black male unemployment hovered around 40 percent well into the 1990s.[37] Unemployment and crime were often linked in New Right discourse, but in characterological terms as a failure in the collective character of recently arrived immigrants. This discourse was part of the shift to the right in British politics, with direct and indirect appeals to white voters, along with calls for law and order. In this sense, Thatcherism represented a total or comprehensive vision of British society and polity, one in which the presumption of racial difference and an emphasis on cultural—if not racial—homogeneity was a central ideational component of its vision of governance.

The lack of state attentiveness to racist violence was evidenced during the Thatcher administration. An arsonist blaze in March 1981 left 13 black youths dead in South London and generated community protest of the perceived indifference by London police at several arsonist attacks of black homes and community centers in South London. These events spurred community members and activists to conduct a march to Central London to protest police unwillingness to investigate the cause of the fire. Three months later, London's Metropolitan Police Department launched Operation Swamp 81, named, conveniently enough, in reference to Margaret Thatcher's famous interview in which she equated swamping with unwanted immigration of those populations who would threaten the British working and middle class way of life. While the majority of British citizens viewed Operation Swamp 81 as an example of successful policing, the operation generated increased distress among black and Asian populations in Britain. Over a six-day period, police stopped 943 people, most of them black, and arrested 118. The vast majority of those stopped were law abiding local residents. The Brixton Riots in April 1981, three months of intermittent protest, were the first major moments of racial politics during Thatcher's first term in office.

During this period, the Conservative party's immigration, nationality, and citizenship policy were consistent with Britain's racial regime. That same year, the British Nationality Act of 1981 was passed, which restricted British nationality to those who resided in the UK and those who had one British parent. Former Commonwealth subjects had no a priori right to enter Britain, an example of the dehistoricization of Britain's imperial legacy. By 1982, the number of British immigrants dropped to 54,000. By this time over 2 million nonwhites were in Britain, about 4 percent of the population, projected to be 6.7 percent by 2000. In addition, the Nationality Act contained a voluntary repatriation plan encouraging Commonwealth subjects who were not from New Zealand, Australia, or Canada to return to their Commonwealth even though in many instances Commonwealth "immigrants" were actually born in Britain. These policies continued during the second and third Thatcher administrations (1983–1987; 1987–1990).[38]

Perhaps the case that best demonstrated the racial regime modalities of British governance is the 1993 Stephen Lawrence case, considered a watershed moment in British racial politics. For the first time in British history, a governmental report acknowledged the existence of institutional racism within British police forces, evidenced in its relations with Afro-Caribbeans and Indo-Pakistanis in Britain; surveillance and harassment were disproportionate across the range of these populations (not just the youth). Indifference and hostility to minority community requests for police assistance in combating hate-based crimes were evidenced in the Stephen Lawrence case. Lawrence, a young black male, was chased, beaten, and ultimately stabbed to death by a group of local white youths with known ties to white racist organizations.

In a classic example of institutionalized racism, Lawrence's friends, also black, were waiting at the bus stop along with Lawrence when the attack took place. Instead of being treated as witnesses who potentially had viable information, they were treated as suspects. Additionally, neighborhood observers provided police with key clues regarding hidden evidence (including bloody clothing and a knife) that Lawrence's attackers had attempted to discard while Stephen Lawrence's friends were being investigated.

The public outcry led to protests, which prompted more aggressive governmental investigation into the possibility of structural, institutional racism not only in the Lawrence case, but in British police departments more generally. In his observations on the Stephen Lawrence case, Stuart Hall provides a definition of institutional racism in the British context that resembles the definition of racial regimes offered at the beginning of this chapter:

> Institutional racism does not require overtly racist individuals; it conceives racism as arising through social processes. . . . [in] institutional

racism . . . *culture* regulates *conduct.* These behavioural norms are carried within the occupational culture of an organization, and transmitted by informal and implicit ways through its routine, everyday practices as an indestructible part of the institutional *habitus.*[39]

Hall emphasizes the interactions between formal and informal institutions that combine to alter deliberation and decision-making processes to produce outcomes based not on available evidence, but on racist logic. The Stephen Lawrence incident, like similar incidents in Britain, France, and the United States, helps illuminate another aspect of institutional racism operative in racial regimes, particularly in instances of policing and the presumption of criminality. One of the hallmarks of institutionalized racism in policing is the difficulty police officials have in considering blacks and members of other nonwhite minority groups as victims of crime, or as law-abiding citizens, because of the accumulation of stereotypical assumptions of their criminality. Stephen Lawrence and his friends were transformed into criminals and potential criminals during the process of the initial police investigation, even when the police were presented with information that corroborated the interpretation of events offered by Lawrence's companions.

The accumulation of racist incidents disproportionately affecting black and brown communities in Britain was a factor in community protest, self-defense, and ultimately retaliation. The 2005 riots in Oldham, Burnley, and Bradford were precipitated by attacks by mobs of white men, some who were members of the National Front, on young Asian men. In retaliation, 500 Asian youths armed with petrol bombs and bricks attacked a pub, torched cars, and fought with police officers, sparked by the attack by white youths who vandalized houses belonging to Asians. In Bradford two racist gangs set upon Asian men after a football match. In response, two white brothers were beaten by twelve Asian men. Failure of police to protect Asians prompted the response by second- and third-generation Asian youths who were born and raised in Britain. Scholars of Britain consider these riots the worst in Britain since the Handsworth, Brixton, and Tottenham uprisings of 1985.

The historical context of riots, police harassment, right wing mobilization in political parties, and social movements, along with quotidian racism, are all factors cited by several important scholars of racism and immigration studies in Britain, and more recently, in interviews with "homegrown terrorists" in Britain. In Britain and France (the latter developed below), many youth who have joined groups committed to terrorist acts are children of immigrants and naturalized citizens who have had either a single, particularly traumatic experience with racism, or recalled constant, low-intensity microaggressions as integral, formative experiences in their lives.[40]

France

In France, the ideology of republicanism has long served as a powerful rhetorical tool to proclaim the French exception, the priority of the category of the citizen over ethno-national, religious, and presumed racial differences. Unlike Britain and the United States, identification of population difference among the citizenry has been actively discouraged. In the French popular imagination, racial categorization of French citizens was a national policy only during the period of the Vichy Regime, administered by the Third Reich during World War II, and thus a foreign imposition. Actual French history, which includes the history of republicanism, is much more complicated, however. Eugenicist thinkers such as René Martial flourished in France, as did the rightist and racist social movement Action Française, both before the Vichy Regime. Anti-Semitism in France can be traced back to the medieval period.

As in the British and US cases, the French government has often described its colonial and imperial past as a mutually beneficial partnership for colonizer and colonized alike; colonial subjects and immigrants were blessed with the *fraternité* and *égalité* of French culture and civilization, while French civilization and culture benefited from the contributions of non-European foreigners. As recently as 1998, then President Jacques Chirac declared that the 150th celebration of the abolition of slavery in the French colonies provided an opportunity for France "to welcome and integrate into the national community successive generations of men and women who have chosen to settle in our land. In return, these men and women, who have a rich culture, a rich history and rich traditions, have given new blood."[41]

There was no mention in Chirac's speech of the true costs—psychic, emotional, and material—of the integration of men and women from many external French départements into the metropolitan center: wars in Saint-Domingue (Haiti), Indochina, and Algeria, among other locales, pitting French colonial and national troops against local populations seeking national sovereignty and an end to colonial rule. The forced labor and production of the enslaved certainly helped drive the emergent maritime economy of France and generate profits for its capitalist class, the bourgeoisie. It is in

the interconnected history of the French metropole and its colonial départements and outposts that the origins of France's racial and ethno-national
regimes can be found.

The relations between France's colonies and its national government
reveal a complicated pattern of what could be characterized as inclusionary discrimination, in which certain ethno-national groups have been more
easily integrated into French society than others. French society contains
elements of the assimilation and segregation models, in addition to unique
features not attributable to either one.[42] Racism without races, to paraphrase
the work of David Theo Goldberg, exists in France. As noted by several
scholars, French governmental officials and public intellectuals across the
ideological spectrum have contrasted the so-called French republican model
with Anglo-Saxon (British and US) models of internal apartheid and spatial
segregation of immigrants and minorities. Silverman notes how the distinction between French and Anglo-Saxon models of immigration and integration have actually obscured how French governmental housing policies
helped create the ghettos (*banlieues*) in the suburbs of Paris that share similar
problems of relative isolation, disproportionately high unemployment, and
tensions between police and residents found in other plural societies.

Consider, by contrast to Chirac's declaration, the lyrics of a song written
by the French rapper Axiom. These lyrics provide some insight into perceptions among an increasing number of French-born residents and citizens of
African, Caribbean, and Maghrebi descent of their experiences as victims of
French racism as the unfulfilled promises of the ideology of republicanism:

> I am French and grew up in the popular neighborhoods,
>
> My grandparents also defended France during the war
>
> My parents they too rebuilt this republic
>
> Remember these workers who were brought from Africa
>
> And their children ignored by the jus soli law
>
> Second class citizens, from birth to school
>
> I accuse thirty years of racism and ignorance
>
> Repression without prevention in France
>
> I accuse your policies, your archaic methods
>
> Centralization, the sole defense of the law of money
>
> Instead of bringing us together because we are all French.[43]

Contrasted with Chirac's statement, the lyrics suggest that French republicanism has failed to integrate nonwhites into French society, coupled with the inability of French people to recognize the role of racism as a differentiating mechanism. Instead, many French nonwhites, youths in particular, experience limitations upon access to greater employment, housing, and educational opportunities and disproportionate police harassment, surveillance, and criminalization.

Between these competing understandings of the meaning of French colonialism and republican assimilation lie several centuries of French history and politics. Not surprisingly, studies of French history and politics relating to colonialism, immigration, racial discrimination, and exclusion in France and its former colonies vary widely not only in focus and quality, but in interpretation. Recent riots and disturbances in France, coupled with revelations by former French colonial officials, police, and military officers provided additional evidence to help distinguish French republican history from its ideological scaffolding. The practice of republicanism by the French state and its citizens has worked far better at integrating some populations than others. Recent scholarship in the past twenty years and increased access to primary materials from several civic, industrial, and governmental sources have provided scholars with more evidence of institutional racism in French politics and society.

The riots of 2005 and 2007 and the 2015 terrorist attacks intensified national discussion in France as well as an emergent recognition that racism is indeed among the complexities of social reality in contemporary French society. Yet, a careful examination of France's colonial and imperial past reveals recurrent patterns of institutional discrimination that have disproportionately and negatively impacted black and brown French citizens and subjects.

The Hippodrome attacks in 2015 generated intense debates about republicanism and multiculturalism. French public opinion ranged from support for republicanism on the right as a solution to communitarian empathies held by nonwhite French and their supporters, to denunciations of republicanism as the unmet promise of integration dangled before a portion of the citizenry whose families have lived in France for several generations but still do not feel French.

As in the Athenian case, explored in the previous chapter, the stakes for French republicanism extend beyond its metropolitan borders. Kurt Raaflaub, in his analysis of available writings after the Persian Wars of the

5th century, concluded that the apologists for Athenian colonization and subjugation of foreign lands and peoples believed they "had not deprived its colonial subjects of freedom, but rather given it to them."[44] Athenian rationalizations of expansion and subjugation resonate in French, British, and US justifications for expansion and colonization based on the premise that even under colonial governance, subject populations would fare better under the rule and tutelage of imperial nation-states with democratic polities.

French republicanism, like the majority of republican ideologies in Latin America (see chapter 3), emphasized citizenship—and therefore public and civic identification—over all other forms of identification. Nation, then, was presumed to trump religious, ethnic, gendered, and other forms of collective identification. And yet in practical terms, distinctions among populations had implicit and explicit legal implications in everyday life. France, known throughout Europe to accept and even encourage waves of European immigration in the 19th and early 20th centuries, imposed stricter immigration controls and popular scrutiny of nonwhite immigration into France. Like Germany, Britain, and Belgium in the post–World War II years, the French government encouraged and subsidized migration from its colonies and départements to offset dwindling labor pools.

In neither the French nor the British cases did nonwhite immigrants enter into culturally neutral environments undergirded by abstract, universalist ideals of national belonging. As noted by Joseph Carens in his critique of allegedly neutral, antidifferentialist renderings of contemporary Canada, assumptions of neutrality and uniformity in society often ignore implicit and explicit cultural bias. Similarly, Weil notes that French republicanism assumes that to be French does not also mean to be Catholic, European, and white. Hence the debates and vitriol around policies and statements about who is, actually, an "immigrant" and who is French. A Breton can be French, but can a North African? Why were Portuguese, Spanish, and Eastern European more readily integrated into French society in the 20th century than Guadeloupeans, Martinicans, Algerians, and Beninois?

With the relative absence of explicit racial and racist language in mainstream media, public statements by governmental officials, and in legislation, scholars of contemporary France have begun to pay closer attention to relative valorization of certain ethnic groups and the derogation or distancing techniques devised to describe less valued groups that are also part of the French nation. Groups who are most often described as part of the national fabric are ethnic, while the groups who are still framed through coded language as somehow not quite French are characterized as other and unassimilable.

The Racial and Ethno-National Regimes of France: Historical Context

Conflicts in contemporary France over the presence of nonwhite populations in French society provides an opportunity to situate contemporary debate and policy about multiculturalism and difference in some historical context. Despite republican proclamations, racial and ethno-national regimes can be identified at different moments in French history, within its colonies and départements , as well as in contiguous territorial France.

The earliest example of such policies can be found in the medieval period under the French monarchy and prior to the era of republicanism. Karen Barkey and Ira Katznelson explore how both English and French monarchies used the threat of expulsion to extort taxes from Jews living within the territory. With promises of time-sensitive state protections, revenues generated from such taxation were crucial to state building. Through a review of state and fiscal policies toward Jews between the 13th and 14th centuries, the authors demonstrate that monarchies in England and France imposed taxes upon Jews as payment for security, which, in essence, was a form of extortion. Jews, "had been important fiscal assets for kings, helping to provide funds for territorial expansion and protection through warfare. They had also been useful as buffers between the crown and society, deflecting fiscal pressures to a widely disliked group."[45] Among the five key points the authors propose for their contribution to literature about state-making and the history of the Jews (specifically expulsions) is to highlight the limitations of "historical sociology's standard chronology of state building in early modern Europe . . . [that] regrettably tends to ignore earlier, precursor innovations in the medieval period."[46]

When we consider the broader implications of their empirics, Barkey and Katznelson's study makes an additional contribution to comparative politics. Revenue extraction, spatial segregation in both society and polity, extrusion and forced migration of targeted groups is characteristic of racial and ethno-national regimes. These regimes require bureaucrats, law, deliberation, ritual, and procedure operating within the framework of governmental authority and of course, overwhelming coercive capacity. Secondly, modern states, in the development of laws, procedures, and institutions,

have often taken their cues from premodern periods and forms of governmental authority in response to crisis and uncertainty. These cues can be
rooted in a historic dislike for specific populations due to cultural aversion,
labor competition, fears of upsetting demographic balance, xenophobia,
and racism, or any combination of these factors. Policies of the past become
guides for state practices in more recent moments of uncertainty.

Policies designed to restrict Jewish participation in French society continued well into the early Republican period. Sephardic and Ashkenazi Jews
were permitted to become French nationals in 1790 and 1791, respectively,
and in accordance with Republican ideals were acknowledged as citizens
of France, not as Jews. Until 1830 however, Jews had to pay a religious tax
directly to the French government. Earlier in 1808, Napoleon decreed Jews
were prohibited from borrowing or lending money. This law was in effect
until 1818. Thus, across the monarchial and medieval eras, through the periods of the First and Second Republic, state restrictions were imposed upon
Jewish participation in the economic and religious life in French society.

Similarly, laws either denying or limiting black civic participation in
France and its colonies also predates the republican period. The Code Noir
(Black Code) adopted into French law in 1685 regulated slave life in the colonies until 1848 when slavery was finally abolished, over 50 years after the successful overthrow of the monarchy installed the First Republic. Slaves were
considered property and, as a consequence, were not entitled to property
rights or the rights of individuals. Slaves attempting to escape were branded
and their ears cropped; a second attempt led to the slave's hamstrings being
cut; a third attempt was met with execution without appeal. As in the Anglo-
phone and Spanish colonies, slaves could not participate in colonial court
and juridical proceedings as claimants or plaintiffs and could not testify
against whites under any circumstances. Although issued by royal decree,
the code was "drafted in the Antilles by the highest officials in the islands,
the Governor-General and the Intendant"[47] who based their conclusions on
firsthand experience with slaves, the plantation economy, and slaveholders
in the French colonies. In this sense, the Code Noir was a very practical law.

The punitive aspects of the Code Noir only represent one aspect of
the code's regulatory aims. As Tyler Stovall notes, the code also included
"proscriptions against assembly, alcohol use, flight and interracial sexual
relations."[48] As anthropologists remind us, regulatory laws and practices
specifically designed to regulate behaviors among subordinated, marginalized populations invariably reveal the actual behaviors of dominant groups
in their relations with them. Sexual unions between slaves and masters were

commonplace in all French colonies, and no more so than in the New World. French colonial officials often lived openly with slave mistresses and so-called mixed race or mulatto women. Léger-Félicité Sonthonax, the colonial administrator of one portion of the French colony, lived openly with a mulatto woman and ultimately prescribed his own demise by freeing slaves without the approval of the metropole.

As in the British and US cases, the gendered component of ethno-national and racial regimes are embedded in structuring dynamics between male and female gendered subjects within dominant and subordinate groups. To put a finer point on this observation, the portion of Code Noir that focuses on miscegenation, much like antimiscegenation laws in many slaveholding locales, is a recognition of the relations (however constituted) between white men and black, mulatto, and in some cases, indigenous and Asian women. Relations between black and mulatto men and white women was considered a far worse transgression of the racial order and prompted more severe coercive responses.

This aspect of the Code Noir also provides evidence of the difficulties in actually managing segregation. A slaveholding society that was originally designed to manage one population (the enslaved) not only had to manage the behaviors of slave owners, but, as a consequence of procreation, also had to manage a third population—mulattos. Mulattos were proof that white French men, whether living in the colonies or in France, had routinely broken this particular prohibition of the Code Noir.

In addition to the code's impact in colonial France, it would also be used in metropolitan France to limit political participation of freed blacks in the 18th century. In practical terms, the application of these laws to free blacks reduced the status of black freedpersons in the republic to little more than slaves.[49] In fact, the code's impact stretched to Canada as well as what became the United States, since it was cited and applied by US and Canadian judges in court cases involving escaped slaves in Canada and in the French settlement of Louisiana. An amended and amplified Code Noir was introduced for the province and colony of Louisiana in 1724 for this purpose. In addition to prohibitions against sexual relations between whites and blacks, the Louisiana codes also called for all slaves to be baptized and educated in Roman Catholicism. Several scholars have noted how, in French as well as other empires with plantation economies, religious instruction and socialization often conflicted with the economic imperatives of slave regimes. In most cases, whether in the French, British, or Spanish colonies, religious worship was subordinated to the production demands of a plantation economy.[50]

Yet there is another, much less explored aspect of the Code Noir that provides further evidence of its regulatory role as a racial and ethno-national regime. The requirement of religious instruction for slaves in the Code Noir was not only intended to indoctrinate the slaves in the selective interpretation of the Bible offered by colonial and monarchial clergy, but to limit the spread of Judaism in the French colonies. In fact, the opening article of the Code Noir specifically instructs French officials to rid its colonies of Jews. This provision in article 1 of the Code Noir was written in 1683, two years prior to the official publication of the code, and just before the French king's decision to ban Jews from the French isles that same year. Palmer suggests that the inclusion of prohibitions against Jews in the Code Noir stems from "the resolution of a long-smoldering controversy surrounding their slaves, their commercial activities and their freedom of conscience in the Antilles."[51] The Jesuits, who opposed the presence of Jews and Huguenots in the Antilles, appealed to the crown and to colonial officials to evict Jews from the region. Several local laws particular to specific islands forbade Jewish commercial activities within the region. The decisions of 1683 and later, and the revocation of the Edict of Nantes in 1685, made anti-Jewish regulations applicable throughout France's colonial dominion in the Caribbean.

Although slavery was abolished by the French in their colonies in 1794 by what is known as the French Convention, Napoleon reinstituted the slave trade in 1802. The most lucrative commodity resulting first from indentured and later slave labor brought France great wealth. The port cities of Bordeaux and Nantes would profit greatly from this trade, and it would help lift, by the 19th century, Bordeaux into an agricultural powerhouse of mostly wine production, fostered in part from the investments of slave and sugar profits. In the 18th century, the ports of Nantes, Bordeaux, La Rochelle, and Le Havre sent out 2,800 ships for the triangular trade that outfitted finished goods from Europe to Africa for trade; then ships were loaded with slaves, who were then brought to the Caribbean to work on the French plantations to produce mostly sugar and rum. During the 18th century alone, scholars estimate 1 million slaves were brought to these islands. By the end of the 18th century, one-eighth of the metropolitan French population made their living in some aspect of the colonial slave trade.[52]

A momentous year in European political history, 1848 was also significant for the creation of the Second French Republic. Slavery in French territories was officially abolished—over forty years after the success of the Haitian Revolution—and Algeria was reorganized as three départements of France. After 1848, Algeria became a host locale for immigrants from the Mediterranean and an outpost for the French government to deport undesirables (political subversives). By 1865, measures to facilitate the naturalization of these immigrants at their demand had been established. In 1870, Algerian Jews became French citizens. In 1889, the law facilitated naturalization and established strong enticements to all European settlers in Algeria to become French citizens.

The indigenous Algerian population did not enjoy the same privileges, however, and were defined by the French government as subjects, not citizens. The period between 1830 and 1845 was what the French government referred to as the period of "pacification" of Algeria, two years before Algeria became a département of France. France's other African holdings— Cameroon, Togo, Mali, Madagascar, Dahomey, Ivory Coast, Upper Volta, Chad, Senegal, Mauritania, the Central African Republic (Congo), and Morocco—were all French colonies that achieved independence during what Eric Hobsbawm has referred to as the glory years of nationalism, between 1955 and 1970. For 19th century Algerians, Muslim law, not French law, provided rules of private conduct. Algerians had to renounce their Islamic civil status and undergo a formal process of naturalization to obtain full nationality. Only a few thousand Algerians who went through the process succeeded in becoming French citizens by the time of Algerian independence in 1962.

Scholars of France who have specialized in the nexus of immigration, citizenship, and colonialism have provided valuable revisionist accounts of the shifting criteria and purpose of French citizenship. Republican ethos notwithstanding, distinctions between types of citizens and subjects of France have existed from the republic's inception. No one policy alone characterizes French immigration, naturalization, and nationalization law, but several together do. Shifts in policy have been affected by war, geopolitical concerns, demography (labor shortages, falling birthrate, foreign occupation, the Vichy regime), and decolonization.

Patrick Weil further notes that the so-called "French exception"—*jus soli*—was not consistent throughout the history of the French republic. It was not until 1889 that jus soli citizenship law applied to all individuals born on French territory. Prior to 1889, the Civil Code of 1804 granted French nationality at birth only to a child born to a French father, either in France or abroad, making residence and bloodlines factors in the determination of citizenship eligibility, and not just accepting the responsibilities associated with French citizenship. Weil's scholarship details how French nationality policy has changed over time in response to varying immigration streams, civil conflict, war, and the transformation of France's colonial relationship with several départements , most notably Algeria. "Each major step in the development of French Nationality law was taken to the detriment of certain categories of French people, leaving them with fewer rights or otherwise worsening their situation."[53]

By the late 19th and early 20th centuries in France, falling birth rates and depopulation led to labor shortages. "Demographic stagnation meant that France had neither the workers to fill its factories and mines nor sufficient means to secure its national defense."[54] Hence, immigrants from Poland, Italy, Czechoslovakia, and other nations of Central Europe poured into France. It is important to note, as in the case of Britain, how French national society and government reacted differently to the wave of European immigrants after World War I and the wave of immigrants from the French colonies after World War II.

Indochina, the Maghreb, and the Colonial Question

Algeria's European democrats, in the framework of the Algerian war, could not as a whole act like their homologues living in France. Democracy in France traditionally lives in broad daylight. In Algeria, democracy is tantamount to treason.[55]

In his account of the internal dynamics of the Algerian war for independence from France, Frantz Fanon provides this observation of the predicament and paradoxes Europeans faced living in Algeria in the moment of war; Fanon tries to articulate their roles as participants in democratic politics as French citizens in colonial France. Under the conditions of colonialism set by the French government, the Algerian nation-state was inconceivable. For the indigenous Algerians and Europeans who supported the revolution, French repression of nationalist aspirations made the practice of democracy impossible; a European could speak her or his mind in France but not in Algeria. Fanon captures one of many contradictions inherent in the colonial-metropolitan relationship; the French presiding over a liberal democratic republic prohibiting freedom of speech and voluntary association among a population in a site that had been seized by force. With force came pacification and the dictation of the conditions of labor and employment, education, legal and juridical codes, emigration, and movement for the subordinated population.

Algeria's increasingly tenuous and conflicted relationship with France during the war for independence underscored the contradictions of France's colonial and imperial policies. To acknowledge the existence of French colonies would have entailed the acknowledgement of the French government as a colonizing power with imperial authority, not the model of republicanism and universalism. The nonrecognition of population variation in France was tied to the nonrecognition of French colonialism, with its own bureaucratic and legal scaffolding that ultimately influenced French domestic and foreign policy. In contrast to the British, who officially declared the post–World War II period as their era of decolonization, the French never publicly acknowledged their colonial inheritances. In this sense, France was more similar to the United States in the latter's tendency to not publicly acknowledge its imperial relationship to several protectorates as well as sovereign powers (Guam, Puerto Rico, the Philippines, and Cuba) well into the late 1950s.

France's "nonwars" within its colonies, particularly Vietnam and Algeria, seeped into metropolitan French politics. First, Algeria's National Liberation Front (FLN) orchestrated attacks within France against French citizens, in effect bringing the colonial conflict (that France refused to acknowledge as a colonial conflict) to the metropole. In response, the French government adapted guerilla warfare tactics that were first utilized against the Viet Minh and applied them against both the civilian population and military personnel allied with the Algerian war for independence. These measures would be adapted once again to police and monitor North African immigrant communities in France after 1962.

Against the backdrop of labor shortages, depopulation, and the needs of industry, France began to encourage North African immigration to France on the eve of Algerian independence. In preparation for the influx of a new immigration stream, the central, local and municipal governments developed housing policies and facilities specifically for the new immigrants. While the North African immigrant population provided much needed labor, recent Algerian independence and attacks on French soil helped generate concerns of increased political and social disorder. As in other examples of state-sponsored immigration, however, these immigrants invariably brought not only their labor but their customs, cuisines, and in several instances, their politics. Thus the French government was forced to draw distinctions among the North African populations, between those born within France proper and those born in Algeria, Tunisia, or Morocco, and those who fought against the French or on the side of the anticolonials. Not only did this policy result in the disproportionate segregation of Maghrebis in Paris suburbs (HLM social housing construction), but it also provided one of the earliest indications that in practical terms the combined policy initiatives in response to the Maghrebi population contradicted republican claims of antidifferentialism.

As Ariane Chebel notes, immigration, nationality, and citizenship law along with colonial rule collided in the years after World War II.[56] Chebel suggests that for much of its history, France has had a nationalization and naturalization policy that addressed the integration and assimilation of distinct ethno-national, regional, and linguistic differences in the territory of France (Breton, Corsica, Occitan, Provence, Basque, etc.) as well as among immigrants from Europe, mostly Italy, Spain, Portugal, Poland, Germany, and Eastern Europe. It has not had an immigration policy designed to incorporate non-European immigrants, many from colonial outposts, into national society.

French labor policies provide an opportunity to explore the racialized dimensions of labor recruitment and, ultimately, immigration policy, which not only contributed to creation of segmented labor markets but ethno-nationally segregated neighborhoods. Patrick Weil and Elisa Camiscioli note how the science of population studies, immigration, and scientific racism combined in the development of theories about the relative value of immigrant streams from distinct countries of origin. Jules Amar, Paul Gueriot, Rene Martial (a eugenicist who enjoyed his professional heyday during the Vichy regime), William Oualid, and several other French social scientists articulated clear preferences for European-origin immigrants, not only for their purported capacity for efficient, productive labor, but the greater likelihood of their assimilation and positive reproduction of a truly French national population.

As noted by Camiscioli, the comparative studies of these and other French scholars of the alleged disparities in employment rates of Belgian and Luxembourg, Swiss, Italian, Czech, Slav, Russian, Polish Armenian, Chinese, Greek, Sub-Saharan, and North African workers provided politically useful data to assess the relative merits of workers, laborers, and fighters during times of peace and times of war. As with Woodrow Wilson, Freeman, along with scholars of the 19th century and earlier who drew comparisons about the political and economic capacities among diverse populations, this cohort of French eugenicist intellectuals revealed the undercurrent of anxiety about nonwhite, non-European immigration into their country. As with Freeman and Wilson (and much earlier, Kant), the taxonomic schemes that hierarchically ordered populations cross-spatially also provided evaluations of the relative merits of various populations within Europe.

Camiscioli, in her detailed review of wartime documents of the Ministries of War, Labor, and Armaments, provides evidence of these correlations. French employers, work supervisors, and representatives of the Ministries of War, Labor, and Armaments consistently placed North Africans and Asians at the lowest end of the racial-labor hierarchy, with Slavs and Greeks on the two rungs above, just below Belgians, Spaniards, and Greeks. Poles and Italians were viewed with relative suspicion, based on data culled from studies that also factored in complexion and linguistic compatibility. Such correlations and hierarchies in France's labor markets led Camiscioli to characterize French immigration debates of the period as "the intertwined fates of universalism and particularism," demonstrating "the clash of a universalist social theory and a racialized labor force."[57] Although the French government never adopted these racialist models, the interaction between public and private interests reveal the extent to which such ideas circulated in society and state.

The racial and ethno-national valuation and differentiation of immigrant labor and residence in France resumed after World War II. In one of the many ironies of French public opinion after World War II, Alec Hargreaves cites public opinion data from a 1971 INED (Institut national d'études démographiques) survey that indicated markedly improved perceptions of Germans among the French population, while Maghrebi and Sub-Saharan Africans were ranked the lowest. Hargreaves draws comparisons with the ability of the French government and people to foster subsequently positive intergovernmental and EU relationships involving Germany, noting that since the Treaty of Friendship signed in 1963 between France and Germany, "both countries have actively sought to overcome past enmities through bilateral programs of cooperation involving the public at large. There have been no comparable investment aimed at overcoming the divisive memories and attitudes inherited from the colonial period."[58]

An often ignored series of policies developed by the French government during the Algerian crisis, however, highlights one of the rare instances of recognition by a French government that a nominally French population had been insufficiently integrated into the French nation-state. In an effort to respond to the Algerian independence movement, several politicians and governmental bureaucrats devised policies that acknowledged the discriminations Algerians faced in France by emphasizing integration. As Todd Shepard noted, scholars of modern France and French imperialism have debated whether this short-lived policy was merely a reiteration of French colonial ideology and not a genuine effort at integration, particularly when the war in Algeria had already gotten underway. Shepard argues that the French government's integration initiatives "were symptomatic of wide-ranging efforts among French politicians and bureaucrats to rethink and refine French state institutions and the relations between those institutions and the people they governed."[59]

The move toward more integrationist policies was partly motivated by modes of recognition: (a) that formal legal equality for Algerians meant little without corresponding commitment to French governmental invest-ments in education, employment, and housing, and (b) discriminatory practices that Algerians experienced in metropolitan France and in Algeria could not be attributed to Nazism, anti-Semitism, or even American forms of racial discrimination. This policy initiative was led by then Interior Min-ister François Mitterrand and further elaborated by Jacques Soustelle, then governor-general of Algeria in 1955.[60] Part of the attempted integrationist strategy was to increase the number of Muslims in civil service posts in Al-geria which, interestingly enough, was a key demand of Algerian nationalists during World War II and the immediate postwar years.

Such policies and public debates help complicate the broad generali-zations offered by political scientists and sociologists who study race and racism in comparative perspective and who have argued that the French government has always been opposed to population-centered affirmative action policies as implemented in the former Soviet Union or the United States. The work of Shepard and other historians of this period provide more documentary evidence of the French government's own comparativist turn in the post–World War II period, when French governmental bureaucrats and intellectuals developed what could be characterized as a comparative imagination of population statecraft, observing how other governments around the world resolve conflicts and problems related to the nexus of population distinction and inequality. During the same period, Mitter-rand and the French government paid close attention to developments in UNESCO, France, and Brazil on matters of cultural pluralism after World War II, in search of ideas and governmental strategies to combat discrim-ination and inequality while at the same time charting a policy direction distinct from the segregationist United States. Brazil, with its ideology of racial democracy, and Mexico, with its state-sponsored *indigenismo*, seemed appropriate alternatives for Mitterrand, Soustelle, and other governmental officials desirous of keeping Algeria French.

Although these efforts by the French government were ultimately unsuccessful *vis* its larger objective, they at a minimum signal an instance where certain sectors of the French government, politicians, and intelligentsia acknowledged the existence of discrimination in French society that could not be traced to anti-Semitism. Subsequent moments in French governance that reveal recognition of homegrown racism in France against Maghrebi and African populations more generally was the Anti-Discrimination Act of 1972.

These issues would reappear in the 1990s, both in internal documents and published reports that acknowledged the existence of racism and racial discrimination, separate and distinct from social discrimination and xenophobia. Didier Fassin attributes this attitude to governmental efforts to contrast with the "situation in the United States, which served as a foil to both condemn racist practice and criticize communitarian drifts."[61] In other words, French republicanism could both acknowledge racism as a problem in French society while denouncing efforts by victims of racial discrimination to organize politically, on a "communitarian basis." In 1994 a law passed explicitly prohibiting "discrimination based on origin." A year earlier, in 1993, the Méhaignerie Law, a restrictive citizenship reform, was adopted. The law modified Article 44 of the citizenship code, changing the jus soli automatic right to citizenship to a system of "will and choice" exclusively for individuals born in France to foreign-born parents. Under this provision those individuals had to actively request citizenship and demonstrate their allegiance to the state at some point between the ages of 16 and 21, with proof of five years of continuous residency. This modification changed the logic of French citizenship that had been instituted in 1889; it granted all individuals born on French territory the birthright to citizenship. In 1997, the Guigou Bill was introduced by the Lionel Jospin government to amend the 1993 law so that children born in France to foreign-born parents could acquire citizenship after five continuous years of residency after the age of 11 (fulfilling certain conditions). However, with this bill, parents could not attain birthright nationality for their children.

The council's 1998 report constituted a "double rupture" in the discourse of official institutions: "It is no longer the attributes of foreigners that are considered responsible for the difficulties foreigners face . . . but the functioning of the French society itself."[62] Mistreatment, harassment, and wage disparities among citizens who were actually French of non-European origin were identified in the report as phenomena separate and distinguishable from the anti-Semitism and xenophobia affecting "colored Frenchmen, and especially those from overseas or of non-European origin." This statement was part of a broader recognition of unequal treatment rooted in racism, which in turn forced the recognition that French society was composed of a highly diverse population and not a monolithic group of undifferentiated citizens. However, Fassin and others argue that these instruments amounted to little more than the formal recognition of racial discrimination in French society, without the French state actively pursuing institutional discrimination. Again, republicanism's aggressively antidifferentialist ethos forbade government tallying of "communitarian statistics" identifying forms of diversity within the French population.

The circumstances and effects of the 2005 and, to a lesser extent, 2007 riots in France are well known. Rather than review the chronology of events leading up to the series of disturbances and riots, the focus here will be on the reactions of the French government. Governmental responses reveal the limitations of the ideological framework of republicanism to address concerns of racism and social exclusion articulated by segments of the nonwhite French population.

Of the three cases, France's national society and polity appear to be on the brink of the most significant changes in how inequality and discrimination are understood. Unlike Britain and the United States, where a documentary record of institutional racism exists in the juridical and legal spheres as evidence of labor market segregation and wage and employment disparities, French governments have only recently acknowledged the existence of institutionalized racial discrimination.

National debate around the riots in 2005 and 2007, as well as the more recent Charlie Hebdo attacks, reveal long-standing normative and ideological positions, but also new fault lines in public and scholarly debate. The Hebdo attacks, as they are referred to in France, have led to redoubled efforts on the French right to associate republicanism with greater immigration restrictions, antidifferentialism, and stronger evidence that minorities, in this instance Muslims and nonwhites from North and Sub-Saharan Africa and the Middle East, should prove their loyalty to the French state. Another sign of the correlation between the French right and republicanism is the renaming of Sarkozy's Union for a Popular Movement (UMP) political party as the Republican Party, a redoubt for those who are steadfast in their belief in republicanism's ability to resolve social tensions and to somehow separate republicanism from racism.[63]

The French left's roots in Marxism as a philosophy of history and a trajectory of liberation have proved inadequate for understanding the role of difference as a source of political, economic, and social inequality critical to the unequal distribution of wages, services, and opportunities, and conversely, as an organizing principle in the dynamic interactions between racist, xenophobic organizations and antiracist ones. As detailed in chapter 4, "the social question" is actually composed of a number of questions or paths to inequality. Racial and ethno-national hierarchy, as detailed in this chapter, is a largely unacknowledged dimension of the social question in France that requires an interpretive lens broader than those provided by republicanism, Marxism, and liberal individualism.

Both the French right and left have been largely unprepared for the emergence of racial conflicts and politics in French society. So-called "communitarian" organizations, namely, organizations created and founded by Francophone black political actors and their allies, have emerged in response to the perceived inabilities of the French right and left to address racism and inequality in French society. Organizations like SOS Racisme, CRAN (Conseil représentatif des associations noires), and Brigade Anti-Negrophobe reflect the development of independent black and antiracist institutions in response to the general absence of strong antiracist agendas in many organizations in the 1960s and 1970s. Such organizations at minimum reflect frustration with existing political parties, their platforms, and their coalitions, wherein "the racial question," as part of the social question, is constantly elided in French politics.[64]

The increase in voluntary associations in France emphasizing communitarian sentiments—specifically, the desire and need of certain members of French society to identify themselves by color, phenotype, or even presumed race, indicate at minimum a frustration with the capacity of existing political parties and social movements to represent the concerns of nonwhite French who have experienced exclusion and discrimination. French republicanism, with its premise of abstract universalism, has often functioned as an ethnos (like other democratic polities) with its own exclusionary mechanisms and regimes.

The United States

As a case of racial and ethno-national regimes operating in conjunction with nominally democratic institutions, norms and processes, the United States is the most studied nation-state in the social sciences. Offered here is an analysis that emphasizes how the racial regimes in US politics have been part of a larger political order: the institutionalization of immigration and citizenship law and regimes.

Much has been written about the circumscribed or second-class citizenship of US African Americans, Asian Americans, and Native Americans in the course of US political history. While the overlapping histories of inequality and exclusion of these populations is well and ably documented, less attention has been given to the linkages among immigration, citizenship, and hierarchy as component parts of racial and ethno-national regimes in the United States. Exclusion from a polity is ultimately a result of politics. Common to African Americans and many immigrant populations in the United States has been the monitoring, surveillance, and restriction of movement by the state. Restrictions and discrimination toward subject populations are part of a more general process of actively structuring and policing the body politic.

As in the previous two cases, ethno-national and racial regimes combined anxieties over pluralization, immigration, and presumed racial difference into laws affecting cohabitation, citizenship, residential and other forms of segregation, and of course, political mobilization. These regimes, formally and informally constituted in law and custom, impacted seemingly unrelated dimensions of civic and private life in the United States. This section will focus on largely neglected aspects of racial and ethno-national regime formation in the United States.

The conjuncture of racial regimes and immigration policy in the US helps illustrate how ethnic and racial categorizations are dynamically related and ultimately determined in—and through—politics. Some populations who are now classified as white or prototypically American were once classified as ethno-national, even racial groups, whose claims on citizenship were suspect. Governmental rationalizations for the exclusion of white ethnic populations usually contained some ethnicized or racialized justification in addition to class, regional, and other factors.

State and federal laws concerning slavery and black insurrection in the 19th and 20th centuries directly influenced the development of national immigration policy, restrictions on the internal movement of black peoples within the United States, and restrictions upon the travel and movement of black citizens or subjects of the United States in other polities. Movement restrictions upon US African American slaves and freedpersons made US African Americans native-born "foreigners." As will be explored below, legal determination of the status of US African Americans as slaves and freedpersons often influenced the legal determination of the immigrant as a potential citizen of the United States.

Roy Garis, an advocate of selective immigration in the 1930s, wrote that "historical facts thus seem to refute the contentions of the past and present advocates of unrestricted immigration that we have always welcomed the immigrant with outstretched arms."[65] The first national Congress of 1790 limited naturalization to "any alien, being a freeborn white person." It was not until 1870 that the 1790 naturalization law was amended to allow African-descended immigrants to apply for citizenship, a mere five years after slave emancipation.[66] Indeed, as in other cases where societies with slave-based economies formally abolished slavery in the 19th century, the cessation of slavery was not followed by an influx of African immigration to former slave-holding societies. More often than not, immigration streams from Europe and Asia emerged after the abolition of the institution of slavery in the fledgling republics of the New World.

The first explicitly racialist immigration laws were directed toward Asian and Pacific Islander peoples. The Chinese Exclusion Act of 1882 was implemented to curtail Chinese immigration on the West Coast. The 1913 Alien Land Law discouraged Japanese immigration. The 1924 Immigration Act used tabulations from the 1890 census and not the more recent 1920 census to further reduce eastern and southern European immigration. The 1924 law extended anti-Asian immigration policies by restricting the immigration of Asians and Pacific Islanders, who were not allowed to become naturalized citizens based upon the 1790 naturalization law.[67]

The 1920 census would be put to political use, however, in subsequent restrictions. The 1920 census eliminated previous census distinctions between "mulatto" and "Negro" and introduced the category of "children of foreign-born." Michael Paul Rogin writes that the 1920 census redefined "the in-between statuses that threatened Anglo-Saxon purity; mulattos were nothing but black; children born of European immigrants in the United States were less than white."[68] Significantly, the 1920 census, and not the 1950 census, was the basis for immigration quota restrictions under the McCarran-Walter Act of 1952. The 1920 census categories would be the basis for immigration quotas until the major revisions in immigration law in 1965, which lifted quotas upon Caribbean immigrants and led to a large upsurge in Caribbean migration to the United States.

While often viewed by scholars of US immigration policy as a significant shift from race-based immigration policy to quotas based upon national origin, the McCarran-Walter Act of 1952 in some important respects continued to maintain the formal as well as tacit parameters of racial and ideological conformity of previous immigration laws. Although it erased the racial restrictions of the 1790 "freeborn white persons" edict, it nonetheless contained significantly higher entry quotas for North European immigrants while maintaining racial restrictions for Asian immigrants, specifically Japanese, Koreans, and Pacific Islanders.

While no explicit restriction of other nonwhite immigrants was in the 1952 act, quota restrictions of 100 people per year were levied upon entrants from the British West Indies—Trinidad, Jamaica, and the Virgin Islands. As islands of the British Commonwealth, proponents of this portion of the bill argued, its quota restrictions were components of Britain's national quota. The author of the bill argued that black immigrants from Haiti and the Dominican Republic were under no such restrictions, since they were sovereign nations and not colonies. Thus, it was argued, the bill did not have a racially discriminatory basis. Those opposed to the act, however, noted that no other immigrant population in the Western Hemisphere had similar quota restrictions.[69]

Most scholars of the McCarran-Walter Act have emphasized its ideological underpinnings in the xenophobic, communist hysteria of the period. The bill's emphasis on quota restrictions, particularly with regard to Asian immigrants (northern and southern Asia, including Australia and New Zealand), was coupled with a desire for a good-neighbor policy to halt the alleged spread of communism throughout Asia. Indeed, much of the debate surrounding the amendment of racial restrictions against Asia-Pacific Triangle peoples focused on the contradictions of excluding members of populations who, as naturalized citizens, had either fought in World War II on the side of the Allied Powers or were descendants of Asian Americans who had lived for several generations in the United States and its territories. Opponents noted the seeming paradox of advocating geo-political consistency during the Cold War (the Good Neighbor Policy) while at the same time upholding racialist criteria for entry into the country, the very criteria the act was supposed to abolish. Their criticisms underscored the need to think of immigration policy not in terms of rhetoric and slogans about democracy, but in the racialized underpinning of actual immigration legislation.

Throughout the debate preceding the House vote on the bill, the racialist and ideological intent of its crafters was made explicit through their rationalization of racial and national restrictions. The significant bias toward northern and western European immigration (84 percent of the total immigration quota per year) was justified by several congressmen with the claim that these immigrants proved to be the most productive citizens, while southern and eastern Europeans were overwhelmingly represented in degenerate, illicit, and ideologically radical acts. For example, in the discussion of an amendment presented on April 23, 1952, to give nations with a quota under

7,000 the unused portions of quotas from nations with greater quota allot-ments, Rep. Wood of Ohio stated that while he was not a follower of Hitler, the idea of racial superiority had some validity. Metaphorically referring to the idea of Aryan racial supremacy, Wood stated, "We cannot tie a stone around its neck and dump it into the Atlantic just because it worked to the contrary in Germany. . . . I believe that possibly statistics would show that the Western European races have made the best citizens in America and are more easily made into Americans."[70] With the unfounded assertion that "possibly statistics" would prove him right, Wood's preference for maintain-ing lower quotas for nonwhite immigrants had blatant echoes of herrenvolk notions of national unity. The amendment was rejected by a vote of 70–25.

While claiming a race-neutral position regarding immigration, several proponents of the McCarran-Walter Act argued that the United States gov-ernment had every right to be racially and ideologically selective in its assess-ment of immigration influx if the nation would be free of both communist menace and racial degradation. In decrying, among other things, racial inte-gration, Rep. Rankin of Mississippi combined the racial-ideological menace that open immigration represented to him when he warned that the influx of "questionable characters swarming into this country" would lead further to-ward racial conflict: "Communism is racial. A racial minority seized control in Russia and in all her satellite countries, such as Poland, Czechoslovakia, and many other countries I could name. Just a little group at the top have control, and they know that if the people of these countries have a chance at them their yellow heads will roll in the sawdust."[71]

Conclusion

In the case of France, republican ideology and public policy operated both as a mobilizing national principle replete with symbols, rituals, myth, and custom, as well as a means to exclude and marginalize populations deemed nonnational and unassimilable into French society and polity. Additionally, successive governments and political officials, along with several generations of French intellectuals on both the right and left, discouraged the forma-tion of state-based institutions designed to combat racial discrimination in employment, housing, education, and other areas of French public life. Consequently, when compared to Britain and the United States, French society and government did not develop robust governmental and paragov-ernmental apparatuses to identify and combat racism against African (North and Sub-Saharan) descended citizens and immigrants.

Parallels can be made between the British and French cases. The period after World War II brought about significant changes in the relationship between the French and British governments, on the one hand, and their colonial territories and dependencies, on the other. Their nominally post-colonial eras augured shifts in immigration, naturalization, and citizenship policy, as well as strategies of containment regarding recently-arrived immigrants, making it difficult for new immigrants, as well as African- and Asian-descended citizens, to integrate and assimilate into these societies, even though these populations spoke and functioned in the primary national language and were socialized in the customs, norms, myths, and rituals of the nation-state.

In contrast, the United States, as a settler nation-state with clearly defined restrictions for indigenous, black, and Asian populations not long after its creation, developed a much more robust set of institutions and governmental practices explicitly designed to administer and facilitate segregation. These restrictions, coupled with the desire of members of these and other groups (most notably, white women), to participate in the US polity, helped generate dynamic tensions between political and social actors who sought to maintain segregation and relatedly, inequality and those actors who through protest and activism fought—sometimes successfully—exclusion and inequality. The United States, more so than the other cases, has had a much more public and popular discussion of the myriad forms of racism in its society and polity. This is not to suggest that the United States has been more successful in combating informal and formal institutional racism, but it has developed more explicit institutional forms that are at once the recognition of racist phenomena and an attempt to deploy strategies that would seek to diminish its presence in US society. Britain has developed the most explicitly racialized governmental apparatuses and policies, through its Race Relation Acts first developed in the 1960s. As several scholars of British racial politics have argued, the "race relations paradigm" has tended to obscure the larger issues intrinsic to British society: immigration and the nature of the welfare state.

Immigration analyzed through the conceptual lens of racial regimes allows us to interpret immigration law in the United States and France formalized in direct response to the need to distinguish between slaves and immigrants, in the US case, and between European immigrants and expatriates, on the one hand, and non-European colonial subjects of Africa, Asia, and the Caribbean, on the other. Most scholars of British immigration acknowledge the drastic shift in political debate, the clamoring within society and polity for stricter controls on immigration and, finally, the response to constituent claims by creating policy and law that sought to restrict immigration and naturalization laws, for fear that Britain would become a nonwhite majority population. In more recent times, anti-immigrant sentiments are also suffused with anxiety over the real and imagined prospects of terrorism within Britain, with a focus on citizens and residents with Middle Eastern, Soviet, and North African histories as objects of increased scrutiny and restrictions.

In all three cases, the prospect of homegrown terrorism has also exposed some of the limitations of racial and ethno-national framing of terrorism suspects. In each case, members of majority populations have signed onto various jihadist manifestos and participated in military operations against their own government representatives, whether in their country of birth or citizenship or abroad. What has also become clear, however, are documented cases in which part of the appeal for disaffected members of minoritized and racialized populations to join groups committed to violent attacks upon members of their own national communities is their own experience with racism within France, Britain, and the United States.

In addition to the lessons learned from the examination of ethno-national and racial regimes in the three countries, this analysis has some broader implications. First, rather than understand these cases as refutations of democracy, they actually highlight the principles of polyarchy, namely, the existence of multiple forms of governance and political rule within democratic polities and societies. Ethno-national and racial differences were rendered politically salient, evidenced in institutional racism and discrimination, the conflicts and clashes between institutions and actors committed to upholding racial and ethno-national regimes and the institutions and actors (governmental and nongovernmental) who seek to overturn such regimes and replace them with more transparent, democratic, and egalitarian institutions.

Second, these exclusionary regimes were a constant and recurrent dimension in each case. At certain moments, they arose under conditions of secrecy. In other instances, these regimes emerged with majority support within both polity and society, as evidenced in highly selective immigration laws and reforms; voting restrictions; residential, spatial and occupational segregation; and marriage and cohabitation restrictions. A unique feature of racial and ethno-national regimes is their combination of formal and informal institutions that in effect suture distinct policy, juridical, and legal spheres. Thus, immigration, carceral, electoral, and property laws, as well as internal migration and movement of specific populations, were prompted by perceived crises in phenomena that seemingly threatened to affect dominant group constituencies. Perception, even more than reality, often guided regime developments. Racial and ethno-national regimes were not just operative in the political arenas deemed—whether formally or informally—as racial or ethno-national, but in most significant arenas of social and political life.

Against this backdrop of institutional history, evolutionary and developmentalist arguments about the temporal dimensions of democratic political development in these countries can be understood as deeply teleological claims rather than historical ones. At issue, as noted in chapter 1, is whether restrictions imposed upon minoritized and racialized populations are reformed or rescinded, allowing them to participate in the polity as full-fledged citizens. At stake here is not whether democratic polities exclude or delimit certain groups of people from their polities, but when, under what conditions, by whom, and from whom? What are the terms and circumstances in which widely disliked groups are targeted for specific state sanctions and policies?

As highlighted at the beginning of this chapter, Freeman's lectures on comparative politics, analyzed in the introduction, suggest a history of the discipline rooted in a quest for science and racial hierarchy. This section places the field's origins, periodization, and telos of political development in a more complicated environment of geopolitical and economic entanglements. Hendrik Spruyt and James Mahoney's conclusions regarding Britain's post–World War II shift to a policy of decolonization can only be affirmed if we ignore the actual policies designed to engineer the outcomes of electoral competition, overthrow governments, and eradicate political actors and movements that attempted to shift policies away from their former colonial overseer. Evidence of these activities on behalf of the British government are not limited to the recent "migrated archives" controversy but in earlier scholarship examining Commonwealth immigration policy and the sabotage of fledgling democratic polities in Guyana, Kenya, and other Commonwealth nation-states after World War II. Both French and British governments sought to distinguish their governmental policies as nonracialist or even antiracist, particularly when compared to the United States. In the case of France, the refusal to compile racial, ethnic, or religious statistics amounted to the state's nonrecognition of the plurality of French society and populations within it, and the prospect of inequality and discrimination based upon differences.

As outlined in this chapter, the paths to political development of many former colonies of the United States, Britain, and France were structured, in part, by the ongoing economic, military and institutional interventions of these major powers. In the case of Britain, metropolitan and colonial state interventions into the electoral politics of Ghana, Guyana, and Kenya directly determined the outcomes of several electoral campaigns for presidential and prime ministerial leadership. In certain instances, support of opposition led to political instability and outright overthrow of democratically elected leadership. The United States' interventions into electoral politics in Nicaragua, Chile, the Dominican Republic, Haiti, South Africa, Congo, Ghana, and other cases were also combined with exerting financial pressures upon their struggling economies to increase the prospects of political instability and their desired political and economic outcomes deemed advantageous to the United States. France's interventions in Algeria, Morocco, Vietnam, the French Republic of the Congo, and Haiti evidenced similar effects upon the national economies and politics of these societies, as both nation-states and former colonies of France.

Finally, the ethno-national and racial regimes of the three countries analyzed in this chapter also serve as a reminder to students of comparative politics that the skepticism necessary for any scientific exploration of politics includes an interrogation of governmental and scholarly proclamations about the organization of history according to governmental proclamation and periodization. Decolonization and the civil rights era are two examples relevant to our cases of received wisdom about periodization that often does not capture the historical complexity of an epoch, nor the tensions between state chronicles and actual political realities between a state's declarations of fealty to democratic practices and its efforts, often successful, to make its history of political inequality disappear.

5

Conclusion

RECONFIGURING COMPARATIVE
POLITICS AND DEMOCRACY

The emphasis on induction, political ethnography, the relationship between ideas and institutions, process tracing, and history in this book should be recognizable to most students of comparative politics. This concluding chapter's objective is to emphasize the continued relevance of history, local knowledge, and context in the study of comparative politics and to identify several research streams that could be developed in the exploration of political phenomena relating to ethno-national and racial regimes. Greater attention to ethno-national and racial hierarchy in politics can enable students of comparative politics to further explore how the study of racial and ethno-national regimes can complement important methodological innovations by feminist scholars in comparative history, sociology, and political science,[1] on the political salience of gender in the development of law, public policy, and civil and human rights. Finally, institutional differentiation that is the result of racial or ethno-national hierarchy within plural societies and polities can provide research opportunities for intraspatial comparison, through the assessment of how institutional variation according to population can enable students of comparative politics to identify group-based patterns of inequality within a national society.

Excavation of the neglected writings of Edward Augustus Freeman on comparative politics will not, on its own, alter how the current generation of comparative politics students approach their field. Those with little or no interest in the history and genealogy of the discipline can readily ignore these findings and proclaim their irrelevance to ultimately mathematical and large N explanations of political phenomena. Yet, as a field, comparative politics (as with most disciplines of the social sciences and humanities) is marked by the preoccupations of its methodological horizons and the limits of those horizons that tend to dominate the field at a given moment. Those horizons are characterized not only by what its objects of inquiry are, but also by what they are not—by what the dictates of its professional mandate discourages as much as what it encourages its practitioners to research. No less than the actors and institutions that are the major preoccupations of comparative politics, students of comparative politics are objects of socialization in their own subject positions (class, gender, nationality, religion, and so on) and modes of professionalization that help determine which phenomena and institutions warrant closer study and which do not.

The dearth of scholarship on slavery and colonialism, or on the relationship between colonialism, imperialism, and comparative politics, reveals more than just neglected subject matter, but an aversion to phenomena whose most important lessons are difficult to quantify. We can dismiss Freeman's preoccupation with comparative politics as the musings of a racist crank of a previous era. Yet Freeman's preoccupations also reveal how racist norms and assumptions can assume institutional form and structure conditions and circumstances of dynamic interaction between differentiated groups.

More broadly, the relationship between racial hierarchy and inequality in democratic polities also forces us to consider competing conceptualizations of democracy. Should a democratic polity concern itself only with its own citizens and institutions, or with the implications of its democratic practices for all members of society? The cases examined in this book reveal how highly functional, democratic polities generate and maintain inequality, specifically ethno-national and racial hierarchy. The generation of inequality did not, in these cases, make the states and governments less efficient. The more central question is whether the differentiating regimes that generate and maintain inequality in democratic societies make democratic polities less democratic. Another way of posing this question is whether it is possible to maintain, in the contemporary world, democratic polities within nondemocratic societies. As global inequality increases, according to most reliable measures and indicators, this is a question that has been raised with greater frequency in the most affluent—and the poorest—societies in the world.

Definitions of democracy have certainly expanded and proliferated since its first iteration in the demos of classical Athens. The nation-state system has experienced several waves of democratic, anticolonial, revolutionary movements: the nonhistorical nations of the late 19th and early 20th centuries and the former colonies and so-called dependencies after World War II. Latin American polities that emerged from the authoritarian periods of the 1950s–1970s, along with the new nation-states that emerged from the collapse of the Soviet Union, also bore the moniker of newly democratic or democratizing polities. More recently the so-called Arab Spring sprung, but with few blooming democratic polities. All of these regions of the world, if not all the nation-states therein, have struggled with Freeman's correlations between race (in whatever guise) and political community.

Freeman's worry for the United States in particular has resonated in many parts of the world, when social and political movements demand that their political leaders resemble them in some fundamental way; whether in attendance at the same mosque, church, or synagogue, the use of the same primary language, phenotypic similarity, or the fuzzy notion of origins. The homologous arrangement of nation, state, people, and leadership is an ideal that has prompted civil wars, secessionist and irredentist movements, and of course, apartheid. The very idea of a two-state solution in the case of Israel underscores the durability of the one people–one state ideal, an ideal that has promoted more heartbreak than political stability.

As explored in chapter 1, population distinction has had political implications from the very first republic to more contemporary democratic polities. Even the most durable and enduring democratic polities have existed within an ethnos, an institutional and normative environment that encourages the life-ways of particular groups often at the expense of other groups in its midst. The United States, France, and Britain, but also contemporary Germany, Switzerland, Belgium, Scandinavia, Ghana, South Africa, Indonesia, and many other countries that have been classified as democratic have exhibited this tendency. Scholarship of these countries and the likelihood of particular groups or subgroups attaining the most preferable positions in the economy, polity, and society attest to the fact of bias, on a continuum ranging from the taken-for-granted nationalization of specific religious and ethnic holidays to mass expulsions. How to make societies less ethnocentric and more ethos-centric is one of the great challenges of balancing pluralism and democracy in contemporary nation-states.[2]

Students of comparative politics have devoted considerable attention to developing methodological approaches and concepts that could capture the institutions, processes, dynamics, and actors deemed central to the development and maintenance of Western liberal democratic polities of the 19th and 20th centuries. Yet neither colonialism nor neocolonialism by the world's major powers has received much attention by scholars of historico-institutionalism in comparative politics.[3] Is it mere coincidence that the most enduring democracies of the contemporary world are the societies and polities that have benefited the most from the transatlantic slave trade? Did slavery, specifically racial slavery, provide the necessary material largesse to make democracy possible for its architects? And is it not also worth considering that some of the most significant civil rights and nationalist movements of the modern world occurred among the slaves, their descendants, and colonial subjects who were the conscripts of Western modernity? The Haitian Revolution, Mau Mau revolt, Algerian War, US Civil Rights Movement, and more contemporary movements for civil rights in France and Britain exemplify the resultant conflicts that emerged as a result of the dynamic relationship between colonizers and colonized, masters and slaves, citizens and noncitizens, and dominant and subordinated groups.

Given the autoreferential character of most methods discussions within the field, with the focus on mathematical precision and predictive capacity (more often than not, as applied to the past!), the actual world of politics barely intrudes, except when the researcher creates a game theoretic model that could be applied and tested in the field using real political actors with carefully controlled inducements and parsing of information to create laboratory-like conditions in which to properly test a hypothesis. These findings are then inserted into a "real" set of political dynamics, where the solution to the hypothetical problem may be posed as a mechanism to resolve real conflicts. Such training in econometric models, game theory, and mathematics, on their own, will not prepare students of comparative politics to understand these real conflicts themselves.

A more informed understanding of contemporary political conflicts might begin, ironically, with a view toward the past, by returning to earlier stages in the field or discipline's history. The return to earlier periods in comparative politics is motivated not by a desire to return to the teleological assumptions about modernity, progress, development, and underdevelopment. Instead, it is prompted by the insight that the field's questions and methods were shaped more by the identification—in theory, law and history—of political problems than by methodological tinkering. Indeed, though some concepts deployed in comparative politics during this period have stood the test of time, most have not.[4] Edward Augustus Freeman's and the Social Science Research Council's respective instantiations of a comparative politics discipline—seventy years apart—both occurred at moments of significant change in regional and inter-state relationships: a world of empires, colonies, nation-states, and multiple economies that are no more.

Political phenomena of world historical or national significance brought into question the ability—or lack thereof—of political scientists to accurately and competently identify and assess the major political problems of an era. As noted in chapter 2, political scientists freely borrowed from other disciplines (not just economics and mathematics) concepts and approaches considered helpful for the enterprise of comparison. Through the interface with other, more established disciplines and knowledge clusters, comparative politics and political science were far more porous at these earlier stages than now. Philosophy, anthropology, and sociology are all disciplines with—pardon the sports metaphor—far deeper benches than political science, at least in terms of their histories as disciplines, and their recognition (at least in sociology and anthropology) that responding to conditions of crisis—from the local to those of world order—required internal assessment of a discipline's, and its practitioners', relation to the world.

The fall of the Soviet Union, civil rights movements, feminism, nationalism, and the Cold War are some of the major issues that have at times posed significant analytic, but also ethico-political, challenges to many practitioners within the discipline. More recently, France, Britain, and the United States also pose challenges to the limited conceptual vocabulary in the field of comparative politics to understand how difference, inequality, institutions, and revolt congeal in societies with democratic polities embedded within.

These equivalents of disciplinary soul searching had varying degrees of impact, contingent, in part, upon the field and subfield in question. The charges levied against comparative politics by members of the Perestroika movement were especially resonant with practitioners who had long railed against more positivist methodologies and approaches that minimized or ignored the role of history, culture, and context in understanding political actors, institutions, and dynamics.[5] World historical events also intervened to force shifts in objects of study: the cessation of the arms race and collapse of the Soviet Union deeply affected what international relations and comparative specialists subsequently studied. Urban riots in 1965 and 2015 helped shape the contours of American politics study. Comparative politics, like political theory, has largely followed a Euro-US axis, with few, isolated reflections on what or how comparative politics (along with "continental" philosophy and political theory) is affected by the postcolonial in Europe and the sunset of multiculturalism across Europe and the United States.

Perestroika and the debates it generated within comparative politics, while important, were only the most recent version of a recurrent set of concerns held by the more qualitatively minded students within the field, particularly those with one foot in area studies at the onset of the Cold War. Perestroika represents the third instance in the professional discipline of comparative politics when some of its practitioners sought to devise methods appropriate to study politically salient phenomena that had not been examined before, and in so doing highlight the shortcomings in approaches to the study of politics that did not emphasize locality, context, and endogenous factors.

In its post-1950s iteration, comparative politics interfaced with area studies in ways that forced its practitioners to consider the methods and conclusions of social scientists in other disciplines. The very language of civic and political culture deployed by the members of the Social Science Research Committee and their students emerged from sustained discussions with area studies specialists, particularly scholars trained in anthropology and sociology, who were interested in the themes of political development in the parts of the world deemed non-Western.

Resistance to both positivist and behavioralist dominance within the profession began at least two generations earlier. Comparative politics and political theory reacted to the narrowing of topical choices and methodological approaches in political science by the 1960s. Both fields had the advantage of a relation to disciplines and professions outside their own; philosophy and classics in the case of political theory, and history, sociology, and especially anthropology in relation to comparative politics. Colonialism, imperialism, decolonization, and the rise and collapse of new political forms (fascism and totalitarianism) were all examined by practitioners in these disciplines.

As noted in chapter 2, regional studies became the site for exchanges between comparative politics, sociocultural anthropology, and sociology (primarily, though not exclusively). A key point of divergence between comparativists across these disciplines was anthropology's self-reflexive acknowledgement of the role of colonialism not only in Western colonial theaters, but in Western political formation and, ultimately, the discipline and practice of anthropology itself. Anthropology's relation to empire, imperialism, and racism was too obvious to ignore.[6] By contrast, as I will outline below, the neglect of colonial rule's impact upon the functioning of Western polities (characterized as either liberal and social democracies or polyarchies) in their administration, governance, and ideological representations of minority and formerly colonial populations has resulted in the neglect of a question that could be central to comparative politics: how did colonial rule influence Western polities?[7] What I offer are some preliminary suggestions about the influences of colonialism, particularly the administration, management, and ideologies of racial and ethnonational hierarchy upon the governments of France, Britain, and the United States, particularly in the 1950s and 1960s, in their treatment of populations defined as minority groups within their territories.

Comparative politics, with the exception of several important students of African and South Asian politics, has largely avoided the legacies of colonialism, racism, and imperialism *within* nation-states even though the institutional imprint of these practices are evident in immigration, citizenship, and naturalization policies, elite formation and reproduction, voting and suffrage, the right to property, and most vividly in certain cases, policing. Below is a preliminary effort to demonstrate how racial and ethno-national regimes provide opportunities for intraspatial comparisons within nation-states to explore variation and continuity in the administration of the populations within a plural society.

Intraspatial Orders, Racial Regimes, and Comparative Politics

From the outset of the comparative politics movement of the 1950s, several political scientists conducting survey research in the so-called developing areas recognized the disjuncture between their research methods and the phenomena, institutions, and actors they encountered in their field sites outside of Western polities. Lloyd and Susanne Rudolph were among the first generation of researchers to enter the field and find their research tools wanting. In collaborative and individual research, both scholars openly questioned the capacity of Western researchers to comprehend how people in developing countries understood politics and political participation.

One of their findings culled from fieldwork was that the category of the individual voter was largely nonexistent in Madras, India, given the role of both patriarchy and collective deliberation in determining electoral choices.[8] Rudolph and Rudolph advocated that the political scientist, no less than the anthropologist, needed interpretive methods of cultural translation to make sense of politics that was not directly attributable to individual voter preferences or the state. In this sense, cultural translation was more than methodological; cultural translation was an epistemological problem.

In a retrospective article in 2005 (a more developed version of her 2004 American Political Science Association Presidential Address), Susanne Rudolph revisited and expanded upon her fieldwork experience in Madras State in 1957.[9] In her more recent article, Rudolph generated key questions about the past and continued relevance of what she refers to as Anglo-American concepts and methods for making political sense of norms, opinions, and behaviors in societies and polities that are only nominally based upon Western political institutions and cultures:

> Without concepts and methods we would not know where to look and what to look for. The question was, and still is, to what extent were these concepts and methods amenable to infiltration, adaptation, modification and transformation by the forms of life and worldview of the alien other.[10]

Just below, she describes what she and Lloyd Rudolph earlier conceptualized as "the imperialism of categories," categories first crafted in Anglo-American research institutions and applied to distinct and unfamiliar political environments. Their skepticism regarding the applicability of survey research methods first devised in the social science environments of elite academic institutions in the United States was first generated by what Alasdair MacIntyre characterized as an epistemological crisis,[11] the moment of recognition that facts and assumptions held as certainties no longer hold true; methods and concepts once considered universally applicable in the explanation of politics no longer made sense.

Rudolph and Rudolph's descriptions of the interpretive challenges they and others experienced in the field resonate with Giovanni Sartori's emphasis on concept clarity (intension and extension) to ensure that comparativists identify the closest empirical approximation for their conceptual containers, coupled with the recognition that concept stretching might render both concept and empirical referent mutually unintelligible.[12] Rudolph and Rudolph's epistemological crisis takes us into deeper conceptual waters where concerns about the very epistemological assumptions of comparative politics can be found. Can we be sure that what we understand as political is also political in other times and places? If so, why?

Different portraits of leadership, charisma, authority, and legitimacy emerged from anthropology and what came to be known as political culture in political science, as comparativists in both disciplines sought to make sense of emergent and waning political institutions at the end of colonial rule in Africa, Asia, and parts of the Caribbean. Through comparison, students of comparative politics had an opportunity to consider a wider range of roles and functions of political actors and institutions across time and space. Was a British king the equivalent of an Omanese sultan, whose political function at times resembles a Nigerian oga, whose role and function more closely resembles a prime minister in a parliamentary democracy, who in turn, more closely approximates a popularly-elected president in a majoritarian democracy, who at times might behave like a raj in colonial India, or even an esteemed cricketer in the Caribbean?

In epistemological terms, Rudolph and Rudolph identified the horizons of the comparative politics enterprise, the limits of its vision. For the structural functionalists, (examined in chapter 2) attention to function rather than façade or symbol enabled the student of politics to apprehend the politically salient in virtually any context. With its postmodern association, the phrase "alien other" deployed by Suzanne Huber Rudolph conveys the assumption of irreducible distinction.

What remains unexplored in the Rudolph's account is how difference in comparative politics is actually understood. Was the alien other a place, a people, a complex of norms and institutions, or some combination of all three? In bringing the gaze of the comparativist (the Rudolphs in this case) under closer scrutiny, we must also consider that the distinctions students of comparative politics search far and wide for might also exist closer to home. This was a belated recognition in the discipline of anthropology, chronicled by practitioners such as James Clifford, Talal Asad, and Paul Rabinow, that anthropology's hubris lay (among other places) in the belief that Western anthropologists could somehow escape othering and colonial tendencies in their interpretations of non-Western peoples and cultures.[13]

The perception of irreducible difference, while often associated with cultural, somatic, and phenotypical characteristics cited to distinguish one group of people from another, is also certainly one of the motivations for politics. When a group of people believes their needs and objectives diverge from those other groups of people, politics, if not conflict, emerges. And in the case of plural societies with any number of groups considered (whether true or not) irreducibly different from one another, either a distinct form of politics is attributed to them, or distinct forms of politics are applied to them. As explored in chapters 2 and 3, distinct modes of governance were devised and deployed to manage discrete populations in both colonial and metropolitan spheres. Thus, to probe Rudolph and Rudolph's claims about comparative politics' relation to the alien other even further, we might ask whether the alien other in the Rudolphs' account is necessarily individuals and groups who inhabit far away places. Could the alien other also be a few blocks, a few neighborhoods away? New Orleans, Flint, Michigan, the South Side of Chicago, and Baltimore, Maryland, are some of the more prominent places amid mainland US geography where the administration of the "alien" other can be identified.

Guillermo O'Donnell and Prospects for Intraspatial Comparison

The question above is a provocation to a research agenda that explores more fully the implications of racial and ethno-national regimes for intraspatial comparison. The outline for a research agenda of this sort was developed by Guillermo O'Donnell, though not with the aim of exploring the correlations of political institutions, spatiality, and ethno-national and racial hierarchies. Unlike many comparativists in political science of his generation who specialized in Latin America, O'Donnell's scholarship acknowledged the plurality of Latin American societies. He was an important contributor to our understanding of the dynamics of democratization in Latin America as well as other regions of the world.

Unlike development and modernization theorists of the previous generations, O'Donnell's perspectives and formulations were anti-teleological; he understood the installation of democratic institutions and practices as neither immanent nor cyclical but the result of political mobilization against authoritarian, oligarchic, and other forms of nondemocratic rule. O'Donnell had a clear understanding of the relationship between politics, economics, and cultural manifestations of democracy, and sought to make sense of the interconnectedness of institutional, material and behavioral dimensions of polyarchy.

Antidemocratic politics and social inequality produced social and political behaviors and cultures of arrogance among elites, on the one hand, and subservience and resignation among popular groups, on the other. In describing state power, for example, O'Donnell emphasizes the distinction between state power and the state apparatus, the latter as an institutional form with various departments, and the state itself "a set of social relations that establishes a certain order, and ultimately backs it with a centralized coercive guarantee, over a given territory. Many of these relations are formalized in a legal system issued and backed by the state."[14]

For those familiar with the literature on the origins of the modern state (Weber in particular), O'Donnell's description above might seem obvious.

Yet O'Donnell's emphasis on the socially constituted origins of the state itself, particularly for what he refers to as "new democracies" in the post-communist era after the collapse of the Soviet Union, serves as a reminder to comparativists of the socio-spatial context of state formation. This article is one of the more suggestive and generative in O'Donnell's scholarship. Its framing provides the possibility of concept extension, including more cases.

As noted in chapter 3, the newly independent nation-states of early 19th century Latin America were forged through coalitions between criollo elites and their supporters among a motley assortment of poorly compensated and noncompensated laborers. Power dynamics were suffused among them in various ways. Legal restrictions imposed upon slaves, freedpersons, and the poor in Latin America limited or prohibited access to formal education and literacy, property, and wealth. For slaves and their descendants, further prohibitions disallowed juridical and legal claims against whites. The Catholic Church devised ingenious ecclesiastic procedures that equated whiteness with Christianity and provided freedpersons with the means to "clean their blood" (*limpieza de sangre*) through payment of a fee that provided a certificate of authenticity as proof that the certificate's bearer had "clean" or "white" blood.[15] Thus, the new states at once enshrined citizens in a national pact while encoding the highly unequal relations between elites and nonelites of the earlier colonial period. Here, there are opportunities for historical comparisons between the types extortionist regimes applied in medieval France and Britain as "protections" for Jews (as discussed in chapter 4) and the caste regimes of colonial Spanish America.

As with the United States and France, the democratic pact forged among Latin American elites with their new governments only partially incorporated the darker-skinned masses and the very poor. Laws, edicts, and decrees either on the eve of independence or soon thereafter served to assure the continued marginality of non- or minimally enfranchised subjects. The conditions of their marginalization were not the same as they were under conditions of enslavement, serfdom, or debt peonage, but were modified under new political, economic, and legal arrangements.

Although this history of Latin America is largely absent in O'Donnell's scholarship on the region, it serves as a backdrop for his broad examination of Latin American politics in the 1970s and 1980s, when it appeared as if South American polities were transitioning from authoritarian rule to a more democratic politics. In trying to explain the variation among cases such as Argentina, Brazil, and Chile, O'Donnell suggested that a new form of polyarchy emerged in Latin America after the exhaustion of dictatorships within the region. On the one hand, these states adopted political democracy, namely representative, competitive electoral politics. On the other hand, however, these electoral forms of democracy were limited in their scope and impact across the spatial totality of the state's domain. O'Donnell and other comparativists would refer to such polities as "uneven democracies," wherein "ineffective states coexist with autonomous, also territorially based spheres of power. States become ostensibly unable to enact effective relations of social life across their territories and their stratification system."[16]

O'Donnell's conclusion is preceded by the following question: "What happens when the effectiveness of the law extends very irregularly (if it does not altogether disappear) across the territory, and the functional relations (including class, ethnic, and gender relations) it supposedly regulates? What influences may this have on what kind of democracy may emerge?"[17].

To emphasize the spatial dimensions of this democratic-polyarchic order, O'Donnell devised a color scheme to identify the spaces in national societies according to their degrees of governability and consistency between state law and creed and according to actual politics. Blue denotes spaces with a high degree of state presence and effectiveness. Green indicates "a high degree of territorial penetration and a significantly lower presence in functional/class terms;"[18] state presence, but without outright hegemony (in the Gramscian sense) and authority over society and polity. Brown signifies spatial conditions with low state presence and penetration. These have a weak infrastructural capacity, such as the delivery of public services like electricity and roads and clearly limited ability to effectively regulate social conditions.

For societies with more brown spaces than blue and green, O'Donnell poses the question, "What kind, if any, of democratic regime can be established over such heterogeneity"[19] in the absence of uniform application of law throughout society? Before proceeding with his analysis, O'Donnell characterizes the new democracies of Latin America (with references to postcommunist and African cases as well) as follows:

> States become ostensibly unable to enact effective regulations of social life across their territories and their stratification systems. . . . The unlawful intervention of the police in poor neighborhoods, the widespread practice of torture and even summary execution of criminal suspects from poor or otherwise stigmatized sectors, the actual denial of rights to women and various minorities . . . reflect not only a severe process

of urban decay, they also express the increasing inability of the state to implement its own regulations.[20]

In Latin America, but also in the cases examined in chapter 4, the contours of uneven democracies can be traced in the outlines of racial and ethno-national regimes. Evidence of color and ethno-nationally based inequalities in Latin America can be found in Chiapas, Mexico (indigenous), Colombia (Afro-Colombian), Nicaragua (Miskitu and Creole), and Brazil (black and brown Brazilians), allowing for clear correlations (if not causal inference) between legacies of enslavement, forced servitude, and tribute and contemporary disparities in education, wealth, health care, mortality rates, and other epidemiological indicators. Such disparities are examined in greater depth and variety in disciplines such as sociology and anthropology, and in regional studies concentrations such as Africana studies and Latin American studies than in political science.[21]

O'Donnell's assessment of 20th century Latin American politics provide a unique opportunity to apply conceptual formulations designed for "southern" nation-states to "northern" polities and societies. We have an opportunity to extend O'Donnell's concept to encompass more cases without doing violence to the concept itself and, in the language of Sartori, devolving into category error. In this instance, the technique employed would be to utilize O'Donnell's definition of a brown area to determine if brown areas exist in nation-states outside of the region, in nations with similar polity arrangements and modes of rule, and finally, in societies that are considered within comparative politics literature as containing more polyarchic—and ultimately democratic—attributes than other societies.

In these and other cases, democracy can be identified as but one form of politics within a polyarchy. Polyarchy more accurately characterizes the diversity of political dynamics, institutions, and behaviors that persist alongside democratic institutions and processes within a single nation-state, and it is for this reason that we can understand polyarchy and democracy as distinct political forms. While the centralizing state authority is democratic and provides, through electoral competition, more horizontal relations among citizens through suffrage, that same authority countenances and is limited by other, nondemocratic modes of governance within its territorial domain. Democratic practices and institutions may predominate in a given society, but is one of several articulations of political life and power. Under these circumstances and conditions, distinctions between formal and informal institutions become blurred.

The challenge and opportunity here is to distinguish between character-istics of newly-democratic societies emerging from authoritarian rule and societies with other types of rule. A state's capacity to extend its authority evenly over disparate populations inhabiting its territory requires more than logistical and organizational efficiencies; it also requires coordinated com-munication, coercion, and administration. The persistence of ethno-national and racial regimes placed limits upon democratization throughout the re-gion, even amid formal transitions of power from authoritarian, military regimes to democratic or transitional civic regimes. Racial regimes combine highly coercive functions with weak infrastructural capacity, social welfare, and tax revenues. Hurricane Katrina in the United States and Brazil in the aftermath of the 2016 Summer Olympics are two examples of the human-made catastrophes that await the sectors of society predominated by racial and ethno-national regimes.

Applying O'Donnell's scheme more broadly to other, more democratic cases, we discover that many societies with political democracy and repub-lican principles, such as France, Britain, and the United States, have their own brown areas, with entire sections of major cities or regions containing many of the elements of dysfunction found in O'Donnell's characterization of new democracies in Latin America. Brown areas in several of O'Donnell's cases are also spaces with histories of highly unequal land ownership and distribution, with much of the territory devoted to manual labor for agri-cultural purposes that relied heavily on peasant, enslaved, and indigenous labor during their respective colonial and early republican periods.

Health Disparities, Life Indicators, Racial Regimes, and Democracy

How can students of comparative politics explore more fully the implications of racial and ethno-national regimes for the institutions and practices of de-mocracy? To push the field of comparative politics further, we would have to go beyond identification of such regimes and delve into their function as institutions that help produce and reproduce inequality. Cross-spatial anal-ysis of urban policing in plural societies is one of several already emerging research streams. Public health, particularly health disparities, may pro-vide opportunities for scholars to undertake cross-spatial and intraspatial analyses that will reveal that the administration and variation of population differentiation have produced health disparities and outcomes. Public health indicators help punctuate the multiplicity of lived experiences under distinct regimes within the same national territory: variances in life expectancy, mental and physical health, education, and employment. It is important to remember that the distinctions within national populations, no less than distinctions between national populations, are the result of politics.

Tables 5.1, 5.2, and 5.3 are an attempt to make sense of disparities between populations identified as citizens within the same national territory. These populations, categorized by national origin and presumed racial or ethno-national distinction, are also identified in government census data by their epidemiological and sociological characteristics. Governmental, nongovernmental, and quasi-state bureaucracies have developed in each society to monitor, count, and assess disaggregated national populations. Offices of minority health, immigration, national integration, antidiscrimination, and inequality exist in each country. In the nongovernmental realm, health service professionals and academics produce their own data on disaggregated populations, as do pollsters and public opinion research organizations that specialize in ascertaining the opinions and beliefs of disaggregated and national populations. When one considers the data amassed by governmental and nongovernmental organizations on populations defined across the

TABLE 5.1. Infant Mortality Rate in the UK and US

Infant mortality rate is the number of infants dying before reaching one year of age, per 1,000 live births in a given year.

	MOTHER'S REGION OF ORIGIN			
	England and Wales	*Africa*	*Pakistan*	*Caribbean*
United Kingdom (2013)	3.6	5.5	7.2	9.0
	MOTHER'S RACE OR ETHNICITY			
	White	*Hispanic*		*Black*
United States (2010)	5.18	5.25		11.46
Baltimore (2013)	6.8	--*		12.5
New York City (2013)	3.0	4.8**		8.3
		*(**Puerto Rican only)*		

* Insufficient data. Data sources: UK data: Office for National Statistics (ONS); US data: T.J. Mathews and M.F. MacDorman, Infant Mortality Statistics from the 2010 Period Linked Birth/Infant Death Data Set. *National Vital Statistics Report* 62(8) 2013; Baltimore data: J. Sharfstein. *Maryland Vital Statistics Annual Report, 2013*. Baltimore, MD: Department of Health and Mental Hygiene, Vital Statistics Administration, 2013; NYC data: R. Zimmerman, W. Li, E. Lee, L. Lasner-Frater, G. Van Wye, B. Freedman, D. Kelley, J. Kennedy, G. Maduro, P. Ong, Y. Sun, *Summary of Vital Statistics, 2013: Infant Mortality*. New York, NY: New York City Department of Health and Mental Hygiene, Office of Vital Statistics, 2014.

TABLE 5.2. Educational Attainment: Secondary School Qualifications in the UK and US

	White	Hispanic	Black
UNITED STATES	85.6%	78.2%	69.4%
Male students	83.5%	74.1%	64.3%
Female students	87.8%	82.6%	74.8%
NEW YORK CITY	76.4%	53.6%	56.0%
Male students	72.4%	48.8%	49.7%
Female students	81.0%	58.6%	62.2%

	White-British	Pakistani	Indian	Black-Caribbean	Black-African
UNITED KINGDOM	57.1%	51.6%	72.1%	45.9%	55.7%
Male students	52.4%	47.8%	69.0%	39.3%	50.6%
Female students	62.1%	55.7%	75.5%	52.4%	60.8%

In the US, measured as percentage of students graduating high school within four years, among public high schools (2012–2013); In the UK, measured as percentage of pupils achieving 5 or more General Certificate of Secondary Education qualification at A*-C including English and Maths at the end of key stage 4 in each academic year (2014–2015).[i]

[i] Data Sources: US data: McFarland, J., Stark, P., and Cui, J. *Trends in High School Dropout and Completion Rates in the United States: 2013* (NCES 2016-117). US Department of Education, Washington, DC: National Center for Education Statistics, 2006. New York City data: Cohorts of 2001 through 2012 (Classes of 2005 through 2016), *Graduation Outcomes*. New York, NY: Department of Education. UK data: Revised GCSE and Equivalent Attainment by Pupil Characteristics in England: 2014 to 2015. London, UK: Department for Education. Found at: https://www.gov.uk/government/statistics/revised-gcse-and-equivalent-results-in-england-2014-to-2015.

TABLE 5.3. Unemployment Rates by Age, Sex, Race/Ethnicity in the UK and the US

Prevalence of the unemployed as a percentage of the labor force

UNITED KINGDOM (JUNE 2015–JUNE 2016)	WHITE	PAKISTANI/BANGLADESHI	BLACK[a]
Overall (16+)	5%	11%	12%
Male	5%	8%	12%
Female	4%	16%	12%
Age 16–24	13%	26%	30%

UNITED STATES (Q4, 2016)	WHITE	HISPANIC	BLACK
Overall (16+)	4%	5.6%	7.9%
Male	4.3%	5.7%	8.6%
Female	3.8%	5.6%	7.3%
Age 20–24	6.6%	8.8%	14.0%

a. Black includes Black Britons, immigrants from Africa and the Caribbean. Bureau of Labor Statistics, U.S. Department of Labor. *Labor Force Statistics from the Current Population Survey 2016*, U.S. Government Printing Office, Washington, DC, 2016.

above-mentioned categories (such as youth, disabled, or elderly) we can consider the cross-cutting forms of disaggregation that have become part of the bureaucratic and demographic common sense of contemporary nation-states. The key point here is that the subdivision of national populations is accompanied by the development of bureaucracies to administer them.

The objective of these tables is to first demonstrate disparities among populations assigned ethno-national and racial characteristics in each country. The boundaries of the populations in question are, at best, approximations rather than conclusive interpretations of data drawn from individual countries and subsequently utilized for cross-spatial assessment. The indices for each population are compared to the indices of the dominant population in each country, as well as individual countries outside of the objects of comparison. For example, according to data compiled by the city of Baltimore as well as individual researchers in the discipline of public health, sections of that city have some of the highest rates of infant and adult mortality, sexually transmitted diseases, and unemployment in the city of Baltimore, the state of Maryland, and in the United States as a whole.[22] Taken further, the epidemiological characteristics of several neighborhoods in West and East Baltimore more closely resemble the epidemiological profiles of countries such as Bangladesh, Sri Lanka, Belize, and Sudan, some of the poorest nation-states on earth. For example, in 2011 there was a 20-year gap in estimated life expectancy at birth between sections of Baltimore city, with life expectancies in some neighborhoods lower than those of Bangladesh and Iran. Data on civic participation (voting, voluntary association) provides further detail on the disparities between minoritized and racialized populations and their more populous and powerful counterparts in national society.

The difficulties and limitations with this type of cross-spatial comparison are threefold. First, the populations under consideration are not identical to one another. Maghrebi, Latino, US African American, British Indo-Pakistani, and Black British have their own histories of immigration, cultural dispositions, occupations, and conflicts within France, Britain, and the United States that render them distinct from each other. Consequently, comparing populations across nation-states can be a bit like comparing apples and oranges, and is the basis for the second qualification. Black across cases, for example, contains a wide diversity in terms of regional and ethno-national subgrouping. Populations in one country that would be considered black are considered African or Caribbean in another and may or may not be considered black. Here we must also distinguish between governmental and popular classification.

In plural societies, government census categorizations generally operate on a narrower continuum than popular, more horizontal forms of identification. For example, in the United States, the biracial movement in the
1980s reflected efforts by US citizens, mostly children of one white and one
black (hence "biracial") parent, to force the government to provide a category that reflected both parents in their genealogy. In 1970s Britain, many
Asian activists and community leaders referred to themselves as black as a
means to identify with the commonalities of experience with xenophobia,
racism, and discrimination at the hands and institutions of the majority and
dominant population, especially during the Thatcher era, even though they
were categorized in census data as Asian, Indian, or Pakistani. In France,
the antidifferentialist policies of republicanism have recently prohibited the
culling and use of what has often been termed ethnic or racial statistics.
Thus, categories such as white, black, African, Asian, or European have
not been used in census classification, even though they are invoked either
directly or euphemistically in popular, daily interactions and descriptions
of French citizenry. The French case, then, poses the greatest interpretive
difficulty for cross-spatial comparison among the three cases because the
official governmental categories for population classification do not closely
resemble the ethno-national, racial, or even religious categorizations operative in the other two cases.

Scholars of ethno-national divisions in French society have devised ingenious ways to circumvent the limitations of data access imposed by governmental criteria for identifying disparities within French society amid
the ideologies of color blindness and republicanism. De facto spatial segregation, for example, has provided opportunities for demographic and ethnographic research to identify neighborhoods, cities, and regions that are
disproportionately Maghrebi and Sub-Saharan African. Other techniques
include identification of origin through surnames. With these tools, scholars
have been able to roughly approximate infant and adult mortality rates, levels
of unemployment, arrest and incarceration rates, and education among spa-
tially discrete populations that could then be broadly correlated with ethno-
national origin. Here, spatiality becomes an important variable in determining the aspects of identification that are socially, epidemiologically, and, in
some instances, politically significant. The riots of 2005 and 2007 exemplify
the relevance of spatiality in identifying the location of hyperpolicing,[23]
harassment of Maghrebi and Sub-Saharan populations, and ultimately, the
response of residents, which resulted in popular manifestations first in these
communities and then spreading to other populations and parts of France.[24]

Finally, very specific experiences often affect how populations react to their social and political environments and consequently how they might be assessed. For example, restrictive citizenship regimes limiting access to suffrage in turn influences voting patterns. Again using Baltimore as an example, the preponderance of lead-paint contamination among populations in East and West Baltimore has resulted in higher rates of developmental disabilities among a segment of the black population in certain parts of the city. We would have to be careful, however, in extending this comparison beyond the confines of Baltimore, and acknowledging that the local conditions in Baltimore for minoritized and racialized populations might be particularly severe, perhaps more so than the conditions of minoritized populations in other parts of the country.

Colonialism Reconsidered

Here we can link intraspatial to cross-spatial comparisons of political institutions, for which practitioners of comparative politics are best known. Many of the politics, norms, and attributes associated with non-Western political systems and governance could be found within Western polities and societies, especially among marginalized populations and the spaces they inhabit. Whether we are referring to Maghrebian populations in metropolitan France, Native American and African American populations in the United States, or Turks and Iranians in post–World War II Germany, Western polities and societies with colonial and apartheid legacies have devised and maintained bureaucratic regimes to monitor, limit, and in certain instances expand minority populations in their societies. These populations inhabited the national territory, but were invariably subject to distinct formal and informal laws, coercive practices, and regulatory and citizenship regimes. Thus, we have not only witnessed how non-Western groups have fared in these societies, but how state bureaucratic growth and expansion, administration, and surveillance practices are linked to the management of marginalized populations.

The comparative literatures on democratization, and more specific literatures on European politics, have also cordoned off much of Euro-US modern political history from the sorts of political analysis reserved for non-Western polities and regimes, thereby reproducing a key blind spot in the literature in comparative politics: the paradox of labeling political systems that simultaneously administered highly egalitarian and unequal political relations as democracies. The governments of countries such as France and Britain, with their vast and diverse colonial populations, devised various administrative and bureaucratic schemes with informal mechanisms, tacit rules and codes, to manage and distinguish between colonial and metropolitan populations and colonial populations of different territories and regions, in addition to distinctions between the free and unfree.

The management of colonial populations bore a variety of costs: economic, political, ethical, moral, and social. Hannah Arendt's key insight into the origins of state racism that arrived on the European theater in the 1920s was the prior development of what she calls racism in action in European colonies—the bureaucratization and institutionalization of racial orders designed to sustain hierarchical relations between Europeans and colonial others. Nominally democratic and republican governments devised bureaucratic, juridical-legal, and normative codes to limit formal and informal interaction, assimilation, and participation of colonial ethno-nationally and racially subordinated subjects within their polities. Thus, societies such as Britain, the United States, France, Belgium, and the Netherlands had two interrelated political developments within their polities, each with their own ministries, bureaus, policy advocates, ideologies, bureaucrats, and managers: the inegalitarian and the egalitarian. Racial and colonial orders represented not only instances of political development in their own right, but an opportunity to examine the existence of polyarchy within formally democratic polities; the existence, within a single polity, of at least a dual system of governance, designed to address distinct populations.

These forms of polyarchy go unrecognized in modes of analysis that privilege the nation-state as a unit of analysis, with its constitutive components (such as the population or the people) largely following the characteristics attributed to them by the intellectuals and elites of the national government. Students of globalization, transnational networks, and immigration, however, complicate understandings of nation-states, their territories, and national populations, as essentially stable and internally coherent. This recent literature evidences the ways in which nation-states and national societies are actually composed of a variety of national and extra-national forms of collective identification, modes of governmentality and regime type.

Contrary to many of his peers, Aristotle questioned the justification for slavery and was concerned about its corrosive effects upon both slaves and citizens in classical Athens.[25] Alexis de Tocqueville, a commentator on democracy in the United States, did not consider the Indian question or the Negro question to have significant import for the practice of US democracy.[26] Myrdal and Beaumont, on the other hand, perceived racial discrimination of

US African Americans as a clear barometer of democracy in an otherwise egalitarian society.[27] A third way of approaching the relationship between racial discrimination and democracy is to consider the circumstances under which barriers to membership are predicated upon racial and ethno-national regimes and the demand for poorly remunerated labor. As noted in chapter 1, democracy is only one form of political rule that has tolerated, in fact benefited from, inequality, but it is also the only form of political rule for which inequality poses challenges to its ideological legitimacy. Racial and ethno-national hierarchies within nation-states in the so-called developed world also provide opportunities to pursue the implications of governance and governmentality, the exercise of state power, and the development of alliances and allegiances that do not correspond neatly—if at all—to the formal boundaries of nation-states. These two modes of hierarchy, when institutionalized via state bureaucracy, provide opportunities to examine how different sectors of national populations are governed differently.

Institutionalism

Katherine Thelen and James Mahoney, as well as Peter Hall, Sven Steinmo, and other scholars of new institutionalism, have focused on "the whole range of state and societal institutions that shape how political actors define their interests and that structure their relations of power to other groups."[28] Thelen, Steinmo and Frank Longstreth's edited volume signaled the birth of an innovative research stream in contemporary comparative politics. They emphasized the changing and dynamic character of institutions not only in their internal machinations, but in their interactions with political actors and norms as well as other institutional forms. In the words of Peter Hall, institutional configuration shapes political interactions.[29] Most scholarship associated with this more recent research stream on institutions tended to focus on bureaucracy, political parties, economic and social policy, and occasionally, gender politics and the welfare state. With the exception of gender politics and the welfare state, much of the topical interest in scholarship on the themes noted above can be traced to earlier research in sociology, political science, and economics on class politics, capitalist development, and state interfaces. With its emphasis on structure, materialism, and history, the new institutionalists avoided the more behavioralist approaches of the previous generation of comparativists, as well as rational choice institutionalism.

As a topic and object of inquiry, racial and ethno-national hierarchy has not generated much attention among the new institutionalists. Their approaches, however, are quite amenable to analyzing the effects of racial and ethno-national hierarchy upon the development and contours of political institutions. We can explore some of the conceptual and theoretical implications of the empirical evidence of racial hierarchy and state formation to underscore two important, but largely ignored phenomena in the literature on new institutionalism: the role of racial theory and ideology in institutional development and change, and the role of states as "race-making" and "race-sustaining" institutions.

Culture, Politics, and Institutions

Unlike anthropologists, political scientists in general do not engage in self-examination of the relationship between a researcher and their object of study. Part of the goal and operative assumptions of many comparativists engaged in large N research is that their research design eliminates or reduces bias in their questions or in data assessment. The assumption here is that large N research design actually guards against the intrusion of an individual researcher's norms into survey questions, responses, and subsequent interpretation. Political scientists who utilize techniques of immersion, phenomenology, grounded or standpoint theory, and political ethnography are among the few who explore how their own subject position might help or hinder access to communities and individuals in the ways that first concerned Rudolph and Rudolph.

As detailed in chapter 2, the retreat from the culture concept as an explanatory variable for political phenomena can partially be attributed to an effort to apply concepts with greater precision and applicability. After World War II, with the race concept largely discredited, the culture concept was utilized by proponents of political culture and behavioralism in political science. The culture concept, however, was more often the source of category error and excessive concept extension, applied to a range of phenomena that could be more profitably housed in other conceptual containers.

Samuel Huntington is perhaps the most prominent political scientist and student of comparative politics whose scholarship has some conceptual continuity with Freeman. Near the end of his life and career he became preoccupied with the culture concept and its implications for political order, the so-called clash of civilizations, and the dangers of multiculturalism in the late 20th century United States. Samuel Huntington's later work resonates with anxieties about the prospect of political instability in societies with populations defined as culturally or racially distinct. In these societies, governments are thought to be less able to protect their citizens and provide for their over-all well-being and to positively interact with other states and governments in the world at large. This larger backdrop provides an opportunity to examine broader trends in the nation-state system that reflect these anxieties; among them is a recurrent preoccupation with the perceived threat and chaos posed by "others"—plural populations in the midst of a national polity.

If there is one preoccupation across Huntington's writings, whether an-alyzing the former Soviet Union or authoritarian Brazil, it is a concern with order and management in society and polity and the conditions under which governments and political leaders manage change or maintain a status quo. Here I focus on some core concepts in two of his later works, which bear more than traces of 19th century thinkers like Edward Augustus Freeman.

According to Huntington, one of the key threats to political order in nation-states is the presence of diverse populations in a single polity. Unlike Freeman, Huntington does not use the word or concept of race. Instead, culture and civilization serve as the indices of irreducible difference that threaten to transform stable, homogeneous societies into cauldrons of chaos and entropy.

Among his prognostications about the future of world order and global politics, Huntington proclaimed in 1993, three years after the fall of the So-viet Union, that countries with large numbers of peoples of different civili-zations will have the greatest likelihood of dismemberment.[30] Even cultur-ally homogeneous countries are susceptible to dismemberment if they "are divided over whether their society belongs to one civilization or another."[31] Huntington refers to such nation-states as "torn countries." Examples in-clude Mexico, Turkey (the worst offender), and the aforementioned Soviet Union.

Clues to Huntington's selective worry about cultural and civilizational assimilation lies in his choice of nations that are most susceptible to dismem-berment. The so-called clash of civilizations has been invoked ever since the reconquest of Spain from the Moors through the Cold War.[32] In Huntington's scheme, Mexico, like Russia and the Soviet Union, and Turkey, are border countries: between East and West (Russia and Turkey), North America and South America (Mexico), Europe and Africa (Spain) or in the case of North-ern Italy, between Central Europe and Southern Europe.

Many erroneous assumptions, when not dismissed on solely historical grounds, warrant further examination and unpacking. Let's begin with his use of the term "civilization," which would appear roughly to mean societies that have influenced, whether directly or indirectly, the formation of norms, values, and laws across time and space. Huntington understands civilizations as internally coherent and culturally homogeneous entities, but this view is contradicted by overwhelming evidence of borrowing, absorption, and assimilation across civilizations and national cultures.

The vast majority of nation-states in the world have plural origins, namely, multiple linguistic, religious, and ethno-national elements, whether they are present in governmental authority or not. Heterogeneity—not homogeneity—has been the rule rather than the exception among national societies governed by states. As noted in a recent book by David Laitin, *Nations, States and Violence*, the assumption that the mere presence of multiple peoples participating in the same polity increases the likelihood of violence is not borne out by close empirical examination.[33] In both empires and settler societies with diverse populations (in their societies, if not their polities), difference, on its own, has rarely been the source of political conflict.

Based on his findings, Laitin concludes that there is no causal relationship between population heterogeneity and violence, just as—unfortunately— there is no causal relationship between difference (what we would now refer to as multiculturalism) and democracy. Huntington, however, like Freeman believed that the presence of specifically differentiated actors leads to disorder and violence. Huntington warns against blanket suspicion of all immigrants, noting that "Americans have tended to generalize about immigrants without distinguishing among them and have focused on the economic costs and benefits of immigration, ignoring its social and cultural consequences."[34] Thus, it is not immigrants per se, or immigrants in general, but specific immigrants that warrant monitoring.

Huntington's concern about the seeming inability of Latinos to assimilate into what he calls "US national identity" is premised upon Latinos' reluctance, by his understanding, to learn English, and their inability or unwillingness to use English as the language of state. The presence of populations in the United States whose primary language is not English, and who conduct their socioeconomic and even political transactions in another language, is neither unprecedented nor peculiar to Latinos. The first constitution of the state of California was bilingual, and Scandinavian languages and Dutch immigrants in New York, Minnesota, and other parts of the Midwest spoke Dutch and Scandinavian at municipal deliberations. These examples of bilingualism and most importantly, multiple languages of state, are not cited by Huntington. In juxtaposing Laitin's findings and Huntington's declarations, we return to the relationship between difference and politics, or more precisely, the point in interpretation when it becomes apparent that the presence of difference per se becomes politically salient in relation to some groups and not others. As Arendt reminds us, foreignness is ultimately a political distinction.

This recognition can be posed in the form of a question: what makes the presence of Hispanics or Latinos—as opposed to French, Dutch, or Russians in Coney Island, New York—different from earlier immigrant streams that brought people, legally or otherwise, into the United States? At different points in US history, various groups were characterized as unassimilable into society, the body politic, or both: Latino migrants, and by inference, Mexican-Americans, in the current moment, the Irish and later Chinese in the 19th century, Italians in the late 19th and early 20th century, Afro-Caribbeans and Africans prior to 1965, and Jews in the 1920s. Common across these groups is their racialization at different points in US history. In the current moment of immigration crises within the EU, the question above can be extrapolated to consider France and Britain.

Culture and civilization in the later writings of Samuel Huntington bear the mark of irreducible difference where culture—like race in earlier periods—is fixed and ontological. The "torn countries" to which Huntington refers, to continue the metaphor, can be repaired only by removal or assimilation of the tear's source; that is, the foreigners seemingly unwilling or incapable of adapting to the dominant linguistic, cultural, and political forms associated with the majority population of the nation-state.

Like Freeman, Huntington deploys a logic of disaggregation to identify specific populations, not randomly chosen, as threats to the integrity of the body politic and bearers of instability, entropy, and chaos in politics. We do not need the language of biology, scripture, apartheid, or Jim Crow to translate the anxiety over very specific forms of difference into state and popular practices designed to forcibly assimilate populations, monitor their presence, or encourage those populations to leave.

David Laitin has sought to address these questions in his scholarship on nationalism and ethnic identity in Somalia and in the former Soviet Union. In his most recent work, Laitin posits that nationalism has cultural origins. His definition of culture, however, is minimalist, neither instrumentalist nor primordial. Culture is what binds people together in both their collective identification (who they are and how they relate to other self-differentiated groups) and their decision-making processes. Laitin utilizes what he characterizes as an equilibrium theory of culture, which operationalizes aspects of perspectives, ideas, and norms associated with group identity and identification and translates these aspects into formal language.[35] Culture is not a spigot variable, but a cluster of specific norms and understandings that motivate, guide, police, and sanction behavior. Laitin states, "No one has an incentive to deviate from either the norms of their cultural group or membership in it."[36]

Political Development and Modernity

Another research stream worth developing is how the recognition of racial and ethno-national regimes can broaden and complicate scholarly understanding of the relationship between democracy and inequality in modern politics. Carles Boix has written widely on the relationship between democracy, democratization, development, and inequality, employing a statistical analysis with large N data to examine the causal relationship between income and democracy, and inequality and development. Like O'Donnell, Boix utilizes a definition of democracy that emphasizes electoral choice and universal suffrage. Boix, however, compares and contrasts the degree of economic inequality in democratic polities over time, through a statistical assessment of income thresholds. Basing his analysis on annual data from political regimes across the world, as well as more global data about inequality, Boix draws strong correlations between development and democratic transitions and stability.

Boix's definition of democracy, the Boix-Rosato measure, has three components: "elections are free and competitive, the executive is accountable to citizens (whether through presidential elections or legislative elections in parliamentary systems) and at least half of the male electorate is enfranchised."[37] By inference, such a definition presupposes the denial of women's suffrage along with the exclusion of 50% of the male population, and is thus closer to Athenian and early 19th century versions of democracy than contemporary ones.

The proliferation of definitions and types of democracy and republicanism since classical Athens, however, requires much greater elaboration of the definition of democracy operative in the Boix-Rosato measure. In the contemporary world, few if any polities with an electoral threshold of 50% of the male population and with the exclusion of women would be considered democratic polities.

Rousseau, among others, provided a more expansive view of democracy as the articulation of a popular will, a view which frightened and enraged conservative thinkers like Joseph de Maistre and Edmund Burke. The French and Haitian revolutions, women's suffrage and feminist movements, civil rights movements of national minorities, anticolonial movements (each briefly considered in chapter 1), and the fall of totalitarian regimes of the former Soviet bloc in the 1990s exemplify the practical expansion of definitions of democracy and those who aspire to its practice. A definition of democracy rooted in Athenian criteria would hardly satisfy the bulk of the world's populations in Asia, Africa, Latin America, and the Middle East whose movements toward voluntary association, electoral transparency, and an end to capricious uses of state violence against dissidents and the poor have no parallel in the ancient world—except for slave revolts. The point here is that democracy, as both practice and concept, is not static. One of the signal changes in both philosophical and empirical explorations of democracy is how populations excluded from full civic participation in societies with highly restrictive citizenship regimes, totalitarian regimes, or both, act as if they have the rights of citizens, whether they have rights or not.

The second part of Boix's explication of the relationship between democracy and development pertains to exogenous factors of geopolitics and the fact that "great powers tend to deal with (and interfere in) the domestic politics of their allies (and, if possible, the allies of their enemies) as a further means of advancing their interests in the international area."[38] In developing this second dimension, Boix argues that democratic hegemons such as the United States end up supporting nondemocratic regimes in world politics because of the potential unreliability of new democracies and changing electoral fortunes. What could be characterized as a "confidence deficit" forms part of the calculus for evaluating risks associated with support for fledgling democracies. Yet there is another possible explanation for a democratic hegemon's support of nondemocratic regimes: the geopolitics of colonial and imperial rule.

The period of decolonization—roughly between 1955 and 1970, when the colonial satellites of the West in Asia, Africa, and parts of Latin America and the Caribbean gained independence from European powers and the United States—receives no mention in Boix's account. The role of Western powers in actually *discouraging* democratization during this period, in cases including India, Ghana, Guyana, Kenya, Algeria, the Dominican Republic, Morocco, Vietnam, and Chile among others, is an important part of the story of political development largely ignored by Western students of comparative politics—influencing not only the entropy and conflicts associated with the global South, but the wealth, rationalization and order of vibrant democratic polyarchies in the North.[39] Some of these examples are explored in chapter 4.

Both prior to and during the Cold War, the United States engaged in direct and indirect conflicts that resulted in low-intensity or outright warfare with a national army or local population for control of, or access to, natural resources such as oil, waterways, diamonds, precious metals, and minerals (e.g., in South Africa, Angola, Congo, Panama). Democratic and sometimes (as in the case of Panama under Noriega) authoritarian regimes actually threatened US, Belgian, and other hegemons' access to these resources.

Indeed, one of the sources of state and private wealth in the formerly imperial nation-states has been resource extraction from the so-called developing world,[40] a factor in the tale of development and underdevelopment that garners no mention in Boix's account, nor in the majority of canonical accounts of the relationship between democracy, capitalism, and political development. As in the case of France's relationship with Haiti, explored in chapter 3, resource extraction enriched the coffers not only of the French government, but the mercantile bourgeoisie. In the case of Britain, the provision of insurance to slave traders helped expand the insurance industry in Britain to global prominence. Lloyd's of London is one notable example. Port cities, cauldrons of trade and commerce, also benefited greatly from the trade in slaves: Nantes, Liverpool, and New York City are all global cities whose growth was aided, in part, by the slave trade.

The positivist response to these and similar claims has been to assert that neither colonialism nor modern slavery can be causally related to the birth or growth of capitalism. Yet if income is isolated from other factors that might contribute to the growth and spread of democracy within and across societies, as it is in Boix's models, then a more historicized account would have to identify both the sources and scale of profit income in early (mercantile) capitalist development that made the regeneration of wealth under industrial and finance capital possible. In other words, by understanding the sources of wealth creation we can better identify the limits of approaches that emphasize a causal relationship between colonialism, capitalism, and democracy. If one society's democracy is premised upon another society's (or population's) impoverishment, poorly remunerated labor, and coercion, then we would have to, at minimum, acknowledge that development and underdevelopment are not only dynamically intertwined, but may also be correlated. Despite some of its problems, dependency theory at least highlighted this entanglement.

Let us briefly consider one example of the relationship between racial slavery, mercantilism, and what some economists have referred to as "democratic capitalism," which can be broadly defined as nonelite based forms of capitalist enterprise. Paul Cabot, of the Cabot family of Boston, helped found the State Street Investment Corporation in 1924 as one of the first investment corporations to undertake a more scientific approach to investing. Their decision to invest—or not—in capitalist ventures was based upon data about a company's financial health (examination of financial ledgers) and prospects for return on investment, not on kinship, ethnic, or status networks. The State Street Investment Corporation was one of the first mutual fund companies in the world, based on the idea that people could invest and withdraw funds at any time, further socializing the risks but also the rewards of capitalist investment.

An admiring biographer writes that Paul Cabot "made professional money management services available to average investors on a democratic basis which, even in the troubles and scandals of recent years . . . has made a major contribution to human happiness."[41] Cabot, the son of Henry Bromfield Cabot, a prominent lawyer and real estate investor, later became treasurer of Harvard University and was directly responsible for the growth of Harvard's endowment.

The capital that helped launch the State Street Investment Corporation was generated via mercantilism, specifically trading in rum and slaves in the 18th century. The Cabots were among a class of European and US capitalists who, amid the French and US political revolutions along with the Industrial Revolution in Britain, generated substantial profit from the slave trade and slave-produced commodities such as sugar and rum. Although much of this story is well known among economists, sociologists, and historians of slavery, its implications for how we study comparative politics remains to be explored.

The impact of racial slavery upon the development of political and economic institutions in Europe, the Americas, and Africa has received little attention by students of comparative politics. Yet from the beginning of the transatlantic slave trade in the early 17th century until its demise in the Americas at the end of the 19th century, the slave trade had significant effects upon a range of political and financial institutions throughout the Atlantic World. This literature could be quite instructive for students of comparative politics seeking to develop new research streams that focus on the relationship between racial hierarchy and political institutions. As noted in an earlier chapter, the causes and effects of racial hierarchy extend well beyond the framing of either "race relations" or racial politics, taking us into territory about the fundamentals of capitalism, political, and economic development. Below is an exploration of scholarship that exposes the ways in which the transatlantic slave trade was integral to mercantile, and ultimately industrial capitalism—the creation of specific industries of trade, commerce, and production.

In the realm of politics, the slave trade and conflicts over its existence generated interstate wars as well as two civil wars (Haiti and the United States), disputes over territorial boundaries and sovereign recognition, as well as intrastate disputes over property, taxation, and territorial jurisdiction. The literature and its implications are too vast to revisit here, so what follows are highlighted areas of inquiry most relevant for the arguments put forth in this book.

Joseph Inikori has produced the most comprehensive accounts of the contribution of the transatlantic slave trade and the labor of Africans and their New World descendants to the emergence of Western capitalist financial institutions and economies as the dominant actors in the global political economy by the 17th century. The central point of Inikori's contribution to understanding the history of capitalist development is in his emphasis on the role of international trade in the Industrial Revolution in England, with comparative references to France, Spain, and Portugal in the 17th through 19th century. He gives examples of the role of international trade and commerce in the robust economies of Asia and the Third World during the latter quarter of the 20th century.[42] Echoing points raised by Walter Rodney, Andre Gunder Frank, Immanuel Wallerstein, and Eric Hobsbawm, Inikori provides ample empirical detail to demonstrate how the triangular trade between Europe, the Americas, and Africa involving textiles, capital investment, and traded human beings generated the bulk of profits plowed into the development of textile industries in England (cotton, silk, wool).[43] For Britain as well as France, slave labor in the Americas provided free labor central to the production of sugar, one of the most profitable commodities in global markets in the 18th and 19th centuries. West Africa became the site for the distribution and sale of finished cottons and linen produced in England from the raw materials produced in the Americas and India. The forced emigration of the enslaved from Africa to the New World contributed to a robust maritime economy and insurance industry that relied heavily upon the shipment of slaves and insurance policies purchased by slave owners and owners of slave ships. Several ports in cities such as New Orleans, New York City, Nantes and Marseilles thrived from the profits garnered by rental use and dockage of slave ships. The profits from the trading, transport, and labor of slaves had distinct but interrelated accruals for capitalist gain and ultimate investment in industrial production and technology. Inikori's argument, like those of

Eric Williams and C.L.R. James before him (along with William Darity, Jr.), has two significant implications for understanding the role of the production and trading of slaves during the Industrial Revolution.

Rather than treat slavery as an antiquated and inefficient mode of production rendered obsolete by industrialization, Inikori's evidence demonstrates how the profits from commodities produced by slave labor provided the capital for investment in new forms of technology (the cotton gin, for example), financial institutions, and emergent industries. The evidence marshaled from primary materials ranging from trader correspondence to national economic data of trading and financial institutions enabled Inikori to refute claims made by an earlier generation of economists such as Douglass North, who argued that the Industrial Revolution was a largely exogenous phenomenon driven by spontaneous technological innovation and subsequent industrialization to meet internal (national) demands for goods and services.[44] Inikori demonstrates that the British economy in the 17th and 18th century was not robust enough to sustain demand for locally produced goods. Economic stagnation in the domestic economy led the British government and entrepreneurs to seek larger markets outside of Britain and ultimately outside of Europe. Two of those burgeoning markets were on the West Coast of Africa and in India.

The term Industrial Revolution has been interpreted differently by various scholars, depending in part upon the emphasis given to particular aspects of the transformation of the English economy in the 18th century. Inikori and others do not dispute the unprecedented (and in this sense revolutionary) transformation in the British economy and manufacturing in this period. What is at stake for Inikori, however, is an explanation of the causes and sources of unprecedented growth in the quality, quantity, and efficiency of mass production. In the case of economies largely based upon subsistence agricultural production, classical economists such as David Ricardo, Adam Smith, and John Stuart Mill considered overseas trade to play a significant role in an increased division of labor as well as opportunities for commodity production. The enslaved, as chattel and productive labor supply, provided the means for European traders and producers to provide commodities for New World, European, and African markets and extend lines of credit to those who traded in slaves and commodities such as sugar and cotton, which in turn allowed the deepening and expansion of profits from these enterprises, as well as an increased capacity to capitalize other economic ventures of trade, production, and entrepreneurship.

The development of the credit industry in Britain is largely the result of financial dealings associated with the slave trade in the 18th century. As examined in detail by Sven Beckert and Seth Rockman, cotton harvested from the Americas was the major raw material for British commodities and the most significant source of public and private wealth in the British economy.[45]

> The labor of enslaved Africans did not only make possible large-scale commodity production for Atlantic commerce in the Americas. It also made possible the expansion of European consumption of these products. A combination of the economies of scale and the below subsistence cost of the labor of enslaved Africans brought down the cost of production and the consumer price of these products. Following from this, the American products changed over time from being luxury products for the European aristocracy and the upper middle class to necessities even for the lower classes. This explains the phenomenal expansion of Atlantic commerce during the period.[46]

For the Spanish and Portuguese, the discovery of silver, gold, and other precious metals in the New World generated significant resources for European markets, utilizing indigenous tribute, indentured, slave, wage, and contract labor to extract these commodities. In several instances of mineral and metal extraction, slave, tribute, wage, and contract labor worked collectively in mines such as those in Potosi, Peru.[47] Thus in both practical and historical terms, slave labor was not an antiquated, anachronistic artifact of precapitalist, preindustrial forms of accumulation, production, and profit, but complementary with capitalist modes of production.[48]

The literature in comparative politics on the development of political institutions in Africa during and after the era of colonialism largely ignores the impact of slavery upon African political development, whether in terms of localized ethnic politics or larger dynamics of territorial sovereignty and political rule over both populations and territory. Africanists in comparative politics have tended to focus on several facets of African colonial and postcolonial politics: property rights, ethnicities, structural adjustment, corruption, and state formation and deformation (failed states). Less attention has been paid to the impact of the triangular slave trade upon African political authority, political institutions, and war on the continent. In the literature on state formation, war is considered an important factor in the genesis of the modern state, first in the creation of landed estates, absolutist monarchies, and ultimately, what came to be described as the modern state—the apparatus that holds a monopoly on the use of force. European raiding of slaves led to the fall of several empires and the rise in states that traded in slaves as a source of revenue—the Dahomey—for example.[49] Warren Whatley and Rob Gillezeau provide empirical material demonstrating the increase of ethnic fragmentation and mistrust in response to the slave trade, and they identify a causal relationship between banditry and absolutism. According to their data, between 1700 and 1850 "a West African person faced a one in five chance of being swept up in the transatlantic slave trade sometime in his [*sic*] life."[50] Absolutism was based in promises of protection against capture by slave traders—among other potential perils—in exchange for political fealty and relinquishing the possibility for greater individual freedoms. As noted by Davidson, "As the slaving state become increasingly a predator, kinship systems were strengthened and elaborated as a means of providing protection against the dangers of the violence created by the slave trade."[51]

Political Deformation

Mahmood Mamdani's *Citizen and Subject* is one of the few books in comparative politics to explore the ways in which colonialism and its legacies impacted the development of political institutions in Africa.[52] Mamdani explicates a dual system under colonial rule that institutionalized colonizer preferences by linking tribal identification with political, economic, and social status. While there has been some debate over the generalizability of Mamdani's findings, we at minimum have a broader, more detailed historical context to explore the impact of Western nation-states and economies upon the development of political institutions on the continent.

One of the interpretive consequences of this consideration is to bring into question much of the "politics of the developing areas" literature, which based its assessments of developing nations' and regions' respective paths to development on a clear distinction between Western and non-Western nation-states and regions of the world. The templates of empire—the spheres of indirect influence and direct intervention by imperial nation-states such as the United States, France, Belgium, Britain, and Portugal have certainly entailed more than formal inter-state relationships.[53] Coups and corrupted elections, politically manipulated shifts in the price of commodities such as oil and guano, and strategic partnerships in global geopolitics complicate the neat distinctions between the developed and developing worlds. The economic and political fortunes of the developed world were, and are, deeply intertwined with the so-called developing world. As outlined in chapter 2, we can trace the evolution of specific laws, amendments, and legal precedents in several distinct nation-states to earlier imperial and colonial maneuvers to minimize the prospect of social and political conflict arising from populations who were never intended to be citizens.

The State's Reputation

Viewed through the lens of entanglement first proposed by the Martinican writer Édouard Glissant,[54] the intertwined fates of so-called developed and developing countries can be considered more dynamically. Formerly known as the Third World, the Global South has provided opportunities for more recent generations of scholars to idealize Western polities and represent shortcomings of political institutions and actors in Asia, Africa, and Latin America as symptomatic of underdeveloped political cultures. Authoritarianism, corruption, tribalism, and nepotism are the oft-cited culprits, as if they exist in these parts of the world and nowhere else.[55]

Yet, given the past 60 years of political turmoil, most recently the so-called Arab Spring, where a number of contemporary conflicts have their origins in the mandates system designed by Britain, France, the United States, and Germany after World War I, it is not an unreasonable question to ask whether comparative politics should focus greater attention on the political deformations introduced into the Global South by the major powers. Here in the gap between proclamations about democracy's export and the realities of democracy's denial by Western powers, scholars might discover yet another research stream in the distinction between how states represent their histories of interaction with other nation-states and regions of the world and how powerful nation-states utilize their power in the global geopolitics and political economy.

As explored in chapter 4, the migrated archives controversy revealed the discrepancy between the information the British government produced about itself—in its very arrangement of archival materials and its socialization of citizens and observers alike—as an exceptionalist, tutelary empire ("commonwealth") and the historical record of the empire as a both hegemonic and brutal enterprise. Other examples from the post–World War II period—Argentina, Brazil, and Chile during and after their authoritarian dictatorships, the French government's manipulation of information about the Algerian struggle for independence, Stalin's crimes against Jews in general and dissidents in particular—each point to statecraft designed to conceal the truth about government deeds that might threaten the state's historical posterity (propriety?).

With the explosion of the internet and technologies of surveillance over the past 20 years or so, scholars and journalists have paid increasing attention to incongruities between "statespeak," the discourses and rhetoric deployed by states to explain and justify domestic and international activities, and their effects upon national citizens and other populations. Scholarly and popular investigation into these discrepancies serves as a reminder of the usefulness of skepticism in the development of a research agenda, in determining the fault lines between rhetorical and policy practices and in discovering new sources of data and information. Certainly the Edward Snowdens and Julian Assanges of the world exemplify the effects of whistleblowers upon international politics in the era of information technology; just as they reveal the incursions powerful states and corporations make upon the privacy of average citizens.

Historical perspective is also important, however, for taking a longer view of the significance of these recent breaches of information and their import—in material and symbolic terms—for how we might understand threats to national security, human rights, and personal safety. The revelations of torture, kidnapping, and assassination of US civil rights workers, nationalist leaders in the British Commonwealth and, in the case of France, in Algeria and Vietnam, were also examples of breaches of information, whether spontaneous or belated, that had symbolic and material consequences for various US, British, and French governments after World War II. Well before hacking into government web pages became the norm, hacking of another sort—the brazen pilfering of confidential state documents by Daniel Ellsberg in the United States and by Catholic church activists against dictatorships in Argentina and Brazil[56]—brought to light details of covert state warfare often directed against its own citizens. These breaches led to efforts at reputation management by states, as well as hunting down and prosecuting perpetrators. The efforts by governments to repress, co-opt, or ignore claims by marginalized populations have become both part of a state's reputation management and the basis for democratic claims.

The abiding question scholars can ask of democratic states in these instances is whether the state's declaration of democracy and transparency should be taken at face value or if it should serve as a motivation for scholarly investigation. A reinvigorated skepticism, one more attuned to matters of difference, could help students of comparative politics generate more critical distance between state proclamations and state practices, particularly in the case of powerful state actors across the political spectrum, whether liberal and social democratic, authoritarian, or totalitarian. Lacking this skepticism, much of the comparative politics diagnoses of and prescriptions for the political ills of the developing areas resembled the foreign policies of the major powers, based in part on their idealization of the politics of the so-called developed world.

The lack of skepticism about a state's claims translates into neglected or ignored research questions. The carceral dimensions of British, French, and US domestic governance, with racialized and minoritized populations disproportionately represented in national prisons, provides a glimpse of one aspect of racial and ethno-national regimes operative in these societies. Comparisons of the carceral dimensions of these states is not a topic encouraged by dissertation advisors in top comparative politics PhD programs.

Clifford Geertz's trenchant observation in his essay on Bali, Indonesia, in which he declared that "symbols are not the effect of state power, but the source of state power" helps underscore[57] how symbols not only function as a source of propaganda (though they often do), but as a source of legitimacy and national unity, particularly during times of crisis. Though certainly not the sole source of state power, symbols are an oft-utilized weapon in a state's arsenal to project power, authority, and legitimacy. As we have regularly witnessed in Russia since the rise of Vladimir Putin, virulent smear campaigns can be just as effective in vanquishing a state's foes as poison or assassination. This dimension of state practice provides research opportunities for political anthropologists and comparativists in political science to examine the ways in which symbols of political power are constitutive of, and constituted in, state power.

In the cases of Britain, France, and the US, the public exposure of racial and ethno-national regimes in national and international discourse generated political crises in both their domestic and foreign policies. Vietnam, the civil rights movement in the United States, the Algerian revolution in France, and the waves of anticolonial mobilization against the British Empire in the 1950s generated crises in state reputation management. Public—and publicized—mistreatment of minorities led to the development of propaganda campaigns in France and the United States designed to downplay the ultimately systemic and institutional nature of state discriminations and repression, whether in local communities within the metropole or in the territories of colonized populations.[58] State reputation management has been one of the governmental responses to the gap between these states' declarations of their ideals and the real consequences of their practices, in this instance, of racial and ethno-national hierarchy and exclusion.[59]

Political anthropology provides several guides for comparative politics. The anthropologists Michel-Rolph Trouillot and Begoña Aretxaga were in some ways Clifford Geertz' methodological successors, in their semiotic interpretations of state practice, the role of the state in the development of national iconography for the creation of national myth, and ideology. James Scott and Lisa Wedeen are among the small cohort of political scientists who have attended to the more semiotic expressions of state power, legitimacy, and authority through comparison.

In "Maddening States," Aretxaga writes that "the state cannot exist without this subjective component, which links its form to the dynamics of people and movements," highlighting the centrality of symbols and semiotics to state power and legitimacy.[60] Like Geertz, Aretxaga calls attention to the state's fictive dimension, producing its own "genre of representation, involving, ritual, gestures, pageantry and ceremony."[61] Particularly repressive regimes, as in the case of Haiti and the colonial regimes of the British Empire, utilize assassinations, kidnapping, disappearances, and imprisonment not only for the purpose of immediate punishment, but as representative symbols of a state's coercive power and the prospect of recurrent expression, scaring away actual and potential dissidents. Aretxaga refers to these state practices as "spectral reality," the material and symbolic expression of state power.[62]

For Trouillot, an ethnography of the state provides an opportunity to trace a state's practices, processes, and effects. The state is neither entirely beholden nor, obversely, autonomous from societal pressures. Moreover, societal pressures upon a state cannot be reduced or always traced to material or economic constraints. In his scholarship on Haiti, as well as in his scholarship on the state as concept and apparatus, Trouillot conceptualizes an ethnography of state power that enables a closer reading of how states administer and mediate the relationship between micro and macro politics.[63] In the case of Haiti, the power and effects of several Duvalier regimes could be witnessed and observed at the local level. Minor bureaucrats and militias associated with the security forces of Papa Doc and his successor, Baby Doc, deployed repertoires of rhetorical and symbolic forms laden with populist imagery, a Negritudean inspired racial and cultural identification, symbolically linking the Duvalierist state to the Haitian peasantry and urban workers.[64] This created a black elite through state patronage and clientelism to accompany the shock troops, the *tonton-makouts*, while brutally suppressing dissent and exploiting the rural peasantry.[65] Trouillot makes clear how power and domination are not solely expressed in coercive forms.

Trouillot and Aretxaga, however, are also preoccupied with state power and its effects on cultural processes during both normal and exceptional times. Both provide ethnographic examples of how state semiotics actually generate and create popular norms, as well as opportunities to contest state domination, in colonial and postcolonial settings. They also represent a methodological departure from Foucault, for whom power is virtually everywhere, with detail of how state power is congealed and generated for purposes of control and domination. Aretxaga's ethnography of the hunger strikes that led to the death of Bobby Sands evidence the conflictual relationship between an occupying power (the British government) and a nationalist movement. Sands and other patriots utilized their very bodies and effluent to contest the state's ability to define them as criminals and not political prisoners. Aretxaga's detailing of conflicts over the distinctions between political prisoners and common criminals, colonial subjects and national citizens, or an army of occupation and a police force have comparative resonance in a variety of civil rights, anticolonial, nationalist movements.

Earlier generations of sociologists and political scientists made important contributions to a more semiotic understanding of the state as a site of normative manufacture. Murray Edelman wrote in *The Symbolic Uses of Politics that* the state

> is an abstraction, but in its name men are jailed or made rich on oil depletion allowances and defense contracts, or killed in wars. . . . Political forms come to symbolize what large masses of men need to believe about the state to reassure themselves. It is the needs, the hopes and the anxieties of men that determine the meanings. . . . Political symbols bring out in concentrated form those particular meanings and emotions which the members of a group create and reinforce in each other.[66]

George Mosse, in his pathbreaking work 40 years ago about the relationship between art, aesthetics, and politics, described what he termed the new politics of the Nazi regime.[67] Borrowing from republican and democratic traditions, the Nazi regime involved the masses in nation-building, making and maintaining the new political order. The masses were not just obedient followers of middle classes and elites; they had their own separate role to play. The new politics drew people into active national political participation through rites and festivals as myths and symbols that gave a concrete expression to the general will.[68]

George Steinmetz has urged scholars to utilize a more maximalist view of states, enabling scholars to comprehend a state's form and functionalities not only as a cluster or apparatus of "coercion wielding organizations," but also as an executor of cultural techniques not reducible to a single class or social formation.[69]

An important technique in the interpretive approaches of Trouillot and Aretxaga is their semiotic decoding of state practices to reveal distinctions between what states represent and their actual activities. The ability of states to represent their practices and justifications as objective renderings of often discordant and internally contradictory interests is a key element of noncoercive power. Whether in the targeting and marginalizing of internal populations in the name of order or crisis, or prosecuting wars upon other populations and territories in the name of "national security," international socialism, or ethnic cleansing, state explanations and justifications for their practices often seek to conceal interests that are not fully acknowledged in official explanations. Here is where skepticism could serve as a core cognitive element in a comparativists' interpretive scheme: doubt regarding a state's ability (particularly a democratic state) to provide a transparent accounting of all its policies and objectives, interests, networks, alliances, and weaknesses.

State mythologies provide opportunities for states to symbolically bind themselves to their citizenry, developing allegiance to the state and its ideals through political socialization.[70] Governments, even democratic ones, deploy strategies of reputation management to conceal or justify the existence of racial and ethno-national regimes. Like few other informal and formal institutional practices, racial and ethno-national regimes provide an opportunity to examine the dynamic interaction between populations subject to those regimes and those groups and institutions that impose them. On the whole, scholars are no less immune to the galvanizing appeals of state mythologies than other members of a society and polity, which might help account for some of the reluctance of students of comparative politics to explore the dark side of their profession.

The path toward the dark side is strewn with histories of exclusion, often with invocations of national security in the name of democracy, in order to keep certain ethno-national, racial, and religious minorities, immigrants, foreigners, and political dissenters, outside the political community, or outside society altogether. These archaeologies of exclusion have histories of their own, at once distinct and intertwined with histories of democracy. The spectre of race, one panel in a larger tapestry of difference, can help illuminate the costs that have been borne by democracy's victims.

Postscript

FROM ATHENS TO CHARLOTTESVILLE

There are times when the crises of an era match a scholar's abiding preoccupations. For students of nationalism, xenophobia, racism, and citizenship, the second decade of the 21st century has provided ample opportunity to observe and examine how ideas and concepts such as those just noted get invoked in actual politics. The bulk of the research and writing for this book was completed before the election of Donald Trump in the United States and the resurgence of authoritarian populism in both the US and Europe. Readers who are not academics or specialists of some sort, however, might still wonder how all of this effort at measured, scholarly investigation into the relationship between democracy and political inequality helps explain our contemporary moment in which social and political movements within nation-states as diverse as South Sudan, Israel, Myanmar, and South Africa in addition to the United States, Britain, and France, have advocated, sometimes strenuously, for the assimilation or outright expulsion of one or more populations from their societies.

To better comprehend the recent upsurge in authoritarian populist, fascistic, and fascist movements that exacerbate racism, chauvinism, and xenophobia, it is important to distinguish between epochal trends, historical patterns, and systemic features within both nationalism and the nation-state system. The spectre of difference has hovered over democratic polities ranging from classical Athens to contemporary nation-states. The fear, the fright of difference is only unknown to those who have not been paying attention.

The quest for homogeneity and the utilization of democratic practices and institutions to manage political inequality are often combined by governments and nationalists during moments of perceived or actual crisis to further marginalize populations that are considered unworthy of participation in the polity or, worse still, membership in society altogether. Threats of war and invasion, economic recession, and a sudden influx of unwelcome migration streams, are all triggers for the urge to population homogenization articulated in politics.

One of the lessons to be drawn from this book is that these recent movements are either rooted in or gain inspiration from movements lodged in other times and places. Some of these inspirations are fascist, or what could be called fascistic, but more broadly steeped in the language of nationhood and statehood, and the role of difference, whether ethno-national, religious, racial, and "civilizational," in marking perceived boundaries between peoples.

The belief that occupants of the category of the citizen, as well as the state which coheres them, must share common cultural and territorial origins can be found in debates in classical Athens, but also in many parts of the world entirely unrelated to Greece. One of the questions posed but unanswered by this book is whether the tendency toward homogeneity is simply an unattractive human trait, to be found wherever and whenever human beings come into some form of political community, or whether certain parts of the world exhibit this tendency more than others. I have sought to provide an answer to whether this tendency, when exhibited in Western nation-states with liberal democratic polities, has impacted how democracy has been practiced therein. How those who are perceived as different from members of the dominant or foundational group (often one and the same) should be treated, not just in social terms, but in political terms, is a core preoccupation of this book. This question encompasses concerns about minority rights as well as the rights of migrants and immigrants.

In terms of immigration, with the exception of the sudden rush of immigrants into a particular country where thousands and in some cases millions of people seek relief from war, mass expulsion, genocide, and famine, the overwhelming majority of cases where immigration is viewed as a problem are not problems of immigration. Instead, they are problems of perception that undergird, explicitly or implicitly, public and private deliberations about the perceived worthiness of particular groups of immigrants. Those perceptions, in turn, are often based on the perceived worthiness of particular groups for labor, residency, assimilation, and, in some cases, participation in the body politic, the political body of the nation, particularly if that nation is based upon republican and democratic principles that expect citizens to actively take part. Within this process of deliberation and reflection, certain populations are considered more worthy of labor than citizenship; others are considered prime candidates for a combination of labor and citizenship, and yet others are deemed unfit for either labor or political participation. Others, for reasons of criminality or ideology (sometimes their definitions overlap) are determined to be unworthy of entry, much less citizenship and residency. Thus, some immigrants enter into many countries without comment (such as Europeans into the United States) while others generate commentary (Syrians in Austria, Latin Americans and Muslims in the US). The fears and anxieties often reveal long-standing ethno-national, religious, and racist biases, which in turn find their way into governmental policy and public debate.

One of the ongoing normative paradoxes of societies with liberal, republican polities is that for all their emphasis on individualism, personal liberties, and freedoms, popular discourses and state logics nevertheless emphasize group distinctions, as evidenced in EU and US policies regarding emigrants from Muslim countries. Thus, the first form of inequality is perceptual discrimination, which precedes discriminations articulated in law and policy. Perceptual group discrimination deployed to distinguish between safe and dangerous immigrants poses obvious and practical dangers to efficient statecraft designed to protect citizens from physical harm. Definitions of trustworthiness, based on race, ethnicity, nationality, or religion in a democratic polity are ultimately unreliable.

By their design (though not intention), immigration and citizenship restrictions based on corporal and origin criteria ultimately misidentify actual threats to a society and its citizens among minority populations, while ignoring internally-generated threats to a society's stability. As I write these words, considerable discussion is ongoing in the United States regarding the prospect of Russian influence in the 2016 US presidential election. At issue is whether the president-elect, or at minimum, the president-elect's campaign personnel, sought and received assistance from the Russian government in influencing the outcome of the election in the president-elect's favor. Regardless of the outcome of the investigations into possible malfeasance (or even treason) attributed to Donald Trump's campaign, there are larger lessons to learn not only about the fragile nature of democracies and threats to their health, but also their sources of support. Among those most devoted to democratic ideals and practices are people who are not formally members of the political community. Conversely, there are those with formal membership in the political community of a democratic polity who are quite likely, even routinely, to betray that community's ideals. In the case of classical Athens, Aristotle is a prime example—as is Fannie Lou

Hamer in the United States or Thereza Santos in Brazil—of people who upheld democratic principles in the very societies and polities that denied them full membership in the polity. In the second instance, we can think of Richard Nixon or Timothy McVeigh in the United States, or the Duke of Windsor in Britain in the 1930s.

In addition to the issue of immigration, there is the matter of a European or Western civilization premised on dream that refuses to die: a dream of unity, if not uniformity, of peoples and nation-states organized under the banner of the West. Blandishments articulated by European heads of state and EU officials about a single European culture, civilization, and core values ring hollow against the backdrop of interstate conflicts—including but not limited to warfare—across 400 years, especially World Wars I and II, the cacophony of languages, and differences in cuisine, taste, economies, topography, and governance within the region.

With Brexit close to becoming a bureaucratic reality, and the breakup of the United Kingdom that might well follow, with Catalan nationalists threatening to secede from Spain, we have two of many political crises that exemplify that the idealized image of a coherent, unified Europe never matched its linguistic, cultural, social, political, and economic diversity. In most European nation-states, the US, and many nation-states in Latin America and Asia, the history is that race, nationality, religion, and ethnicity have helped determine who shall enter and who shall not, who can reside and who cannot, and ultimately, who can be a full citizen and who cannot.

On the eve of the white nationalist demonstrations and counterprotests in Charlottesville, Virginia, on August 14, 2017, right wing nationalists, fascists, and Nazi sympathizers gathered in front of several monuments to the Confederacy that had been targeted for demolition. Their chilling, well-rehearsed chant will be familiar to those who viewed the video footage compiled by the reporter embedded in the crowd of mostly male white nationalists who marched through the streets with torches and shouted in unison, "ground and soil," "we will not be replaced," and "the Jews will not replace us." In a country with a remarkable lack of historical memory, the words and deeds of white nationalist protestors that evening were often interpreted by everyday citizens, pundits, and politicians alike as "unprecedented" expressions of "pure evil." Yet, anyone with any historical knowledge of the US civil rights movement or the fascist and antifascist mobilization of World War II will recognize the invocations of whiteness, anti-Semitism, and Nazism in Charlottesville in 2017 as a composite echo of previous periods in

US history: the invocation of a political community in search of a following, drenched in racist ideology.

One of the spokespeople who received the most attention for several days after the events in Charlottesville revealed to an interviewer his dream of an ethno-state, presumably a nation-state in which the governed and the government were racially unified. This particular racist vision as civic imaginary bears traces of the vision of Edward Augustus Freeman and Woodrow Wilson, two of several advocates of democracy, political modernity, and racial hierarchy examined in several chapters of this book. Yet the invocations of the white racists in Charlottesville also contained elements of an older, ancient series of associations which, as we have discovered, can be traced back to classical Athens of the 5th century BCE—of blood and soil. In 2017, these white nationalists proclaimed their inheritance of not only the soil of the United States, but the polity as well, notwithstanding the fact that the Jews, Blacks, Latinos and others prohibited from sharing their ethno-state could also make similar claims to the same blood and soil in the United States. Their very language of "replacement" suggested that the hoped for polity of white nationalists was one in which citizens were born, not made. No amount of religious conversion or socialization could compensate for the inherent limitations of the excluded groups.

Their criteria for a white nationalist civic imaginary also included a warning of the dangers of miscegenation between white women and non-Aryan men, with a clearly articulated desire to protect their women from the clutches of Jews and blacks. As in the case of classical Athens, this particular articulation of autochthony reveals male anxieties over women's sovereignty over their own bodies, the corporal sovereignty and autonomy of women in relation to men, and ultimately, patriarchy, paternity and citizenship.

There are limits in drawing parallels between the 2017 events in Charlottesville and classical Athens, between the exhortations of fascists and neo-fascists with the intellectuals, playwrights, and citizens of Athens regarding the most preferable form of political life. Yet several formal and substantive parallels can be drawn in a more generalizable consideration of the relationship between myth and politics. First, myths are often implicated in power dynamics and politics, since they often have served to justify the condition of human beings in relation to other human beings, regardless of the fact that myths often have no basis in the history of any individual or collectivity. Human beings come into existence through procreation. People become citizens through politics, not nature and certainly not the soil. Second, the linkage of autochthony, blood and soil with citizenship, whether in Athens,

Nazi Germany, or the contemporary United States, ultimately entails the disenfranchisement of an extant group of citizens, and the categorical exclusion of groups of people who would otherwise be eligible for citizenship.

The mythos of the new autochthonists like their predecessors in the 1920s through the 1940s in Germany, Italy, Argentina, Brazil and in the United States, is to make the racial imaginary coterminous with the civic imaginary. The central problem these acted-upon desires would require is the removal, marginalization, or eradication of those excluded from participation in the polity. This project would require the disenfranchisement of Blacks, Jews, Asian Americans, Latinos, and indigenous peoples (whose relationship to US citizenship has its own tortured history). The disenfranchisement of a portion of the US citizenry would be similar to the disenfranchisement of millions of Jews in Nazi Germany, Poland, Austria, and Italy in the 1930s and 1940s. Such a project would entail significant costs—political, social, moral, psychological, ethical—to white nationalists and opponents alike, in the effort to remake US society and polity. In 2017, the world witnessed the lengths some white nationalist groups will go to publicize if not implement their vision of political community in the United States. We have also seen the lengths that proponents of an ethos-centered vision of democracy will go to in countering the ethnos-centered vision of political community in Boston, Phoenix, and other cities in the aftermath of Charlottesville. This is the "real" United States. There is no other.

The lesson I would like to emphasize here for our contemporary moment is that population homogeneity, like the category of the foreigner and citizen, is a political artifact, not something we find ready-made in the world. So much of the origin tales told by various ultranationalist and xenophobic movements is mythical, not historical. Common to the city-states of the classical era and the nation-states of the modern world is their emphasis on origins, and marks of difference among their populations, to distinguish citizen from noncitizen. The nation-state system, a constitutive unit of modern politics, has provided the administrative and territorial template for political actors to correlate the body politic with actual bodies, to distinguish the members of the polity from the mass of bodies in society.

Here is where we can identify what Antonio Gramsci termed "philosophical sediment," traces of disparate, often dominant ideas of a previous era reactivated in a subsequent era. This sediment becomes the firmament for what Gramsci referred to as the folklore of the future, in this context, the common sense racist and xenophobic understandings of the dangers to be had not only by so-called race mixture or miscegenation, but the coexistence of equal and unequal actors in the same polity; certain foreigners, not all foreigners, pose dangers; miscegenation can negatively impact society and polity and thus civilization.

On the other hand, more liberal justifications for less restrictive immigration policies and an embrace of multiculturalism often misrepresent past immigration and citizenship regimes in triumphalist narratives of diversity and inclusion. Ironically, contemporary anti-immigrant movements in many nation-states more accurately reflect the history of immigration policies, controls, and debates than do more liberal arguments. For example, former President of the United States Barack Obama stated on numerous occasions the oft-cited cliché that the United States was—and is—a nation of immigrants, to which we can respond by noting that Japanese internment during World War II, the Asian Exclusion Act, and the Alien and Sedition Acts determined which racial, ethno-national, and ideological others were interpreted as potential dangers and not potential or actual citizens. It will be more accurate to restate this homily in the following way: that most nation-states with histories of significant immigration have selectively accepted migration flows from certain parts of the world more readily than from other parts. Some immigrant groups have been more readily integrated into national societies than others. This restatement would probably not serve a political candidate well on the campaign trail, but it is closer to the truth.

Whether in the United States or Europe, the new autochthonists share a common, problematic relation to the past: their longed for past was—and is—invariably crowded with people who lived in the same territory, who were, for one reason or another, not them. Those people must be assimilated and incorporated into the nation-state or removed, "pacified," or exterminated. Thus, to return to the actual past, that past of state legitimation and the churning formation of different nationalities, ethnicities, and languages into a "national population" would require the reenactment of policies of empire—genocide, centralization, relocation, and removal of the others—to create the homogeneity—the myth of homogeneity—that contemporary nationalists and xenophobes crave.

The nation-state conjoins a loyal, national population residing in a territory to a unitary state that presides over both territory and population. Unlike earlier moments in human history where towns, villages, kinship, empires, principalities, and nomads were far more recognizable modes of human community than nation-states, nation-states provide containers to situate governments and populations within the same territorial unit.

The quest for homogeneity links immigration, citizenship, and racial regimes into a holistic vision of a political community. This vision is steeped in the hope that homogeneity will eclipse the need for politics. If everyone was the same, there would be no need to negotiate difference. Racial, religious, and ethno-national homogeneity will somehow beget unanimity and the obsolescence of politics. The trace of this belief oddly enough links the advocates for a wall between Mexico and the United States to the advocates for a caliphate. The quest for unanimity—whether among the advocates for a caliphate, "America for Americans," or for a "Europe for Europeans"—must necessarily be a rejection of the individual and a very impoverished understanding of the idea of a people.

Both right and most liberal pundits ignore a simple fact: the nation-state has *always* been a container populated by an ever-evolving assortment of nationalities, languages, migrants, and religions. Diversity on its own will not produce democracy, no more than homogeneous societies will. If this were the case, then Saint-Domingue could have avoided a costly anti-imperialist war for national independence, if only mulattos, free people of color, big whites, and small whites valued their respective differences.

The second assumption of contemporary autochthony claims is that national minorities and immigrants, especially semiskilled and unskilled workers, are taking jobs away from hard working members of the dominant group, particularly its working class sectors. These increasingly marginal segments of dominant demographic groups are often represented in populist rhetoric as the original or foundational population, the standard by which all subsequent immigrant groups must measure. Except in most cases, the original population was also a plural population that is, composed of multiple ethnic, linguistic, and religious groups. This is certainly the case with the United States, France, Britain, Germany, and even smaller European nation-states like Switzerland, Italy, Spain, Portugal, and Belgium. With few exceptions, the overwhelming majority of nation-states, city-states, colonies, or principalities in the world's history were founded with more than one readily identifiable population.

The disagreements within Europe regarding who is, and who can be, a European and even more specifically, who can and cannot cross national and regional boundaries, generated another set of questions: Shall we let any of these outsiders in, and if so, which ones? By what criteria shall we include some people and exclude others? Once allowed in, who should be encouraged to leave, and who should be encouraged to stay?

How people answer these questions in vastly distinct places in the world will help determine whether an ethos or an ethnos of democracy ultimately prevails in what is often referred to as the West.

APPENDIX

TABLE A.1. Political Prohibitions on People of African Descent in Latin America and the Caribbean, 1805–1900

	Slavery Abolished	Literacy Requirements	Property Ownership/ Professional Occupation Requirements	Exclusion of Servants, Day/ Wage Laborers, and/or Debtors
Argentina	1853	X	X	X
Bolivia	1861	X	X	X
Brazil	1888	X	X	X
Chile	1823	X	X	X
Colombia	1852	X	X	X
Costa Rica	1824	X	X	X
Cuba	1886	X	X	X
Dominican Republic	1822	X (until 1865)	X	
Ecuador	1851	X	X	X
El Salvador	1824	X	X	X
Federal Republic of Central America	1824		X	X
Guatemala	1824	X	X	X
Haiti				
Honduras	1824	X (until1894)	X	X
Mexico	1829	X (until 1857)		
Nicaragua	1824	X (until 1893)	X	X
Panama	1852	X	X	X
Paraguay	1869	X (until 1870)		X
Peru	1854	X	X	X
Puerto Rico		X	X	X
Uruguay	1842	X	X	X
Venezuela	1854	X	X	X

Note: see Loveman, Brian, pp 115–145.

TABLE A.2. Affirmative Action Policies in Latin America and the Caribbean (1991–2008)*

	Quotas for Education, Public Labor Force, and/or Legislative Representation	Collective Land Rights	Antidiscrimination Laws
Argentina			
Bolivia			
Brazil	X	X	
Chile			
Colombia	X	X	
Costa Rica			
Cuba			
Dominican Republic			
Ecuador		X	
El Salvador			
French Guinea			
Guatemala		X	
Haiti			
Honduras		X	
Jamaica			
Mexico			
Nicaragua		X	
Panama			X
Paraguay			
Peru			
Puerto Rico			
Uruguay			
Venezuela			

*Not including laws prohibiting racial discrimination, such as those passed in the 1940s in Cuba and Venezuela and those in Peru (see Cottrol, 2013: 283-288)

Countries of Latin America and the Caribbean from 1805 to the end of the century that created literacy, property, and other laws specifically designed to limit or prohibit voting and other forms of political participation of freed blacks, slaves, and their descendants.

Country		Type of Laws
Argentina	Yes	**I. Citizenship limited to:** free men, married or over the age of 20, and literate. Denied to women, slaves, illiterates, servants, wage workers, line infantrymen, and debtors (1826 Art. 4, 6, ratified by subsequent constitutions, see for instance 1831). **II. Public office holding limited to:** citizens, with property, or in professional occupations. Denied to women, slaves, illiterates, and the propertyless (1819 Art. 5, 9; ratified by subsequent constitutions, see for instance 1826). **III. Voting rights limited to:** citizens. Denied to women, slaves, servants, wage workers, and illiterates (1826 Art. 13).
Bolivia	Yes	**I. Citizenship limited to:** men, married or over the age of 21, literate, and in professional occupations. Denied to women, domestic servants, illiterates, and debtors (1826, Art. 14, 18. Ratified by subsequent constitutions, see for instance 1831 Art. 12; 1834 Art. 12; 1839 Art. 12; 1871 Art.24; 1880 Art. 33). **II. Public office holding limited to:** literate citizens, requirement of property ownership or professional occupation were added in the 1831 Constitution. Denied to women, domestic servants, illiterates, and the propertyless (1826 Art. 17, 24, 42; 1831 Art. 13, 35, 42, 97, 112, 115, 135; 1834 Art. 35, 43; 1839 Art. 28,72, 100; 1843 Art. 21, 25, 47; 1851 Art. 57, 61, 88; 1880 Art. 57, 62). **III. Voting rights limited to:** citizens. Denied to women, domestic servants, the unemployed, and illiterates (1826 Art. 14–19).
Brazil	Yes	**I. Citizenship limited to:** free men. Denied to slaves and women (1824 Art. 6). **II. Public office holding limited to:** citizens with property or in professional occupations. Denied to slaves, women, and the propertyless (1824 Art. 45, 75). **III. Voting rights limited to:** literate citizens. Denied to women, manumitted slaves, servants, and the propertyless (1824 Art. 90–97).
Chile	Yes	**I. Citizenship limited to:** men, married and 21 years old or unmarried and over the age of 25, literate, with property or in professional occupations. Denied to women, domestic servants, debtors, illiterates and the propertyless (1833 Art. 8–11). **II. Public office holding limited to:** citizens with voting rights, property owners (1833, Art. 21, 32, 60,85,126) **III. Voting rights limited to:** men, married and 21 years old or unmarried and over the age of 25, literate, with property of in professional occupations. Denied to women, domestic servants, illiterates, the propertyless, and debtors (1833 Art. 8–11)
Colombia	Yes	**I. Citizenship limited to:** free men, married or over the age of 21, literate, with property or in professional occupations. Denied to women, slaves, domestic servants, day-laborers, illiterates, the propertyless, and debtors (1830, Art. 9, 14, 15, 16) Slavery is abolished in 1852 and subsequent constitutions drop restriction of citizenship to free peoples (1886 Art. 22). **II. Public office holding limited to:** citizens with property or in professional occupations. Denied to women, slaves, and the propertyless

Continued on next page

Country		Type of Laws
		(1830 Art. 50, 62, 122, 129, 1886 Art. 94, 100, 133, 150) **III. Voting rights limited to:** citizens with property. Denied to women, slaves, servants, day-laborers, illiterates and the propertyless (1830, Art. 22; 1889 Art. 173).
Costa Rica	Yes	See *Federal Republic of Central America* for prior laws. **I. Citizenship limited to:** men, married, or over the age of 20, or in professional occupations or other means of subsistence. Denied to women, domestic servants, the propertyless, and debtors (1844 Art. 60, 61). **II. Public office holding limited to:** citizens, literate, with property. Denied to domestic servants, women, illiterate, and the propertyless (1844 Art. 63, 97, 120, 133). **III. Voting rights limited to:** men over 25, married or widowers, with property. Denied to women and the propertyless (1844 Art. 80).
Cuba	Yes	Spanish colony until 1898. **I. Citizenship limited to:** free men, born of two Spanish parents, and literate. Citizenship may be available to those with African lineage under special circumstances. Denied to slaves, women, illiterates (Cádiz Constitution of 1812, Art. 5, 18–25). Restrictions on Afro-Cuban political organizations (*cabildos*).
Dominican Republic	Yes	**I. Citizenship limited to:** men (1844 Art. 7–14) **II Public office holding limited to:** men with property. Denied to women and the propertyless (1844 Art. 48, 62, 141, 150) **III. Voting rights limited to:** men, with property or professional occupations. Denied to women and the propertyless (1844 Art. 160).
Ecuador	Yes	**I. Citizenship limited to:** men, married or over the age of 22, literate, and with property or in professional occupations. Denied to women, domestic servants, illiterates, the propertyless, and debtors (1830 Art.12) **II. Public office holding limited to:** men over 30 with property or profession. Denied to women, illiterates and the propertyless (1830 Art.24) **III. Voting rights limited to:** citizens over the age of 25 with property or in professional occupations. Denied to women, illiterates, and the propertyless (1830 Art. 16).
El Salvador	Yes	See *Federal Republic of Central America* for prior laws. **I. Citizenship limited to:** men, over the age of 21, who are heads of household, or are literate, or own property. Denied to women, domestic servants, illiterates, the propertyless, the unemployed, and debtors (1841 Art. 4–8) **II. Public office holding limited to:** men, literate, with property. Denied to women, domestic servants, illiterates and the propertyless (1841 Art.11).
Federal Republic of Central America	Yes	**I. Citizenship limited to:** men, married or over the age of 18, with property or in professional occupations. Denied to women, domestic servants, debtors, and slave traffickers (1824 Art. 13, 14, 21). **II. Public office holding limited to:** citizens (1824 Art 22, 90, 110, 130, 133). **III. Voting rights limited to:** citizens (1824 Art. 24).
Guatemala	Yes	See *Federal Republic of Central America* for prior laws. **I. Citizenship limited to:** men, over the age of 21 or over the age of 18 if in the military, with property or in professional occupations. Denied to women, the unemployed, and debtors (1851 Art. 1; 1879 Art. 8; 1886 Art. 8) **II. Public**

Country		Type of Laws
		office holding limited to: citizens, over the age of 21 or over the age of 18 if in the military, with property or in professional occupations. Denied to women, the unemployed, and debtors (1851 Art. 1, 2; 1879 Art. 8, 9, 49, 65, 81) **III. Voting rights limited to:** citizens, over the age of 21 or over the age of 18 if in the military, with property or in professional occupations. Denied to women, the unemployed, and debtors (1879 Art. 8, 9).
Haiti	No	No constitutional measures to limit or prohibit the political participation of freed blacks or their descendants (1805 Constitution).
Honduras	Yes	See *Federal Republic of Central America* for prior laws. **I. Citizenship limited to:** men, over the age of 18 if married or degree-holding, over the age of 20 otherwise, with property or in professional occupations. Denied to women, domestic servants, illiterates, and the propertyless (1865 Art. 13–16). **II. Public office holding limited to:** citizens, with property or degree-holding. Denied to domestic servants, women, illiterate, and propertyless majorities (1865 Art. 23, 31, 37, 53,). **III. Voting rights limited to:** citizens (1865 Art. 18; 1880 Art. 35, 36).
Mexico	No	**I. Citizenship limited to:** men, married or over the age of 21. Denied to women (1857 Art. 34). **II. Public office holding limited to:** citizens. Denied to women (1824 Art. 19, 24, 28, 76 1857 Art. 56, 77,93). **III. Voting rights limited to:** citizens. Denied to women. Establishment of additional qualifications delegated to state legislatures (1824 Art. 9).
Nicaragua	Yes	See *Federal Republic of Central America* for prior laws. **I. Citizenship limited to:** men, over the age of 18 if married or degree-holding, over the age of 20 otherwise, with property or in professional occupations. Denied to women, debtors, slave traffickers, and the propertyless (1858 Art. 8–10). **II. Public office holding limited to:** citizens, heads of household, property requirements for the presidency and for senators (1858 Art. 28–31). **III. Voting rights limited to:** citizens (1858 Art. 9).
Panama	Yes	Part of Colombia until 1903. **I. Citizenship limited to:** free men, married or over the age of 21, literate, with property, or in professional occupations. Denied to women, slaves, domestic servants, day-laborers, illiterates, the propertyless, and debtors (1830, Art. 9, 14, 15, 16). Slavery is abolished in 1852 and subsequent constitutions drop restriction of citizenship to free peoples (1886 Art. 22). **II. Public office holding limited to:** citizens with property or in professional occupations. Denied to women, slaves, and the propertyless (1830 Art. 50, 62, 122, 129, 1886 Art. 94, 100, 133, 150). **III. Voting rights limited to:** citizens with property. Denied to women, slaves, servants, day-laborers, illiterates, and the propertyless (1830, Art. 22; 1889 Art. 173).
Paraguay	No	**I. Citizenship limited to:** men over the age of 18. Denied to women and debtors (1870 Art. 35–41) **II. Public office holding limited to:** citizens, Christians. Denied to women (1870 Art. 46, 89, 111) **III. Voting rights limited to:** Men over 18. Denied to women, debtors, and deployed members of the armed forces. (1870 Art. 38, 39).

Continued on next page

Country		Type of Laws
Peru	Yes	**I. Citizenship limited to:** men, married or over the age of 25, literate, with property or in professional occupations. Denied to women, servants, debtors, the unemployed, illiterates, the propertyless, and slave traffickers (1823 Art. 12, 17, 24; 1856 36) **II. Public office holding limited to:** citizens, with property or in professional occupations. Denied to women, servants, debtors, the unemployed, illiterates, and the propertyless (1823 Art. 22; 1856 Art. 46, 74, 105) **III. Voting rights limited to:** citizens, with property, or in professional occupations. Denied to women, servants, debtors, the unemployed, illiterates, and the propertyless (1823 Art. 34, 43, 75; 1856 Art. 37).
Puerto Rico	Yes	Spanish colony until 1898. **I. Citizenship limited to:** free men, born of two Spanish parents and literate. Citizenship may be available to those with African lineage under special circumstances. Denied to slaves, women, illiterates (Cádiz Constitution of 1812, Art. 5, 18–25).
Uruguay	Yes	**I. Citizenship limited to:** free men, married or over the age of 20, and literate. Denied to women, slaves, servants, day-laborers, illiterates, line infantrymen, and debtors (1830 Art. 6–12). **II. Public office holding limited to:** citizens, with property, or in professional occupations. Denied to women, slaves, illiterates, and the propertyless (1830 Art. 10, 24, 30, 74, 87, 93, 119). **III. Voting rights limited to:** citizens. Denied to women, slaves, and illiterates (1830 Art. 9).
Venezuela	Yes	**I. Citizenship limited to:** free men, married or over the age of 21, literate, with property or in professional occupations. Denied to women, slaves, domestic servants, illiterates, the propertyless, and debtors (1830 Art. 10, 14–16; ratified by subsequent constitutions, see for instance 1874, 1881). **II. Public office holding limited to:** citizens, over the age of 21, literate, with property or in professional occupations. Denied to women, slaves, domestic servants, illiterates, the propertyless, and debtors (1830 Art. 13, 52, 62, 126, 135, 145). **III. Voting rights limited to:** citizens, over the age of 21, literate, with property, or in professional occupations. Denied to women, slaves, domestic servants, illiterates, the propertyless, and debtors (1830 Art. 13, 27).

CHART A.2: Existence of Affirmative Action Policies (1)

Country		Type of Policy
Argentina	No	
Bolivia	No	
Brazil	Yes	Establishment of quotas for public education and public labor; collective rights to land granted to Quilombos (Transitory Disposition of Brazilian Constitution, Art. 68); creation of SEPPIR (Special Secretary of Racial Equality Political Promotion in 2003); criminalization of racist practices (1988 Constitution, Art. 5, incise 41)
Chile	No	
Colombia	Yes	Establishment of quotas for education, congressional representation, collective rights to land, autonomy (1991 Constitution, Law 70 of 1993)
Costa Rica	No	
Cuba	No	
Dominican Republic	No	
Ecuador	Yes	Collective rights to land, self-government (Law 46 of 2006; Article 11.2 of the 2008 Constitution)
El Salvador	No	
Guatemala	Yes	Collective rights to land (Acuerdo Gubernativo No. 22, January 12, 2004)
Haiti	No	
Honduras	Yes	Collective rights to land (Executive Order 09–2007)
Jamaica	No	
Mexico	No	
Nicaragua	Yes	Collective rights to land (Law 443 of 2013)
Panama	No	
Paraguay	No	
Peru	No	
Puerto Rico	No	
Uruguay	Yes	Establishment of quotas for public education and public labor (Law 19.122 of 2013)
Venezuela	No	

(1) I did not include laws prohibiting racial discrimination, such as those issued in the 1940s in Cuba and Venezuela, and those in Perú and explained by Cottrol, 2013, 283–288.

NOTES

Introduction

1. Hannah Arendt, *Imperialism: Part Two of The Origins of Totalitarianism* (San Diego: Harcout Brace Jovanovich, 1968), 161.

2. See, for example, Ira Katznelson, *Black Men, White Cities: Race, Politics, and Migration in the United States, 1900–30, and Britain, 1948–68* (Chicago: University of Chicago Press, 1976); *When Affirmative Action Was White: An Untold History of Racial Inequality in Twentieth-Century America* (New York: W.W. Norton, 2005); Anthony W. Marx, *Making Race and Nation: A Comparison of South Africa, the United States, and Brazil* (Cambridge, New York: Cambridge University Press, 1998); Melissa Nobles, *The Politics of Official Apologies* (New York: Cambridge University Press, 2008); Mark Q. Sawyer, *Racial Politics in Post-Revolutionary Cuba* (Cambridge: Cambridge University Press, 2006).

3. David D. Laitin, *Nations, States, and Violence* (Oxford: Oxford University Press, 2007).

Chapter 1: Edward Augustus Freeman and the Dawn of Comparative Politics

1. Natalie Melas, *All the Difference in the World: Postcoloniality and the Ends of Comparison* (Stanford: Stanford University Press, 2007), xi.

2. Charles Chauncey Shackford, "'Comparative Literature' Lecture Delivered at Cornell University," in *The Proceedings of the University Convocation* (Albany: State University of New York, 1876), 266.

3. Ibid.

4. Arend Lijphart, "Comparative Politics and the Comparative Method," *The American Political Science Review* 65, no. 3 (1971): 687.

5. Ibid.

6. On conceptual methodologies see: Gary Goertz, "Concept Intension and Extension," in *Social Science Concepts: A User's Guide* (Princeton: Princeton University Press, 2006); David Collier and James E. Mahon, Jr., "Conceptual 'Stretching' Revisited: Adapting Categories in Comparative Analysis," *The American Political Science Review* 87, no. 4 (1993): 845–55; Giovanni Sartori, "Concept Misformation in Comparative Politics," *The American Political Science Review* 64, no. 4 (1970): 1033–53.

7. Lijphart, "Comparative Politics and the Comparative Method," 687.

8. Edward Augustus Freeman, *Comparative Politics: Six Lectures Read Before the Royal Institution* (London: Macmillan and Co., 1873), 19.

9. Ibid., 35–36.

10. E. E. Evans-Pritchard, *The Comparative Method in Social Anthropology* (London: University of London, Athlone Press, 1963), 5–6.

11. Freeman, *Comparative Politics: Six Lectures Read Before the Royal Institution*, 1.

12. Ibid., 14.

13. Ibid., 12.

14. Ibid., 35.

15. Ibid., 81.

16. Ibid., 82–83.

17. Peter Novick, *That Noble Dream: The 'Objectivity Question' and the American Historical Profession* (Cambridge: Cambridge University Press, 1988).

18. C.J.W. Parker, "The Failure of Liberal Racialism: The Racial Ideas of E.A. Freeman," *The Historical Journal* 24, no. 4 (1981): 825–46.

19. Otto Bauer, *The Question of Nationalities and Social Democracy*, ed. Ephraim Nimni (Minneapolis: University of Minnesota Press, 2000).

20. Edward Augustus Freeman, "Race and Language," in *Essays: English and American*, ed. Charles W. Eliot (New York: P. F. Collier & Son, 1909), 242.

21. Ibid., 243.

22. Edward Augustus Freeman, *The Life And Letters of Edward A. Freeman, Vol. II* (London: Macmillan and Co., 1895), 242.

23. Edward Augustus Freeman, *Some Impressions of the United States* (London: Longmans, Green, & Co., 1883), 142.

24. Ibid., 146.

25. See, for example: Aline Helg, *Our Rightful Share: The Afro-Cuban Struggle for Equality, 1886–1912* (Chapel Hill: University of North Carolina Press, 1995); *Liberty & Equality in Caribbean Colombia, 1770–1835* (Chapel Hill: University of North Carolina Press, 2004); W.E.B. Du Bois, *Black Reconstruction: An Essay Toward a History of the Part which Black Folk Played in the Attempt to Reconstruct Democracy in America, 1860–1880*, 1st ed. (New York: Harcourt, Brace, and Co., 1935); Steven Hahn, *A Nation Under Our Feet: Black Political Struggles in the Rural South, From Slavery to the Great Migration* (Cambridge: Belknap Press of Harvard University Press, 2003); Thomas C. Holt, *The Problem of Freedom: Race, Labor, and Politics in Jamaica and Britain, 1832–1938* (Baltimore: Johns Hopkins University Press, 1992); David Barry Gaspar and David Patrick Geggus, eds., *A Turbulent Time: The French Revolution and the Greater Caribbean* (Bloomington: Indiana University Press, 1997).

26. H. Morse Stephens, "Review of *The Life and Letters of Edward A. Freeman* by W.R.W. Stephens," *The Annals of the American Academy of Political and Social Science* 7 (1896): 113–14.

27. Woodrow Wilson, *The Papers of Woodrow Wilson, Vol. 2*, ed. Arthur Stanley Link (Princeton: Princeton University Press, 1967), 74.

28. Ibid., 74–75.

29. "Stray Thoughts from the South (22 February, 1881)," in *The Papers of Woodrow Wilson, Vol. 2*, ed. Arthur Stanley Link (Princeton: Princeton University Press, 1967), 27.

30. *The State: Elements of Historical and Practical Politics* (Boston: D. C. Heath & Co., 1889), 1.

31. Ibid., 1–2.

32. Mark Mazower, *No Enchanted Palace: The End of Empire and the Ideological Origins of the United Nations* (Princeton: Princeton University Press, 2009).

33. Desmond S. King and Rogers M. Smith, "Racial Orders in American Political Development," *The American Political Science Review* 99, no. 1 (2005): 75–92; Robert Vitalis, "Birth of a Discipline," in *Imperialism and Internationalism in the Discipline of International Relations*, eds.

David Long and Brian C. Schmidt (Albany: State University of New York Press, 2005), 159–82; Charles W. Mills, *The Racial Contract* (Ithaca: Cornell University Press, 1997).

34. Vicky L. Morrisroe, "Sanguinary Amusement: E.A. Freeman, The Comparative Method and Victorian Theories of Race," *Modern Intellectual History* 10, no. 1 (2013): 56.

Chapter 2: Race Development, Political Development

1. Charles Edward Merriam, "Recent Tendencies in Political Thought," in *A History of Political Theories, Recent Times: Essays on Contemporary Developments in Political Theory*, eds. Harry Elmer Barnes and Charles Edward Merriam (New York: The Macmillan Company, 1924), 1.

2. Ibid.

3. James Bryce, *Modern Democracies* (London: The Macmillan Company, 1921).

4. Merriam, "Recent Tendencies in Political Thought," 17.

5. Ibid., 19.

6. Ibid., 27.

7. Vijay. Prashad, *The Darker Nations: A People's History of the Third World* (New York: New Press, 2007), 44–79; Georges Balandier, "La Situation Coloniale: Approche Théorique," *Cahiers Internationaux de Sociologie* 11 (1951).

8. Martin Robison Delany, *The Condition, Elevation, Emigration, and Destiny of the Colored People of the United States* (New York: Arno Press, 1968).

9. Clifford Geertz, *The Interpretation of Cultures: Selected Essays* (New York: Basic Books, 1973), 327.

10. For anthropologists' collaboration with US national security policy in Latin America, see A. Peter Castro, "Collaborative Researchers or Cold Warriors? The Origins, Activities, and Legacy of the Smithsonian's Institute of Social Anthropology," *Journal of International & Global Studies* 2, no. 1 (2010): 56–82. On the relationship between US Cold War policies and ideologies and social science research on "political development", see Irene L. Gendzier, *Managing Political Change: Social Scientists and the Third World* (Boulder: Westview Press, 1985), 39–62; Samuel P. Huntington, *Political Order in Changing Societies* (New Haven: Yale University Press, 1968); Sara Berry, "Unsettled Accounts: Stool Debts, Chieftaincy Disputes and the Question of Asante Constitutionalism," *The Journal of African History* 39, no. 1 (1998).

11. See Chalmers Johnson's spirited defense of area studies against charges of increasing irrelevance and parochialism made by more mathematically oriented political scientists (Robert Bates in particular) , "Preconception vs. Observation, or the Contributions of Rational Choice Theory and Area Studies to Contemporary Political Science," *PS: Political Science and Politics* 30, no. 2 (1997): 170–74.

12. See Jomo Kenyatta, *Facing Mount Kenya: The Tribal Life of the Gikuyu* (London: Secker and Warburg, 1956); Frantz Fanon, *The Wretched of the Earth* (New York: Grove Press, 1968); Hồ Chí Minh, *On Revolution: Selected Writings, 1920–66*, ed. Bernard B. Fall (New York: Praeger, 1967); Mao Zedong, *Mao's Road to Power: Revolutionary Writings 1912–1949*, ed. Stuart R. Schram (Armonk: M.E. Sharpe, 1992); *The Writings of Mao Zedong, 1949–1976*, eds. Michael Y. M. Kau and John K. Leung (Armonk: M.E. Sharpe, 1986).

13. Some of the biggest names in anthropology, sociology and political science by the 1970s were involved in what would be characterized as area studies research; to name several, Immanuel Wallerstein and Giovanni Arrighi (Sociology), Georges Balandier (Anthropology), and Basil Davidson (History). In Davidson's case, as a military and tactical advisor to Samora Machel and Amilcar Cabral in their war against Portuguese colonialism in Mozambique, Angola and Guinea

Bissau. Several generations of comparativists in political science first built their reputations as scholars who devised innovative research methodologies to conduct survey and ethnographic research in Africa: Robert Bates, David Laitin, David Easton, Gabriel Almond, Henry Bienen and Crawford Young conducted their early research in Africa before shifting research sites. Martin Kilson, Pearl Robinson, Richard Joseph and Willard Johnson were part of a very small cohort of black political scientists who studied African politics.

14. Frederick Cooper and Ann Laura Stoler, eds., *Tensions of Empire Colonial Cultures in a Bourgeois World* (Berkeley: University of California Press, 1997). Aside from justifications for West-sponsored coups d'état by Cold War apologists, the most thoughtful scholarship of the era collectively points to the efforts of the US, Britain, Belgium and France in particular to undermine governments that pursued policies which would have threatened foreign profit streams which commenced soon after the Scramble for Africa (1884–1914), the era which inaugurated what historians have referred to as the New Imperialism of Western powers when Belgium, Britain, France, Germany (and Italy, Portugal, and Spain to a far lesser extent) agreed at the Berlin Conference of 1884–1888 to divide up the African continent and respect the geo-political boundaries of European influence on the continent.

15. As subsequent generations of anthropologists crafting their own critical histories of their discipline and the subfield of political anthropology pointed out, many anthropological claims about the peculiar character of non-Western polities were the result of Western anthropological projection. Evans-Pritchard's claim that the Nuer practiced a form of anarchy in the absence of centralized state power and legitimacy was belied by his own ethnography, which provided a detailed (for the era of anthropology) account of how alliances, feuds and disputes were negotiated and resolved respectively by custom, kinship networks and autochthonous modes of authority. As in many European societies, the king or chief *was* political society, and the distinction between the political and the social was more analytic than real. The so-called "primitive" states under examination—the Nuer, Bemba, Ankole, and the Bantu among them—were quite complex. Few would call political rule under King Leopold, Napoleon or Louis XIV primitive or simple. What often differentiated African political systems from their European counterparts was scale and scope, and temporal distinctions. African independence movements inaugurated the era of state power in Africa a little more than 60 years ago, a very narrow band of time when compared to European state formations.

16. See: Basil Davidson, *Africa in Modern History: The Search for a New Society* (London: Allen Lane, 1978); *Let Freedom Come: Africa in Modern History*, 1st American ed. (Boston: Little, Brown and Co., 1978); *The People's Cause: A History of Guerrillas in Africa* (London: Longman, 1981); *Modern Africa* (London: Longman, 1983); *The Black Man's Burden: The Myth of African Tribalism and the Curse of the Nation-State*, 1st ed. (New York: Times Books/Random House, 1992).

17. *The Black Man's Burden: The Myth of African Tribalism and the Curse of the Nation-State*, 55–56.

18. Ibid., 63.

19. Ibid., 57.

20. Eric J. Hobsbawm and Terence O. Ranger, eds., *The Invention of Tradition* (Cambridge: Cambridge University Press, 1983).

21. Lloyd I. Rudolph and Susanne H. Rudolph, "Surveys in India: Field Experience in Madras State," *The Public Opinion Quarterly* 22, no. 3 (1958).

22. Evans-Pritchard, *The Comparative Method in Social Anthropology*, 3. It is more than coincidental that eight years earlier, Evans-Pritchard was one of a group of anthropologists (along with John Whiting, Beatrice Whiting, Kimball Romney and John Roberts) who participated in

a seminar at Stanford's Center for the Advanced Study for the Behavioral Sciences, 1956–1957 with the political scientist Gabriel Almond. Anthropology provided the key concepts for Gabriel Almond's article on the comparative study of political systems, "Comparative Political Systems", which Almond presented at the conference "The Comparative Methods in the Study of Politics", held in June 1955 at Princeton University.

23. Ibid.

24. There are interesting parallels that could be explored in further research on the iconographies of fear utilized by Western powers and imperialist intellectuals in response to prospects—real and imagined—of political sovereignty among black and brown populations in Asia, Africa and Latin America. As noted by Georges Balandier, *Political Anthropology*, trans. A. M. Sheridan Smith (New York: Pantheon Books, 1970) Western opponents of African and Asian independence movements often warned of the increased likelihood of race war, in the form of revenge politics initiated by the brown and black worlds against Europeans, if Western powers allowed their colonial subjects to enact political freedom and sovereignty. Relatedly, similar warnings of political misrule and revenge against former white masters plagued Haiti in the years immediately following independence. There are parallels here with the US case as well, in which many notable historians of Reconstruction treat the period as a "lost" moment in Southern history characterized by black misrule, corruption and dysfunction, rather than an effort by black office holders to uphold the national laws of the US constitution regarding the universality of the franchise, public education, social services, and efforts to curtail the advances of racist paramilitary organizations which, in purely Weberian terms, challenged the monopoly of coercive sanction that was supposed to be the exclusive province of the US government. For more, see: W. E. B. Du Bois, *Black Reconstruction: An Essay toward a History of the Part Which Black Folk Played in the Attempt to Reconstruct Democracy in America, 1860–1880* (New York: Russell & Russell, 1960). Edmund S. Morgan, *American Slavery, American Freedom: The Ordeal of Colonial Virginia*, 1st ed. (New York: Norton, 1975); Hahn, *A Nation Under Our Feet: Black Political Struggles in the Rural South, From Slavery to the Great Migration*.

25. Edmund Ronald Leach, *Political Systems of Highland Burma: A Study of Kachin Social Structure* (Boston: Beacon Press, 1965).

26. E. E. Evans-Pritchard and Meyer Fortes, eds., *African Political Systems* (London: Oxford University Press, 1940), xii..

27. Balandier, *Political Anthropology*, vii.

28. Ibid., vii–viii.

29. Evans-Pritchard and Fortes, *African Political Systems*, 2.

30. Evans-Pritchard, *The Comparative Method in Social Anthropology*.

31. Ibid., 6.

32. Ibid., 16.

33. Richard Brody, "Interview with Gabriel Almond," in *Political Science in America: Oral Histories of a Discipline*, eds. Michael A. Baer, Malcolm E. Jewell, and Lee Sigelman (Lexington: University Press of Kentucky, 1991), 129.

34. Ibid., 132.

35. Gabriel A. Almond, "Introduction: A Functional Approach to Comparative Politics," in *The Politics of the Developing Areas*, eds. James Smoot Coleman and Gabriel A. Almond (Princeton: Princeton University Press, 1960), 10.

36. Ibid., 11.

37. Ibid., 12.

38. Ibid., 64.

39. Ibid.

40. George W. Stocking, *Race, Culture, and Evolution: Essays in the History of Anthropology* (Chicago: University of Chicago Press, 1982).

41. Ibid., 265.

42. Gabriel A. Almond, "Political Development: Analytical and Normative Perspectives," *Comparative Political Studies* 1, no. 4 (1969): 459.

43. "Introduction: A Functional Approach to Comparative Politics," 64.

44. "Political Development: Analytical and Normative Perspectives," in *Political Development: Essays in Heuristic Theory* (Boston: Little, Brown and Co., 1970), 273.

45. Freeman, *Comparative Politics: Six Lectures Read Before the Royal Institution*, 303.

46. James Mahoney and Dietrich Rueschemeyer, eds., *Comparative Historical Analysis in the Social Sciences* (Cambridge: Cambridge University Press, 2003); Barbara Geddes, *Paradigms and Sand Castles: Theory Building and Research Design in Comparative Politics* (Ann Arbor: University of Michigan Press, 2003); Gerardo L. Munck and Richard Snyder, *Passion, Craft, and Method in Comparative Politics* (Baltimore: Johns Hopkins University Press, 2007).

47. Karl Marx, "The Materialist Conception of History (1859)," in *Selected Writings in Sociology & Social Philosophy*, eds. T. B. Bottomore and Maximilien Rubel (New York: McGraw-Hill, 1964), 52.

48. Almond, "Introduction: A Functional Approach to Comparative Politics," 64.

Chapter 3: Society and Polity, Difference and Inequality

1. Freeman, *Some Impressions of the United States*, 142.

2. Paulin Ismard, *Democracy's Slaves: A Political History of Ancient Greece* (Cambridge and London: Harvard University Press, 2017).

3. See Christopher W. Blackwell, "Athenian Democracy; A Brief Overview," *Demos*, Feb. 28, 2003. http://www.stoa.org/projects/demos/article_democracy_overview?page=4 .

4. Kurt A. Raaflaub, *The Discovery of Freedom in Ancient Greece* (Chicago: University of Chicago Press, 2004).

5. Ibid., 16.

6. Susan Sara Monoson, *Plato's Democratic Entanglements: Athenian Politics and the Practice of Philosophy* (Princeton: Princeton University Press, 2000).

7. David D. Laitin, *Nations, States, and Violence* (Oxford: Oxford University Press, 2007).

8. Eric Voegelin, *The New Science of Politics: An Introduction* (Chicago: University of Chicago Press, 1952); Charles Edward Merriam, *The New Democracy and the New Despotism* (New York: McGraw-Hill, 1939), 4.

9. Susan Lape, *Race and Citizen Identity in the Classical Athenian Democracy* (Cambridge: Cambridge University Press, 2010), 8.

10. Demetra Kasimis, "The Tragedy of Blood-Based Membership: Secrecy and the Politics of Immigration in Euripides's Ion," *Political Theory* 41, no. 2 (2013): 234.

11. Lape, *Race and Citizen Identity in the Classical Athenian Democracy*, 7–19.

12. Denise Eileen McCoskey, *Race: Antiquity and Its Legacy* (Oxford: Oxford University Press, 2012).

13. Edward Augustus Freeman, *Historical Essays* (London: Macmillan, 1871).

14. Joan Wallach Scott, *Feminism and History* (Oxford: Oxford University Press, 1996), ix.

15. Charles Tilly, *Durable Inequality* (Berkeley: University of California Press, 1998).

16. The social question, as it came to be known in postrevolutionary France through the writings of Proudhon, was a recognition of the enduring forms of socio-economic inequality amid

the established democratic order of republican France. See Pierre-Joseph Proudhon, *What is Property?* (Cambridge: Cambridge University Press, 1994); Donald R. Kelley and Bonnie G. Smith, "What Was Property? Legal Dimensions of the Social Question in France (1789–1848)," *Proceedings of the American Philosophical Society* 128, no. 3 (1984): 200–30.

17. Hannah Arendt, *On Revolution* (New York: Viking Press, 1963), chapter 2.

18. *The Promise of Politics*, 1st ed. (New York: Schocken Books, 2005).

19. Ibid., 116.

20. Ibid.

21. *On Revolution*, 71.

22. Ibid., 72, 74. Of course what is interesting here is the absence of any mention of the Haitian Revolution, which belies the limits of the bourgeois imagination for total societal transformation, since the abolition of slavery would have signaled the obliteration of one of the great sources of wealth of the revolutionary elite.

23. The history of revolutions is replete with examples of renewed marginalization of less empowered groups: consider women and homosexuals in the Cuban and Chinese Revolutions, for example.

24. Enrique D. Dussel, *Twenty Theses on Politics*, trans. George Ciccariello-Maher (Durham: Duke University Press, 2008).

25. Benedict Anderson, *Imagined Communities: Reflections on the Origin and Spread of Nationalism*, rev. ed. (London: Verso, 2006).

26. Jim Sidanius, Yesilernis Peña, and Mark Sawyer, "Inclusionary Discrimination: Pigmentocracy and Patriotism in the Dominican Republic," *Political Psychology* 22, no. 4 (2001).

27. For example, Juliet Hooker, *Race and the Politics of Solidarity* (Oxford: Oxford University Press, 2009); Edmund T. Gordon, *Disparate Diasporas: Identity and Politics in an African Nicaraguan Community* (Austin: University of Texas Press, 1998); Helg, *Our Rightful Share: The Afro-Cuban Struggle for Equality, 1886–1912; Liberty & Equality in Caribbean Colombia, 1770–1835*.

28. David Barry Gaspar and David Patrick Geggus, eds. *A Turbulent Time: The French Revolution and the Greater Caribbean* (Bloomington: Indiana University Press, 1997).

29. Ira Berlin, *Many Thousands Gone: The First Two Centuries of Slavery in North America* (Cambridge: Belknap Press of Harvard University Press, 1998).

30. C.L.R. James, *The Black Jacobins: Toussaint L'Ouverture and the San Domingo Revolution*, 2d ed., rev. ed. (New York: Vintage Books, 1989), 71.

31. Ibid., 70.

32. See Lynne Hunt's nuanced introduction that contextualizes key themes in debates and primary texts on the topic of human rights in the French Revolution. *The French Revolution and Human Rights: A Brief Documentary History* (New York, Boston: Bedford Books), 1996.

33. Ibid., 116–118.

34. Laurent Dubois, *Haiti: The Aftershocks of History* (New York: Metropolitan Books, 2012) 25.

35. James, *The Black Jacobins: Toussaint L'Ouverture and the San Domingo Revolution*, 73.

36. Pradine Linstant, *Recueil général ges lois et actes du gouvernement d'Haïti depuis la proclamation de son indépendance jusqu'à nos jour* (Paris: A. Durand, 1886).

37. Patrick Bellegarde-Smith, *Haiti: The Breached Citadel*, rev. and updated ed. (Toronto: Canadian Scholars' Press, 2004), 69.

38. On the ethical state, see: Immanuel Kant, *To Perpetual Peace: A Philosophical Sketch*, trans. Ted Humphrey (Indianapolis: Hackett Publishing Company, 2003), 41; Antonio Gramsci, *The Gramsci Reader: Selected Writings, 1916–1935* (New York: New York University Press, 2000), 234.

39. Michel-Rolph Trouillot, *Haiti, State Against Nation: The Origins and Legacy of Duvalierism* (New York: Monthly Review Press, 1990), 49.

40. Ibid., 51.

41. Ibid., 48.

42. Emília Viotti da Costa, *Crowns of Glory, Tears of Blood: The Demerara Slave Rebellion of 1823* (New York: Oxford University Press, 1994), xiii.

43. Ibid., 19.

44. See also Rebecca J. Scott, *Slave Emancipation in Cuba: The Transition to Free Labor, 1860–1899* (Princeton: Princeton University Press, 1985); William Max Nelson, "The Atlantic World," in *The Atlantic World*, eds. D'Maris Coffman, Adrian Leonard, and William O'Reilly (Abingdon: Routledge, 2015), 650–66; William Max Nelson, "Making Men: Enlightenment Ideas of Racial Engineering," *The American Historical Review* 115, no. 5 (2010): 1364–94.

45. Da Costa, *Crowns of Glory, Tears of Blood: the Demerara Slave Rebellion of 1823*, 235.

46. Ibid., 236.

47. Rebecca J. Scott, "Paper Thin: Freedom and Re-enslavement in the Diaspora of the Haitian Revolution," *Law and History Review* 29, no. 4 (2011): 1061–87; Walter Johnson, "COMMENT: Resetting the Legal History of Slavery: Divination, Torture, Poisoning, Murder, Revolution, Emancipation, and Re-enslavement," *Law and History Review* 29, no. 4 (2011): 1089–95.

48. Readers should consult the following scholarship for country specific and regional accounts of these dynamics in early 19th century independence movements, and in the region more generally: George Reid Andrews, *Afro-Latin America, 1800–2000* (New York: Oxford University Press, 2004); Helg, *Liberty & Equality in Caribbean Colombia, 1770–1835*; Winthrop D. Jordan, *White Over Black: American Attitudes Toward the Negro, 1550–1812*, 2nd ed. (Chapel Hill: University of North Carolina Press, 2012); Leslie B. Rout, *The African Experience in Spanish America, 1502 to the Present Day* (Cambridge: Cambridge University Press, 1976); Scott, *Slave Emancipation in Cuba: The Transition to Free Labor, 1860–1899*; Richard C. Wade, *Slavery in the Cities: The South, 1820–1860* (London: Oxford University Press, 1970); Winthrop R. Wright, *Café con Leche: Race, Class, and National Image in Venezuela*, 1st ed. (Austin: University of Texas Press, 1990).

49. Helg, *Liberty & Equality in Caribbean Colombia, 1770–1835*, 163.

50. Jordan, *White Over Black: American Attitudes Toward the Negro, 1550–1812*, 375.

51. Ibid., 386.

52. Gaspar and Geggus, *A Turbulent Time: The French Revolution and the Greater Caribbean*.

53. Jordan, *White Over Black: American Attitudes Toward the Negro, 1550–1812*, 377.

54. Alfred N. Hunt, *Haiti's Influence on Antebellum America: Slumbering Volcano in the Caribbean* (Baton Rouge: Louisiana State University Press, 2006), 108.

55. Michael Mullin, *Africa in America: Slave Acculturation and Resistance in the American South and the British Caribbean, 1736–1831* (Urbana: University of Illinois Press, 1992), 226.

56. Hunt, *Haiti's Influence on Antebellum America: Slumbering Volcano in the Caribbean*, chapter 4.

57. See Sterling Stuckey, *Slave Culture: Nationalist Theory and the Foundations of Black America* (New York: Oxford University Press, 1987), 146. For example, Stuckey writes that one of the catalytic events in black nationalist Henry Highland Garnet's life was the day his family was forced to flee their home in New York because they were pursued by Maryland bounty hunters seeking to return them to slavery in Maryland. One sister, who was caught, was eventually freed on the grounds that she was a freeperson in New York even though she was classified as a slave in Maryland. For the free black population in many Northern states, freedom was both a contingent and revocable condition. To punctuate matters, various states devised illiteracy tests and exit and entry taxes to discourage the influx of black freepersons and limit—if not outlaw entirely—participation of blacks in the polity.

58. Ibid., 382, 90.

59. James Tyndale Mitchell and Henry Flanders, eds., *The Statutes at Large of Pennsylvania from 1682–1801* (Harrisburg: State Printer of Pennsylvania, 1896).

60. See "An Act to Afford Relief to Certain Distressed French Emigrants," ibid., 1795.

61. Judges of the Supreme Court of the United States. 1849. *Opinions of the Judges of the Supreme Court of the United States, in the Cases of "Smith vs. Turner," and "Norris vs. The City of Boston." In Senate, March 20, 1849*. Washington, DC: Office of the Printer to the Senate.

62. Ibid., 168.

63. Mr. Justice Wayne's opinion states, "The States have the right to turn off paupers, vagabonds, and fugitives from justice, and the States where slaves have a constitutional right to exclude all such as are, from a common ancestry and country, of the same class of men." Ibid., 170–1.

64. Benjamin Chew Howard, *Report of the Decision of the Supreme Court of the United States and the Opinions of the Judges Thereof, in the Case of Dred Scott Versus John F. A. Sandford. December Term, 1856* (New York: D. Appleton & Company, 1857), 403.

65. Merriam is making an implicit argument for situating power relations and hierarchies in a semiotic order in which objects of representation (such as phenotype, dress, and gestures) became markers of political distinction. In the case of revolutionary France, one of the popular reactions against the haut bourgeoisie and ancien regime was the emphasis on modes of dress, demeanor, and public habits that distinguished workers and peasants from members of the elite. Among criteria, for example, to determine whether people were true peasants, artisans, and workers and not members of the haut bourgeoisie and ancien regime masquerading as citizens of the Republic included inspecting and feeling the hands of individuals suspected of elite status and loyalties to determine whether their livelihoods involved manual labor. The coarseness or tenderness of hands helped determine a person's eligibility for the guillotine. Merriam, *The New Democracy and the New Despotism*, 24.

66. See Kasimis, "The Tragedy of Blood-Based Membership: Secrecy and the Politics of Immigration in Euripides's Ion." Jill Frank, "Citizens, Slaves and Foreigners: Aristotle on Human Nature, *The American Political Science Review* 98, no. 1 (February 2004).

67. See Frank, "Citizens, Slaves and Foreigners: Aristotle on Human Nature," pp. 91–104. Frank emphasizes, contra Merriam, that Aristotle's analysis of a slave's "cringing gesture" may be a reflection of fear (well-warranted given the violence of masters) and so a mark of relationality and not an identitarian mark of inferiority or superiority in the alleged ways blackness or Aryan features were alleged to be (correspondence, 8/4/2017).

68. Merriam, *The New Democracy and the New Despotism*, 24.

69. Robert Alan Dahl, *Polyarchy: Participation and Opposition* (New Haven: Yale University Press, 1971).

70. Ibid., 8.

71. William I. Robinson, *Promoting Polyarchy: Globalization, US Intervention, and Hegemony* (Cambridge: Cambridge University Press, 1996).

72. Dahl, *Polyarchy: Participation and Opposition*, 93.

73. Ibid., 95.

74. See: David J. Garrow, *Protest at Selma: Martin Luther King, Jr., and the Voting Rights Act of 1965* (New Haven: Yale University Press, 1978); Taylor Branch, *Parting the Waters: America in the King Years, 1954–63* (New York: Simon and Schuster, 1988); Katznelson, *Black Men, White Cities: Race, Politics, and Migration in the United States, 1900–30, and Britain, 1948–68*.

75. By his own admission, Dahl's choice of terminology is quite arbitrary, evident in his interpretation and deployment of the concept of hegemony. For Plekhanov, hegemony was largely organizational leadership and domination of a political agenda by a singular group—the proletariat. For Gramsci, hegemony mostly referred to a combination of domination and consent,

with the singular group, whether the bourgeoisie or proletarian vanguard), assuming leadership without a primary reliance upon coercion. Dahl's use of hegemony reads more closely to the concept of domination, which, while involving leadership, is less reliant upon the development of consent among contending political actors.

76. See Viotta da Costa, *Crowns of Glory, Tears of Blood*. She introduces the concept of "conservative liberalism" to characterize the political behaviors of Brazilian and Latin American elites who sought all the economic benefits of capitalism and industrialization without the political implications of republicanism, egalitarianism, and liberal ideals regarding freedom of speech and voluntary association.

77. Thanks to Danielle Allen and Nolan McCarty for their insightful questions in conversation and draft comments on this point in the *Egalitarianisms* seminar 2014–2015, School of Social Science, Institute for Advanced Study, Princeton, NJ.

78. Rogers Brubaker, *Citizenship and Nationhood in France and Germany* (Cambridge: Harvard University Press, 1992).

79. Du Bois, *Black Reconstruction: An Essay Toward a History of the Part which Black Folk Played in the Attempt to Reconstruct Democracy in America, 1860–1880*, vii.

80. Arendt, *The Promise of Politics*, 6.

81. Jeffrey A. Winters, *Oligarchy* (Cambridge: Cambridge University Press, 2011), 73, footnote 7.

82. Ibid.

83. Ibid., 73.

84. See, for example, Joanna Innes and Mark Philps (eds.), *Reimagining Democracy in the Age of Revolutions: America, France, Britain & Ireland, 1750–1850* (Oxford University Press, 2013).

Chapter 4: Racial and Ethno-National Regimes in Liberal Polities

1. Etienne Balibar and Immanuel Maurice Wallerstein, *Race, Nation, Class: Ambiguous Identities*, trans. Chris Turner (London: Verso, 1991).

2. Fredrik Barth, ed. *Ethnic Groups and Boundaries: The Social Organization of Culture Difference* (Boston: Little, Brown & Co., 1969).

3. For further reading, see: David Healy, *The United States in Cuba, 1898–1902: Generals, Politicians, and the Search for Policy* (Madison: University of Wisconsin Press, 1963); Nick Nesbitt, *Universal Emancipation: The Haitian Revolution and the Radical Enlightenment* (Charlottesville: University of Virginia Press, 2008); Isar P. Godreau, *Scripts of Blackness Race, Cultural Nationalism, and U.S. Colonialism in Puerto Rico* (Urbana: University of Illinois Press, 2015); Kelvin A. Santiago-Valles, *"Subject People" and Colonial Discourses: Economic Transformation and Social Disorder in Puerto Rico, 1898–1947* (Albany: State University of New York Press, 1994); Paul A. Kramer, *The Blood of Government: Race, Empire, the United States, and the Philippines* (Chapel Hill: University of North Carolina Press, 2006).

4. Michael Omi and Howard Winant, *Racial Formation in the United States: From the 1960s to the 1980s* (New York: Routledge & Kegan Paul, 1986).

5. King and Smith, "Racial Orders in American Political Development," 75.

6. Ibid., 78.

7. Tianna S. Paschel, *Becoming Black Political Subjects: Movements and Ethno-Racial Rights in Colombia and Brazil* (Princeton: Princeton University Press, 2016); Omi and Winant, *Racial Formation in the United States: From the 1960s to the 1980s*; David Theo Goldberg, *The Racial*

State (Malden: Blackwell Publishers, 2002); Michael Burleigh and Wolfgang Wippermann, *The Racial State: Germany, 1933–1945* (Cambridge: Cambridge University Press, 1991).

8. Holt, *The Problem of Freedom: Race, Labor, and Politics in Jamaica and Britain, 1832–1938.*

9. Huw Bennett actually extends his revisionist argument to consider some of the contemporary implications of the colonial and imperial army framing of the Mau Mau revolt as a conflict between nonstate "combatants" (the Mau Mau), on the one hand, and the British government on the other. Because much of international law, particularly the Universal Declaration of Human Rights, emphasized genocidal conflicts between states, systemic state violence targeting specific populations within a national or colonial territory generated less debate—and less law. There are connections to explore between the indeterminate legal status of the Mau Mau as "terrorists" (the term used by British colonial and imperial governance and military) and the determination of jihadists as "enemy combatants" during the presidential administration of George W. Bush. In the French case, three former French generals in Indochina who became police personnel after the Indochina conflict were tried and convicted in French courts for crimes against humanity— in a French Court, not The Hague. Huw C. Bennett, *Fighting the Mau Mau: The British Army and Counter-Insurgency in the Kenya Emergency* (Cambridge: Cambridge University Press, 2013).

10. Gretchen Helmke and Steven Levitsky, "Informal Institutions and Comparative Politics: A Research Agenda," *Perspectives on Politics* 2, no. 4 (2004): 726.

11. Ibid., 728.

12. Ibid.

13. Ibid., 731.

14. See: Almir de Oliveira Junior and Veronica Couto de Araujo Lima, "Seguranca Publica e Racismo Institucional," pp. 21–26, Boletim de Analise Politico Institucional, Publicado por Instituto de Pesquisa Economica Aplicada (IPEA), Rio de Janeiro, 2013, 4th ed., 2013; Fernando Urrea-Giraldo, Gustavo Bergonzoli Pelaez, Bladimir Carabali Sinisterra, and Victor Hugo Munoz Villa, "Patrones de Mortalidad Comparativos Entre Cali y el Valle en Poblacion Afrodescendiente y Blanca Mestiza. Censo 2005 y 2010," presented at Seminario International Estadisticas Etnico-Raciales Recientes en Colombia y America Latina. Cali, Noviembre 19–21, 2014; Jan Hoffman French, "Rethinking Police Violence in Brazil: Unmasking the Public Secret of Race: Critical Debates," *Latin American Politics and Society* 55, no. 4 (2013): 161–81; *Legalizing Identities: Becoming Black or Indian in Brazil's Northeast* (Chapel Hill: University of North Carolina Press, 2009); Melissa Nobles, *Shades of Citizenship: Race and the Census in Modern Politics* (Stanford: Stanford University Press, 2000).

15. Perhaps the most prominent example of scholarship that portrays British empire and imperialism as kinder and gentler than other forms of modern empire is Naill Ferguson's *Empire* (Penguin, 2003). Recent revisionist accounts of British imperial histories in Asia, Africa, Latin America, and the Caribbean suggest otherwise. See, for example, Caroline Elkins, *Imperial Reckoning: The Untold Story of Britain's Gulag in Kenya*, 1st ed. (New York: Henry Holt, 2005); David Anderson, *Histories of the Hanged: the Dirty War in Kenya and the End of Empire*, 1st American ed. (New York: W.W. Norton, 2005); Bennett, *Fighting the Mau Mau: The British Army and Counter-Insurgency in the Kenya Emergency.* See also Jock McCulloch, *Colonial Psychiatry and "The African Mind"* (Cambridge: Cambridge University Press, 1995).

16. Bennett, 60.

17. Erving Goffman, *The Presentation of Self in Everyday Life*, 1st ed. (New York: Anchor Books, 1959).

18. As Bennett, Elkins, Anderson, and Jock McCullogh concluded in their assessments of the British counterinsurgency campaign among the Kikuyu to ferret out Mau Mau participants and sympathizers, claims of atrocities among the British expatriate community by Mau Mau

participants were often exaggerated and ultimately dwarfed by the documented assassinations, starvation, rape, and torture by British colonial troops and indigenous collaborators.

19. Hendrik Spruyt, *Ending Empire: Contested Sovereignty and Territorial Partition* (Ithaca: Cornell University Press, 2005); *The Sovereign State and its Competitors* (Princeton: Princeton University Press, 1994); James Mahoney, *Colonialism and Postcolonial Development Spanish America in Comparative Perspective* (Leiden: Cambridge University Press, 2010).

20. Spruyt, *Ending Empire: Contested Sovereignty and Territorial Partition*, 7.

21. Helg, *Our Rightful Share: The Afro-Cuban Struggle for Equality, 1886–1912*.

22. Spruyt, *Ending Empire: Contested Sovereignty and Territorial Partition*, 2 (listed as footnote 7 in text). Here the analytic emphasis is on history rather than periodization.

23. Todd Shepard, *The Invention of Decolonization: The Algerian War and the Remaking of France* (Ithaca: Cornell University Press, 2008).

24. The controversy revealed some of the anxieties of state officials who were involved about the lack of transparency in releasing documents which, by British law, should have been declassified after 30 years. Internal documents and correspondence between governmental officials, and between government officials and a broader public—journalists and scholars included—revealed that bureaucratic distinction between colonial (indirect) and metropolitan (national territory) could not shield Britain from potential damage to its liberal, democratic reputation by the release of these and other files. In a letter dated 24 February 2011, Anthony Cary, a British public official enmeshed in the controversy, offered his assessment in both diagnostic and prescriptive terms in a letter to Professor Salmon. According to Cary, the netherworld status of the files could in part be attributed to misinformation circulating through the bureaucracy about the largely redundant nature of the archives (containing birth records and marriage licenses already documented elsewhere), but also, more crucially, whether declassified colonial records formed part of a properly British public record, namely a public composed of British citizens, not Commonwealth subjects or their colonial administrators.

After reviewing several key email exchanges and correspondence, Cary concluded that part of the neglect and delay in rendering these materials public was that those opposed to releasing the files concluded (ingenuously, according to Cary) that "they were *not* UK public records within the meaning of the Public Records Act. They were records of the former Colonial Government Administration most of which, but for concern over their safety, would have been handed over to the incoming government on independence."

Thus, according to this perspective, neither Kenyan colonial subjects nor newly independent nation-states of the British Commonwealth constituted part of the British public. By this interpretation, British citizens, particularly those resident in British sovereign territory, constituted the true public. Cary also notes, however, concerns by several officials that release of the documents could not only embarrass Her Majesty's Government, but compromise the statecraft efforts of members of the police and military, as well as informers and sources of intelligence information. Rather than treating the history of British colonialism and imperialism separately from liberal democracy based on criteria of spatial and bureaucratic/administrative distinctions, the administration of colony and metropole can be assessed together as part of a single—if seemingly contradictory and misleading—state and polity. Imperial governance was never far from governance of the nation-state. See Anthony Cary, "The Migrated Archives: What Went Wrong and What Lessons Should We Draw?" (London: Foreign and Commonwealth Office, 2011).

25. William Roger Louis, *British Strategy in the Far East, 1919–1939* (Oxford: Clarendon Press, 1971).

26. Cited in Louis, Imperial Conference Minutes, Secret, 20 June 1921, 1st meeting, CB 32/2.

27. Imperial Conference of 1921, pp. 28–29, Right Hon. W.F. Massey, Prime Minister, New Zealand.

28. George Nathaniel Curzon, *Problems of the Far East: Japan, Korea, China*, 3rd ed. (London: Longmans, Green & Co., 1894).

29. Mazower, *No Enchanted Palace: The End of Empire and the Ideological Origins of the United Nations*.

30. Ashley Jackson, "The Empire/Commonwealth and the Second World War," *Round Table* 100, no. 412 (2011): 67.

31. Black settlement actually begins much earlier in Britain, as early as the 17th century in Liverpool. For more on the discussion of nonwhite immigration in Britain, see: John Solomos, *Race and Racism in Britain*, 3rd ed. (Hampshire: Palgrave Macmillan, 2003); Stephen Small, *Racialized Barriers: The Black Experience in the United States and England in the 1980s* (London: Routledge, 1994); *Police and People in London: A Group of Young Black People* (London: Policy Studies Institute, 1983); Paul Gilroy, *"There Ain't No Black in the Union Jack": The Cultural Politics of Race and Nation* (London: Hutchinson, 1987).

32. See Robert Miles, *Racism and Political Action in Britain* (London: Routledge & Paul, 1979); Robert Miles and Annie Phisacklea, *White Man's Country: Racism in British Politics* (London: Pluto Press, 1984).

33. John Rex, *Race, Colonialism and the City* (London: Routledge, 2013); John Rex and David Mason, eds., *Theories of Race and Ethnic Relations* (Cambridge: Cambridge University Press, 1986); Michael Banton, *Race and Immigration* (London: New Society, 1976); *The Coloured Quarter: Negro Immigrants in an English City* (London: Cape, 1955).

34. For example, John Solomos, *Black Youth, Racism and the State: the Politics of Ideology and Policy* (Cambridge: Cambridge University Press, 1988); Stuart Hall, *The Hard Road to Renewal: Thatcherism and the Crisis of the Left* (London: Verso, 1988).

35. Margaret Thatcher, "T.V. Interview for Granada's World in Action," Margaret Thatcher Foundation, 1978.

36. Hall, *The Hard Road to Renewal: Thatcherism and the Crisis of the Left*.

37. Ambalavaner Sivanandan, "A Different Hunger: Writings on Black Resistance" (London: Pluto Press, 1982); "Race, Class and the State: The Black Experience in Britain," *Race & Class* 17, no. 4 (1976): 347–68.

38. Hall, *The Hard Road to Renewal: Thatcherism and the Crisis of the Left*, 190.

39. Hall, *The Had Road to Renewal: Thatcherism and the Crisis of the Left*, 195.

40. Ironically, the French and US governments have begun to pay attention to the recurrent appearance of "The Autobiography of Malcolm X" in Parisian suburbs and in the hands of US born converts to fundamentalist versions of Islam that promote violence against the West. In France, "hip-hop and the rhetoric of Black Power and Malcolm X are deployed by minority youth in the country's *banlieues* to mock the ideas of colorblindness and secularism." See Hisham Aidi, "The Music of Malcolm X," *The New Yorker*, February 28, 2015.

41. From a *Le Monde* newspaper article (April 24, 1998) quoted in David Macey, *Frantz Fanon: A Life* (London: Granta Books, 2000).

42. Maxim Silverman, *Deconstructing the Nation: Immigration, Racism, and Citizenship in Modern France* (New York: Routledge, 1992); François Dubet, *Immigrations: Qu'en savons-nous?* (Paris: La Documentation Franqaise, 1989); Elisa Camiscioli, *Reproducing the French Race: Immigration, Intimacy, and Embodiment in the Early Twentieth Century* (Durham: Duke University Press, 2009); Gérard Noiriel, *The French Melting Pot: Immigration, Citizenship, and National Identity* (Minneapolis: University of Minnesota Press, 1996); Jacques Barou, "L'espace Immigré ou Comment les Rendre Invisibles," *Politique Aujord'hui* 4 (1984); Ralph Schor, *L'Opinion Française et les Ètrangers en France:1919–1939* (Paris: Sorbonne 1985).

43. Axiom, "Ma Lettre au Président," Universal Music Division, Mercury Records (2006).

44. Raaflaub, *The Discovery of Freedom in Ancient Greece*, 175.

45. Karen Barkey and Ira Katznelson, "States, Regimes, and Decisions: Why Jews were Expelled from Medieval England and France," *Theory and Society* 40, no. 5 (2011): 476.

46. Ibid., 477.

47. Vernon Valentine Palmer, "The Origins and Authors of the Code Noir," *Louisiana Law Review* 56, no. 2 (1995): 364–407.

48. Tyler Stovall, "Race and the Making of the Nation: Blacks in Modern France," in *Diasporic Africa: A Reader*, ed. Michael Angelo Gomez (New York: New York University Press, 2006), 205.

49. Ibid.

50. Riddell William Renwick, "Le Code Noir," *The Journal of Negro History* 10, no. 3 (1925): 321–23.

51. Palmer, "The Origins and Authors of the Code Noir," 382.

52. See C.L.R James, J.E. Inikori, and Stanley L. Engerman. *The Atlantic Slave Trade: Effects on Economies, Societies, and Peoples in Africa, the Americas, and Europe* (Durham: Duke University Press, 1992).

53. Patrick Weil, *How to be French: Nationality in the Making Since 1789*, trans. Catherine Porter (Durham: Duke University Press, 2008), 194.

54. Jeremy Jennings, "Citizenship, Republicanism and Multiculturalism in Contemporary France," *British Journal of Political Science* 30, no. 4 (2000): 579.

55. Frantz Fanon, "Algeria's European Minority," in *A Dying Colonialism* (New York: Grove Press, 1965), 150.

56. Ariane Chebel d'Appollonia, *Frontiers of Fear Immigration and Insecurity in the United States and Europe* (Ithaca: Cornell University Press, 2012).

57. Camiscioli, *Reproducing the French Race: Immigration, Intimacy, and Embodiment in the Early* Twentieth *Century*, 52.

58. Alec G. Hargreaves, *Multi-Ethnic France: Immigration, Politics, Culture and Society*, ed. Alec G. Hargreaves, 2nd ed. (New York: Routledge, 2007), 299.

59. Todd Shepard, "Thinking Between Metropole and Colony: The French Republic, 'Exceptional Promotion', and the 'Integration' of Algerians, 1955–1962," in *The French Colonial Mind: Mental Maps of Empire and Colonial Encounters*, ed. Martin Thomas (Lincoln: University of Nebraska Press, 2011), 299.

60. Ibid.

61. Didier Fassin, "L'Invention Française de la Discrimination," *Revue Française de Science Politique* 52, no. 4 (2002). Translation by Lauren Bovard.

62. Ibid.

63. Nonna Mayer, "The French National Front," in *The New Politics of the Right : Neo-Populist Parties and Movements in Established Democracies*, eds. Hans-Georg Betz and Stefan Immerfall (New York: St. Martin's Press, 1998), 11–26.

64. Herrick Chapman and Laura Levine Frader, eds., *Race in France: Interdisciplinary Perspectives on the Politics of Difference* (New York: Berghahn Books, 2004); Trica Danielle Keaton, "Racial Profiling and the 'French Exception,'" *French Cultural Studies* 24, no. 2 (2013): 231–42; Trica Danielle Keaton, T. Denean Sharpley-Whiting, and Tyler Edward Stovall, *Black France/ France Noire: The History and Politics of Blackness* (Durham: Duke University Press, 2012); Abdoulaye Gueye, "Manufacturing Blackness at the Turn of 20th Century France," in *Becoming Minority: How Discourses and Policies Produce Minorities in Europe and India*, eds. Jyotirmaya Tripathy and Sudarsan Padmanabhan (New Delhi: SAGE Publications, 2014); "The Labyrinth to Blackness: On Naming and Leadership in the Black Associative Space in France," *French Cultural Studies* 24, no. 2 (2013): 196–207.

65. Roy L. Garis, *Immigration Restriction: A Study of the Opposition to and Regulation of Immigration into the United States* (New York: Macmillan, 1927), 33.

66. For a comparison of black and white immigration, as well as black attitudes toward the entry of white and nonwhite immigrants into the United States, see: Lawrence H. Fuchs, *The American Kaleidoscope: Race, Ethnicity, and the Civic Culture* (Middletown: Wesleyan University Press, 1990).

67. United States Cong. Senate. *An Act to Establish an Uniform Rule of Naturalization.* First Cong. 2nd sess. Chapter III. Washington: Government Printing Office, March 26, 1790.

68. Michael Paul Rogin, *Blackface, White Noise: Jewish Immigrants in the Hollywood Melting Pot* (Berkeley: University of California Press, 1996), 101.

69. See "Revision of Laws Relating to Immigration, Naturalization and Nationality," *Congressional Record.* 82nd Congress. Vol. 98, April 23, 1952, p. 4306.

70. Ibid., 4314–16.

71. Ibid., 4320.

Chapter 5: Conclusion

1. Gary Goertz, *Tale of Two Cultures: Qualitative and Quantitative Research in the Social Sciences*, ed. James Mahoney (Princeton: Princeton University Press, 2012); Ann Shola Orloff, *The Politics of Pensions: A Comparative Analysis of Britain, Canada, and the United States, 1880–1940* (Madison: University of Wisconsin Press, 1993); *Perverse Politics? Feminism, Anti-Imperialism, Multiplicity*, eds. Raka Ray and Evren Savci (Bradford, West Yorkshire: Emerald Group Publishing, 2016); Scott, *Feminism and History*; Lisa Wedeen, *Ambiguities of Domination: Politics, Rhetoric, and Symbols in Contemporary Syria* (Chicago: University of Chicago Press, 1999); *Peripheral Visions: Publics, Power, and Performance in Yemen* (Chicago: University of Chicago Press, 2008).

2. Joseph H. Carens, *Culture, Citizenship, and Community: A Contextual Exploration of Justice as Evenhandedness* (Oxford: Oxford University Press, 2000); *Equality, Moral Incentives, and the Market: An Essay in Utopian Politico-Economic Theory* (Chicago: University of Chicago Press, 1981); *The Ethics of Immigration* (New York: Oxford University Press, 2013); Will Kymlicka, *Politics in the Vernacular: Nationalism, Multiculturalism, and Citizenship* (Oxford: Oxford University Press, 2001); *States, Nations and Cultures* (Assen: Van Gorcum, 1997).

3. Daron Acemoglu and James A. Robinson, *Why Nations Fail: The Origins of Power, Prosperity and Poverty* (London: Profile, 2012); *Economic Origins of Dictatorship and Democracy* (Cambridge: Cambridge University Press, 2006).

4. On science as noncumulative knowledge production, see for example Thomas S. Kuhn, *The Structure of Scientific Revolutions*, 2nd ed. (Chicago: University of Chicago Press, 1970); Imre Lakatos and Alan Musgrave, eds., *Criticism and the Growth of Knowledge* (Cambridge: Cambridge University Press, 1970).

5. Johnson, "Preconception vs. Observation, or the Contributions of Rational Choice Theory and Area Studies to Contemporary Political Science," 170–74.

6. See for example: James Clifford and George E. Marcus, eds., *Writing Culture: The Poetics and Politics of Ethnography* (Berkeley: University of California Press, 1986); Melville J. Herskovits, *The American Negro: A Study in Racial Crossing* (Bloomington: Indiana University Press, 1968); Talal Asad, *Anthropology & The Colonial Encounter* (Amherst: Humanity Books, 1998); Veena Das, ed. *The Word and the World: Fantasy, Symbol, and Record* (New Delhi: SAGE, 1986); Arjun Appadurai, "The Colonial Backdrop," *Afterimage* 24, no. 5 (1997).

7. Arend Lijphart, *The Trauma of Decolonization: The Dutch and West New Guinea* (New Haven: Yale University Press, 1966).

8. Lloyd I. Rudolph and Susanne Hoeber Rudolph, *The Modernity of Tradition: Political Development in India* (Chicago: University of Chicago Press, 1967).

9. Susanne Hoeber Rudolph, "The Imperialism of Categories: Situating Knowledge in a Globalizing World," *Perspectives on Politics* 3, no. 1 (2005).

10. Ibid.

11. See Alasdair C. MacIntyre, *Selected Essays* (Cambridge: Cambridge University Press, 2006).

12. Sartori, "Concept Misformation in Comparative Politics," 1033–53.

13. Asad, *Anthropology & The Colonial Encounter*; Clifford and Marcus, *Writing Culture: The Poetics and Politics of Ethnography*; Paul Rabinow, "Discourse and Power: On the Limits of Ethnographic Texts," *Dialectical Anthropology* 10, no. 1/2 (1985): 1–13.

14. Guillermo O'Donnell, "On the State, Democratization and Some Conceptual Problems: A Latin American View with Glances at Some Postcommunist Countries," *World Development* 21, no. 8 (1993): 135.

15. Op. cit. Helg; Sherwin K. Bryant, *Rivers of Gold, Lives of Bondage: Governing Through Slavery in Colonial Quito* (Chapel Hill: University of North Carolina Press, 2014).

16. O'Donnell, 138.

17. Ibid.

18. Ibid., 139.

19. Ibid., 138.

20. Ibid., 138–39.

21. For example, Godreau, *Scripts of Blackness Race, Cultural Nationalism, and U.S. Colonialism in Puerto Rico*; Paschel, *Becoming Black Political Subjects: Movements and Ethno-Racial Rights in Colombia and Brazil*; Hooker, *Race and the Politics of Solidarity*; Charles R. Hale, *Más que un Indio/More than an Indian: Racial Ambivalence and Neoliberal Multiculturalism in Guatemala* (Santa Fe: School of American Research Press, 2006); Gordon, *Disparate Diasporas: Identity and Politics in an African Nicaraguan Community*.

22. For more information, see: Baltimore City Health Department. Neighborhood Health Profiles. Baltimore, MD: Baltimore City Health Department, 2011. https://health.maryland.gov/vsa/Documents/13annual.pdf.

23. Didier Fassin and Eric Fassin, eds., *De la Question Sociale à la Question Raciale? Représenter la Société Française* (Paris: Découverte, 2006).

24. Didier Fassin, *Enforcing Order: An Ethnography of Urban Policing* (Cambridge: Polity Press, 2013).

25. Frank, 2004.

26. Aristotle, *The Politics* (Cambridge: Cambridge University Press, 1988); Alexis de Toqueville, *On Democracy in America* (New York: Sheba Blake Publishing, 2014).

27. Gunnar Myrdal, *An American Dilemma: the Negro Problem and Modern Democracy* (New York: Harper & Brothers, 1944); Gustave de Beaumont, *Marie; or, Slavery in the United States: A Novel of Jacksonian America* (Baltimore: Johns Jopkins University Press, 1958).

28. Sven Steinmo, Kathleen Ann Thelen, and Frank Longstreth, eds., *Structuring Politics: Historical Institutionalism in Comparative Analysis* (Cambridge: Cambridge University Press, 1992), 2.

29. Peter A. Hall, ed. *The Political Power of Economic Ideas: Keynesianism Across Nations* (Princeton: Princeton University Press, 1989).

30. Samuel P. Huntington, "The Clash of Civilizations?" *Foreign Affairs* 72, no. 3 (1993): 11.

31. "The Hispanic Challenge," *Foreign Policy*, no. 141 (2004): 3.

32. Aristide R. Zolberg, *A Nation by Design: Immigration Policy in the Fashioning of America* (New York: Russell Sage Foundation, 2006).

33. Laitin, *Nations, States, and Violence*.

34. Huntington, "The Hispanic Challenge," 31.

35. See Edward Schatz, ed. *Political Ethnography: What Immersion Contributes to the Study of Power* (Chicago: University of Chicago Press, 2009), 713–28; Lisa Wedeen, "Conceptualizing Culture: Possibilities for Political Science," *The American Political Science Review* 96, no. 4 (2002).

36. Laitin, *Nations, States, and Violence*, viii.

37. Carles Boix, "Democracy, Development, and the International System," *The American Political Science Review* 105, no. 4 (2011): 810.

38. Ibid., 814.

39. See also John M. Hobson, *The Eurocentric Conception of World Politics: Western International Theory, 1760–2010* (Cambridge: Cambridge University Press, 2012).

40. Holt, *The Problem of Freedom: Race, Labor, and Politics in Jamaica and Britain, 1832–1938.*

41. Michael R. Yogg, *Passion for Reality: The Extraordinary Life of the Investing Pioneer Paul Cabot* (New York: Columbia University Press, 2014).

42. J. E. Inikori, *Africans and the Industrial Revolution in England: A Study in International Trade and Economic Development* (Cambridge: Cambridge University Press, 2002).

43. Andre Gunder Frank, *Reorient: Global Economy in the Asian Age* (Berkeley: University of California Press, 1998); Immanuel Maurice Wallerstein, *The Modern World-System: Capitalist Agriculture and the Origins of the European World-Economy in the Sixteenth Century* (New York: Academic Press, 1976); E.J. Hobsbawm, *Industry and Empire: From 1750 to the Present Day* (New York: New Press, 1999); Inikori, *Africans and the Industrial Revolution in England: A Study in International Trade and Economic Development.*

44. Douglass C. North and Robert Paul Thomas, *The Rise of the Western World: A New Economic History* (Cambridge: Cambridge University Press, 1973).

45. Sven Beckert and Seth Rockman (eds.), *Slavery's Capitalism: A New History of American Economic Development* (University of Pennsylvania Press, 2017).

46. See Inikori, *Africans and the Industrial Revolution in England*, 481; and J.E. Inikori and Stanley L. Engerman, *The Atlantic Slave Trade: Effects on Economies, Societies, and Peoples in Africa, the Americas, and Europe* (Durham: Duke University Press, 1992). Although not the focus of this study, consumption habits in Europe changed significantly as result of this triangular relationship between slaves, commodities, and production. See Sidney Wilfred Mintz, *Sweetness and Power* (New York: Viking, 1985); Ralph A. Austen and Woodruff D. Smith, "Private Tooth Decay as Public Economic Virtue: The Slave-Sugar Triangle, Consumerism, and European Industrialization," *Social Science History* 14, no. 1 (1990): 95–115.

47. Robin Blackburn, *The American Crucible: Slavery, Emancipation and Human Rights* (London: Verso, 2013); Greg Grandin, *Empire of Necessity: Slavery, Freedom, and Deception in the New World*, 1st Picador ed. (New York: Picador, 2015); Edward E. Baptist, *The Half Has Never Been Told: Slavery and the Making of American Capitalism* (New York: Basic Books, 2014).

48. There are certain parallels to be drawn between racial slavery in the 17th–19th centuries and contemporary sectors of economies reliant upon various forms of coerced labor. Contemporary examples of sweat shop and forced labor—present-day slavery—emphasize the discrepancy between the conditions of labor: poorly remunerated workers often laboring in unsafe and unsanitary conditions who nevertheless produce commodities that are invariably sold in capitalist marketplaces that, through advertising techniques, remove any trace of the highly unequal and often unlawful conditions under which these commodities were produced.

49. John K. Thornton, "African Soldiers in the Haitian Revolution," *The Journal of Caribbean History* 25, no. 1 (1991); Robin Law, "King Agaja of Dahomey, the Slave Trade, and the Question of West African Plantations: The Embassy of Bulfinch Lambe and Adomo Tomo to England, 1726–32," *The Journal of Imperial and Commonwealth History* 19, no. 2 (1991); Inikori and Engerman,

The Atlantic Slave Trade: Effects on Economies, Societies, and Peoples in Africa, the Americas, and Europe; Berry, "Unsettled Accounts: Stool Debts, Chieftaincy Disputes and the Question of Asante Constitutionalism"; Kwame Y. Daaku, *Trade and Politics on the Gold Coast, 1600–1720: A Study of the African Reaction to European Trade* (Oxford: Clarendon Press, 1970).

50. Warren Whatley and Rob Gillezeau, "The Impact of the Transatlantic Slave Trade on Ethnic Stratification in Africa," *The American Economic Review*, Vol. 101, No. 3, Papers and Proceedings of the One Hundred Twenty Third Annual Meeting of the American Economic Association (May 2011) 571–576. Warren Whatley, "The Transatlantic Slave Trade and the Evolution of Political Authority in West Africa," in *Africa's Development in Historical Perspective*, eds. Emmanuel Kwaku Akyeampong et al. (2012), 471.

51. Davidson, *The Black Man's Burden: The Myth of African Tribalism and the Curse of the Nation-State*.

52. Mahmood Mamdani, *Citizen and Subject: Contemporary Africa and the Legacy of Late Colonialism* (Princeton: Princeton University Press, 1996).

53 . Peter James Hudson, *Bankers and Empire: How Wall Street Colonized the Caribbean* (Chicago: University of Chicago Press, 2017)

54. Édouard Glissant, *Caribbean Discourse: Selected Essays*, trans. J. Michael Dash (Charlottesville: University Press of Virginia, 1989).

55. Boaventura de Sousa Santos, *Epistemologias do Sul* (São Paulo: Cortez, 2010).

56. Archdiocese of Sao Paulo, "Torture in Brazil: A Report," ed. Joan Dassin (New York: Vintage Books, 1986); Argentina's National Commission on Disappeared People, "Nunca Mas, Never Again: A Report" (London: Faber and Faber, in association with Index on Censorship, 1986); Daniel Ellsberg, "Papers on the War," (New York: Pocket Books, 1972).

57. Geertz, *The Interpretation of Cultures: Selected Essays*.

58. See Azza Salama Layton, "International Pressure and the U.S. Government's Response to Little Rock," *The Arkansas Historical Quarterly* 56, no. 3 (1997): 257–72; Gay Seidman, *Beyond the Boycott: Labor Rights, Human Rights, and Transnational Activism* (New York: Russell Sage Foundation, 2007).

59. One of the striking elements of world politics after World War II is the number of national governments that have issued formal apologies for past acts: the Japanese government's apology for the Japanese military's exploitation of Korean females as "comfort women" during Japan's occupation of Korea; the German government and the state of Israel; the governments of New Zealand and Australia's apologies over past treatment of its indigenous population; and the Brazilian and Argentine governments' official apologies for the disappeared, the tortured, and the violated, during their respective years of authoritarian rule. This paradox of chronicling state practices of coercion, surveillance, and extralegal activity both within and external to the territory and dominion of the nation-state conjuncture is perhaps best summed up by William DeVine, a retired CIA operative who was, by his account, instrumental in supporting opposition to the democratically elected national government of Chile under president Salvador Allende: "Covert action is a very important instrument to statecraft." Chile was his first professional assignment, and he recalled having to reproduce a receipt for an informant to convey his activities, proof in his view of statecraft, not gangsterism. "We were not rogues. We had to produce receipts." *Time*, June 16, 2014, "10 Questions: Thirty-two Year Veteran of the CIA Jack Devine on Edward Snowden, Recruiting Traitors and Shoe Phones," p. 60.

60. Begoña Aretxaga, *States of Terror: Begoña Aretxaga's Essays*, ed. Joseba Zulaika (Reno: Center for Basque Studies, University of Nevada, Reno, 2005).

61. ibid.

62. Ibid., 263.

63. Trouillot, *Haiti, State Against Nation: The Origins and Legacy of Duvalierism*; "Global Transformations: Anthropology and the Modern World" (New York: Palgrave Macmillan, 2003).

64. *Haiti, State Against Nation: The Origins and Legacy of Duvalierism.*

65. Robert Fatton, *Haiti's Predatory Republic: The Unending Transition to Democracy* (Boulder: Lynne Rienner Publishers, 2002).

66. Murray J. Edelman, "The Symbolic Uses of Politics," (Urbana: University of Illinois Press, 1985), 2, 111.

67. George L. Mosse, *Masses and Man: Nationalist and Fascist Perceptions of Reality* (New York: H. Fertig, 1980).

68. Ibid., 2.

69. George Steinmetz, ed. *State/Culture: State-Formation After the Cultural Turn* (Ithaca: Cornell University Press, 1999).

70. There is an ample literature on the topic of the state's role in socialization of masses into the rhetoric, ideals, and practices of citizenry. Among them, Eugen Weber, *Peasants into Frenchmen: The Modernization of Rural France, 1870–1914* (Stanford: Stanford University Press, 1976).

BIBLIOGRAPHY

Acemoglu, Daron, and James A. Robinson. *Economic Origins of Dictatorship and Democracy*. Cambridge: Cambridge University Press, 2006.

———. *Why Nations Fail: The Origins of Power, Prosperity and Poverty*. London: Profile, 2012.

Aidi, Hisham. "The Music of Malcolm X." *The New Yorker*, February 28, 2015.

Almond, Gabriel A. "Introduction: A Functional Approach to Comparative Politics." In *The Politics of the Developing Areas*, edited by James Smoot Coleman and Gabriel A. Almond. Princeton: Princeton University Press, 1960.

———. "Political Development: Analytical and Normative Perspectives." *Comparative Political Studies* 1, no. 4 (1969): 447–69.

Anderson, Benedict. *Imagined Communities: Reflections on the Origin and Spread of Nationalism*. 2nd ed. London: Verso, 2006.

Anderson, David. *Histories of the Hanged: The Dirty War in Kenya and the End of Empire*. 1st American ed. New York: W. W. Norton, 2005.

Andrews, George Reid. *Afro-Latin America, 1800–2000*. New York: Oxford University Press, 2004.

Appadurai, Arjun. "The Colonial Backdrop." *Afterimage* 24, no. 5 (March 1997): 4–7.

Arendt, Hannah. *Imperialism: Part Two of the Origins of Totalitarianism* [in English]. San Diego: Harcourt Brace Jovanovich, 1968.

———. *On Revolution*. New York: Viking Press, 1963.

———. *The Promise of Politics*. 1st ed. New York: Schocken Books, 2005.

Aretxaga, Begoña. *States of Terror: Begoña Aretxaga's Essays*. Edited by Joseba Zulaika. Reno: Center for Basque Studies, University of Nevada, Reno, 2005.

Aristotle. *The Politics*. Cambridge: Cambridge University Press, 1988.

Asad, Talal. *Anthropology & the Colonial Encounter*. Amherst: Humanity Books, 1998.

Austen, Ralph A., and Woodruff D. Smith. "Private Tooth Decay as Public Economic Virtue: The Slave-Sugar Triangle, Consumerism, and European Industrialization." *Social Science History* 14, no. 1 (1990): 95–115.

Axiom, *Ma Lettre au Président*, Universal Music Division, Mercury Records (2006).

Balandier, Georges. "La Situation Coloniale: Approche Théorique." *Cahiers Internationaux de Sociologie* 11 (1951): 44–79.

———. *Political Anthropology*. Translated by A. M. Sheridan Smith. New York: Pantheon Books, 1970.

Balibar, Etienne, and Immanuel Maurice Wallerstein. *Race, Nation, Class: Ambiguous Identities*. Translated by Chris Turner. London: Verso, 1991.

Banton, Michael. *The Coloured Quarter: Negro Immigrants in an English City* [in English]. London: Cape, 1955.

———. *Race and Immigration* [in English]. London: New Society, 1976.

Baptist, Edward E. *The Half Has Never Neen Told: Slavery and the Making of American Capitalism*. New York: Basic Books, 2014.

Barkey, Karen, and Ira Katznelson. "States, Regimes, and Decisions: Why Jews Were Expelled from Medieval England and France." *Theory and Society* 40, no. 5 (2011): 475–503.

Barou, Jacques. "L'espace Immigré Ou Comment Les Rendre Invisibles." *Politique Aujord'hui* 4 (1984): 115–23.

Barth, Fredrik, ed. *Ethnic Groups and Boundaries: The Social Organization of Culture Difference*. Boston: Little, Brown & Co., 1969.

Bauer, Otto. *The Question of Nationalities and Social Democracy*. Edited by Ephraim Nimni. Minneapolis: University of Minnesota Press, 2000.

Beaumont, Gustave de. *Marie; or, Slavery in the United States: A Novel of Jacksonian America* [in English]. Baltimore: Johns Hopkins University Press, 1958.

Beckert, Sven, and Seth Rockman (eds.). Slavery's Capitalism: A New History of American Economic Development. Philadelphia: University of Pennsylvania Press, 2017. Bellegarde-Smith, Patrick. *Haiti: The Breached Citadel*. Rev. and updated ed. Toronto: Canadian Scholars' Press, 2004.

Bennett, Huw C. *Fighting the Mau Mau: The British Army and Counter-Insurgency in the Kenya Emergency*. Cambridge: Cambridge University Press, 2013.

Berlin, Ira. *Many Thousands Gone: The First Two Centuries of Slavery in North America*. Cambridge: Belknap Press of Harvard University Press, 1998.

Berry, Sara. "Unsettled Accounts: Stool Debts, Chieftaincy Disputes and the Question of Asante Constitutionalism." *The Journal of African History* 39, no. 1 (1998): 39–62.

Blackburn, Robin. *The American Crucible: Slavery, Emancipation and Human Rights*. London: Verso, 2013.

Blackwell, Christopher W., "Athenian Democary: A Brief Overview, Demos, Feb 28 2003. http://www.stoa.org/projects/demos/article_democracy_overview?page=4

Boix, Carles. "Democracy, Development, and the International System." [In English]. *The American Political Science Review* 105, no. 4 (November 2011): 809–28.

Bourdieu, Pierre, and Loïc Wacquant. "On the Cunning of Imperialist Reason." *Theory, Culture & Society* 16, no. 1 (1999/02/01): 41–58.

Branch, Taylor. *Parting the Waters: America in the King Years, 1954–63*. New York: Simon and Schuster, 1988.

Brody, Richard. "Interview with Gabriel Almond." In *Political Science in America: Oral Histories of a Discipline*, edited by Michael A. Baer, Malcolm E. Jewell and Lee Sigelman. Lexington: University Press of Kentucky, 1991.

Brubaker, Rogers. *Citizenship and Nationhood in France and Germany*. Cambridge: Harvard University Press, 1992.

Bryce, James. *Modern Democracies*. London: The Macmillan Company, 1921.

Burleigh, Michael, and Wolfgang Wippermann. *The Racial State: Germany, 1933–1945*. Cambridge: Cambridge University Press, 1991.

Camiscioli, Elisa. *Reproducing the French Race: Immigration, Intimacy, and Embodiment in the Early Twentieth Century*. Durham: Duke University Press, 2009.

Carens, Joseph H. *Culture, Citizenship, and Community: A Contextual Exploration of Justice as Evenhandedness*. Oxford: Oxford University Press, 2000.

———. *Equality, Moral Incentives, and the Market: An Essay in Utopian Politico-Economic Theory*. Chicago: University of Chicago Press, 1981.

———. *The Ethics of Immigration*. New York: Oxford University Press, 2013.

Carey, Christopher. *Democracy in Classical Athens*. 2nd ed. London: Bloomsbury, 2017.

Cary, Anthony. "The Migrated Archives: What Went Wrong and What Lessons Should We Draw?" 22. London: Foreign and Commonwealth Office, 2011.

Castro, A. Peter. "Collaborative Researchers or Cold Warriors? The Origins, Activities, and Legacy of the Smithsonian's Institute of Social Anthropology." *Journal of International & Global Studies* 2, no. 1 (2010): 56–82.

Chapman, Herrick, and Laura Levine Frader, eds. *Race in France: Interdisciplinary Perspectives on the Politics of Difference*. New York: Berghahn Books, 2004.

Chebel d'Appollonia, Ariane. *Frontiers of Fear, Immigration and Insecurity in the United States and Europe*. Ithaca: Cornell University Press, 2012.

Chí Minh, Hồ. *On Revolution: Selected Writings, 1920–66*. Edited by Bernard B. Fall. New York: Praeger, 1967.

Clifford, James, and George E. Marcus, eds. *Writing Culture: The Poetics and Politics of Ethnography*. Berkeley: University of California Press, 1986.

Collier, David, and James E. Mahon, Jr. "Conceptual 'Stretching' Revisited: Adapting Categories in Comparative Analysis." [In English]. *The American Political Science Review* 87, no. 4 (December 1993): 845–55.

Cooper, Frederick, and Ann Laura Stoler, eds. *Tensions of Empire Colonial Cultures in a Bourgeois World*. Berkeley: University of California Press, 1997.

Cottrol, Robert J. *The Long, Lingering Shadow: Slavery, Race, and Law in the American Hemisphere*. Athens: University of Georgia Press, 2013.

Curzon, George Nathaniel. *Problems of the Far East: Japan, Korea, China*. 3rd ed. London: Longmans, Green & Co., 1894.

Da Costa, Emília Viotti. *Crowns of Glory, Tears of Blood: The Demerara Slave Rebellion of 1823*. New York: Oxford University Press, 1994.

Daaku, Kwame Y. *Trade and Politics on the Gold Coast, 1600–1720: A Study of the African Reaction to European Trade*. Oxford: Clarendon Press, 1970.

Dahl, Robert Alan. *Polyarchy: Participation and Opposition*. New Haven: Yale University Press, 1971.

Das, Veena, ed. *The Word and the World: Fantasy, Symbol, and Record*. New Delhi: Sage, 1986.

Davidson, Basil. *Africa in Modern History: The Search for a New Society*. London: Allen Lane, 1978.

———. *The Black Man's Burden: The Myth of African Tribalism and the Curse of the Nation-State*. 1st ed. New York: Times Books/Random House, 1992.

———. *Let Freedom Come: Africa in Modern History*. 1st American ed. Boston: Little, Brown and Co., 1978.

———. *Modern Africa*. London: Longman, 1983.

———. *The People's Cause: A History of Guerrillas in Africa*. London: Longman, 1981.

Delany, Martin Robison. *The Condition, Elevation, Emigration, and Destiny of the Colored People of the United States*. New York: Arno Press, 1968.

de Sousa Santos, Boaventura. *Epistemologias Do Sul*. São Paulo: Cortez, 2010.

de Toqueville, Alexis. *On Democracy in America*. New York: Sheba Blake Publishing, 2014.

Dubet, François. *Immigrations: Qu'en Savons-Nous?* Paris: La Documentation Française, 1989.

Dubois, Laurent. *Avengers of the New World*. Cambridge, MA, and London, England: Belknap, 2004.

———. *A Colony of Citizens: Revolution and Emancipation in the French Caribbean, 1787–1804*. Chapel Hill and London: University of North Carolina Press, 2004.

———. *Haiti*. New York: Metropolitan Books, 2012.

Du Bois, W.E.B. *Black Reconstruction: An Essay toward a History of the Part Which Black Folk Played in the Attempt to Reconstruct Democracy in America, 1860–1880*. 1st ed. New York: Harcourt, Brace and Co., 1935.

Dussel, Enrique D. *Twenty Theses on Politics*. Translated by George Ciccariello-Maher. Durham: Duke University Press, 2008.

Edelman, Murray J. *The Symbolic Uses of Politics*. Urbana: University of Illinois Press, 1985.

Elkins, Caroline. *Imperial Reckoning: The Untold Story of Britain's Gulag in Kenya*. 1st ed. New York: Henry Holt, 2005.

Ellsberg, Daniel. *Papers on the War*. New York: Pocket Books, 1972.

Evans-Pritchard, E.E. *The Comparative Method in Social Anthropology*. London: University of London, Athlone Press, 1963.

Evans-Pritchard, E.E., and Meyer Fortes, eds. *African Political Systems*. London: Oxford University Press, 1940.

Fanon, Frantz. "Algeria's European Minority." In *A Dying Colonialism*. New York: Grove Press, 1965.

———. *The Wretched of the Earth*. New York: Grove Press, 1968.

Fassin, Didier. *Enforcing Order: An Ethnography of Urban Policing*. Cambridge: Polity Press, 2013.

———. "L'invention Française de la Discrimination." *Revue Française de Science Politique* 52, no. 4. (2002): 403–23.

Fassin, Didier, and Eric Fassin, eds. *De la Question Sociale à la Question Raciale?: Représenter la Société Française*. Paris: Découverte, 2006.

Fatton, Robert. *Haiti's Predatory Republic: The Unending Transition to Democracy*. Boulder: Lynne Rienner Publishers, 2002.

Frank, Andre Gunder. *Reorient: Global Economy in the Asian Age*. Berkeley: University of California Press, 1998.

Freeman, Edward Augustus. *Comparative Politics: Six Lectures Read before the Royal Institution* [in English]. London: Macmillan and Co., 1873.

———. *Historical Essays*. London: Macmillan, 1871.

———. *The Life and Letters of Edward A. Freeman, Vol. II*. London: Macmillan and Co., 1895.

———. "Race and Language." In *Essays: English and American*, edited by Charles W. Eliot. New York: P. F. Collier & Son, 1909.

———. *Some Impressions of the United States*. London: Longmans, Green, & Co., 1883.

French, Jan Hoffman. *Legalizing Identities: Becoming Black or Indian in Brazil's Northeast*. Chapel Hill: University of North Carolina Press, 2009.

———. "Rethinking Police Violence in Brazil: Unmasking the Public Secret of Race; Critical Debates." *Latin American Politics and Society* 55, no. 4 (Winter 2013): 161–81.

Fuchs, Lawrence H. *The American Kaleidoscope: Race, Ethnicity, and the Civic Culture*. Middletown, CT: Wesleyan University Press, 1990.

Garis, Roy L. *Immigration Restriction: A Study of the Opposition to and Regulation of Immigration into the United States* [in English]. New York: Macmillan, 1927.

Garrow, David J. *Protest at Selma: Martin Luther King, Jr., and the Voting Rights Act of 1965*. New Haven: Yale University Press, 1978.

Gaspar, David Barry, and David Patrick Geggus, eds. *A Turbulent Time: The French Revolution and the Greater Caribbean*. Bloomington: Indiana University Press, 1997.

Geddes, Barbara. *Paradigms and Sand Castles: Theory Building and Research Design in Comparative Politics*. Ann Arbor: University of Michigan Press, 2003.

Geertz, Clifford. *The Interpretation of Cultures: Selected Essays*. New York: Basic Books, 1973.

Gendzier, Irene L. *Managing Political Change: Social Scientists and the Third World*. Boulder: Westview Press, 1985.

Gilroy, Paul. *"There Ain't No Black in the Union Jack": The Cultural Politics of Race and Nation.* London: Hutchinson, 1987.

Glissant, Édouard. *Caribbean Discourse: Selected Essays.* Translated by J. Michael Dash. Charlottesville: University Press of Virginia, 1989.

Godreau, Isar P. *Scripts of Blackness: Race, Cultural Nationalism, and U.S. Colonialism in Puerto Rico.* Urbana: University of Illinois Press, 2015.

Goertz, Gary. "Concept Intension and Extension." In *Social Science Concepts: A User's Guide.* Princeton: Princeton University Press, 2006.

———. *Tale of Two Cultures: Qualitative and Quantitative Research in the Social Sciences.* Edited by James Mahoney. Princeton: Princeton University Press, 2012.

Goffman, Erving. *The Presentation of Self in Everyday Life.* 1st ed. New York: Anchor Books, 1959.

Goldberg, David Theo. *The Racial State.* Malden: Blackwell Publishers, 2002.

Gordon, Edmund T. *Disparate Diasporas: Identity and Politics in an African Nicaraguan Community.* Austin: University of Texas Press, 1998.

Gramsci, Antonio. *The Gramsci Reader: Selected Writings, 1916–1935.* New York: New York University Press, 2000.

Grandin, Greg. *Empire of Necessity: Slavery, Freedom, and Deception in the New World.* 1st Picador ed. New York: Picador, 2015.

Green, Peter. *The Greco-Persian Wars.* Berkeley, Los Angeles, London: University of Califrornia Press, 1996.

Gueye, Abdoulaye. "The Labyrinth to Blackness: On Naming and Leadership in the Black Associative Space in France." *French Cultural Studies* 24, no. 2 (2013): 196–207.

———. "Manufacturing Blackness at the Turn of Twenty Century France." In *Becoming Minority: How Discourses and Policies Produce Minorities in Europe and India*, edited by Jyotirmaya Tripathy and Sudarsan Padmanabhan. New Delhi: SAGE Publications, 2014.

Hahn, Steven. *A Nation under Our Feet: Black Political Struggles in the Rural South, from Slavery to the Great Migration.* Cambridge: Belknap Press of Harvard University Press, 2003.

Hale, Charles R. *Más Que un Indio/More Than an Indian: Racial Ambivalence and Neoliberal Multiculturalism in Guatemala.* Santa Fe: School of American Research Press, 2006.

Hall, Peter A., ed. *The Political Power of Economic Ideas: Keynesianism across Nations.* Princeton: Princeton University Press, 1989.

Hall, Stuart. *The Hard Road to Renewal: Thatcherism and the Crisis of the Left.* London: Verso, 1988.

Hargreaves, Alec G. *Multi-Ethnic France: Immigration, Politics, Culture and Society.* Edited by Alec G. Hargreaves. 2nd ed. New York: Routledge, 2007.

Healy, David. *The United States in Cuba, 1898–1902: Generals, Politicians, and the Search for Policy.* Madison: University of Wisconsin Press, 1963.

Helg, Aline. *Liberty & Equality in Caribbean Colombia, 1770–1835.* Chapel Hill: University of North Carolina Press, 2004.

———. *Our Rightful Share: The Afro-Cuban Struggle for Equality, 1886–1912.* Chapel Hill: University of North Carolina Press, 1995.

Helmke, Gretchen, and Steven Levitsky. "Informal Institutions and Comparative Politics: A Research Agenda." *Perspectives on Politics* 2, no. 4 (2004): 725–40.

Herskovits, Melville J. *The American Negro: A Study in Racial Crossing.* Bloomington: Indiana University Press, 1968.

Hobsbawm, E.J. *Industry and Empire: From 1750 to the Present Day.* New York: New Press, 1999.

Hobsbawm, Eric J., and Terence O. Ranger, eds. *The Invention of Tradition.* Cambridge: Cambridge University Press, 1983.

Hobson, John M. *The Eurocentric Conception of World Politics: Western International Theory, 1760–2010.* Cambridge: Cambridge University Press, 2012.

Hoffmann, Odile. *Política e Identidad: Afrodescendientes en México y América Central*. México, D.F.: Instituto Nacional de Antropología e Historia, 2010.

Holt, Thomas C. *The Problem of Freedom: Race, Labor, and Politics in Jamaica and Britain, 1832–1938*. Baltimore: Johns Hopkins University Press, 1992.

Hooker, Juliet. "Afro-Descendant Struggles for Collective Rights in Latin America: Between Race and Culture." *Souls* 10, no. 3 (2008/09/12): 279–91.

———. *Race and the Politics of Solidarity*. Oxford: Oxford University Press, 2009.

Hudson, Peter James, Bankers and Empire: How Wall Street Colonized the Caribbean. Chicago: University of Chicago Press, 2017.

Hunt, Alfred N. *Haiti's Influence on Antebellum America: Slumbering Volcano in the Caribbean*. Baton Rouge: Louisiana State University Press, 2006.

Hunt, Lynn, editor and translator. *The French Revolution and Human Rights*. Boston and New York: Bedford Books, 1996.

Huntington, Samuel P. "The Clash of Civilizations?" *Foreign Affairs* 72, no. 3 (1993): 22–49.

———. "The Hispanic Challenge." *Foreign Policy*, no. 141 (2004): 30–45.

———. *Political Order in Changing Societies*. New Haven: Yale University Press, 1968.

Inikori, J.E. *Africans and the Industrial Revolution in England: A Study in International Trade and Economic Development*. Cambridge: Cambridge University Press, 2002.

Inikori, J.E., and Stanley L. Engerman. *The Atlantic Slave Trade: Effects on Economies, Societies, and Peoples in Africa, the Americas, and Europe*. Durham: Duke University Press, 1992.

Ismard, Paulin. *Democracy's Slaves: A Political History of Ancient Greece*. Cambridge and London: Harvard University Press, 2017.

Jackson, Ashley. "The Empire/Commonwealth and the Second World War." *Round Table* 100, no. 412 (2011): 65–78.

James, C.L.R. *The Black Jacobins: Toussaint L'ouverture and the San Domingo Revolution*. 2d ed., rev. ed. New York: Vintage Books, 1989.

Jennings, Jeremy. "Citizenship, Republicanism and Multiculturalism in Contemporary France." *British Journal of Political Science* 30, no. 4 (2000): 575–98.

Johnson, Chalmers. "Preconception vs. Observation, or the Contributions of Rational Choice Theory and Area Studies to Contemporary Political Science." *PS: Political Science and Politics* 30, no. 2 (1997): 170–74.

Johnson, Walter. "Comment: Resetting the Legal History of Slavery; Divination, Torture, Poisoning, Murder, Revolution, Emancipation, and Re-Enslavement." *Law and History Review* 29, no. 4 (2011): 1089–95.

Jordan, Winthrop D. *White over Black: American Attitudes toward the Negro, 1550–1812*. 2nd ed. Chapel Hill: University of North Carolina Press, 2012.

Kant, Immanuel. *To Perpetual Peace: A Philosophical Sketch*. Translated by Ted Humphrey. Indianapolis: Hackett Publishing Company, 2003.

Kasimis, Demetra. "The Tragedy of Blood-Based Membership: Secrecy and the Politics of Immigration in Euripides's Ion." *Political Theory* 41, no. 2 (2013): 231–56.

Katznelson, Ira. *Black Men, White Cities: Race, Politics, and Migration in the United States, 1900–30, and Britain, 1948–68* [in English]. Chicago: University of Chicago Press, 1976.

———. *When Affirmative Action Was White: An Untold History of Racial Inequality in Twentieth-Century America* [in English]. New York: W. W. Norton, 2005.

Keaton, Trica Danielle. "Racial Profiling and the 'French Exception.'" *French Cultural Studies* 24, no. 2 (2013): 231–42.

Keaton, Trica Danielle, T. Denean Sharpley-Whiting, and Tyler Edward Stovall. *Black France/France Noire: The History and Politics of Blackness*. Durham: Duke University Press, 2012.

Kelley, Donald R., and Bonnie G. Smith. "What Was Property? Legal Dimensions of the Social Question in France (1789–1848)." *Proceedings of the American Philosophical Society* 128, no. 3 (1984): 200–30.

Kenyatta, Jomo. *Facing Mount Kenya: The Tribal Life of the Gikuyu*. London: Secker and Warburg, 1956.

King, Desmond S., and Rogers M. Smith. "Racial Orders in American Political Development." *The American Political Science Review* 99, no. 1 (2005): 75–92.

Kramer, Paul A. *The Blood of Government: Race, Empire, the United States, and the Philippines*. Chapel Hill: University of North Carolina Press, 2006.

Kuhn, Thomas S. *The Structure of Scientific Revolutions*. 2nd ed. Chicago: University of Chicago Press, 1970.

Kymlicka, Will. *Politics in the Vernacular: Nationalism, Multiculturalism, and Citizenship*. Oxford: Oxford University Press, 2001.

———. *States, Nations and Cultures*. Assen: Van Gorcum, 1997.

Laitin, David D. *Nations, States, and Violence*. Oxford: Oxford University Press, 2007.

Lakatos, Imre, and Alan Musgrave, eds. *Criticism and the Growth of Knowledge*. Cambridge: Cambridge University Press, 1970.

Lape, Susan. *Race and Citizen Identity in the Classical Athenian Democracy*. Cambridge: Cambridge University Press, 2010.

Lasso, Marixa. *Myths of Harmony: Race and Republicanism During the Age of Revolution, Colombia 1795–1831*. Pittsburgh, PA: University of Pittsburgh Press, 2007.

Law, Robin. "King Agaja of Dahomey, the Slave Trade, and the Question of West African Plantations: The Embassy of Bulfinch Lambe and Adomo Tomo to England, 1726–32." *The Journal of Imperial and Commonwealth History* 19, no. 2 (1991/05/01): 137–63.

Layton, Azza Salama. "International Pressure and the U.S. Government's Response to Little Rock." *The Arkansas Historical Quarterly* 56, no. 3 (1997): 257–72.

Leach, Edmund Ronald. *Political Systems of Highland Burma: A Study of Kachin Social Structure*. Boston: Beacon Press, 1965.

Lijphart, Arend. "Comparative Politics and the Comparative Method." *The American Political Science Review* 65, no. 3 (1971): 682–93.

———. *The Trauma of Decolonization: The Dutch and West New Guinea*. New Haven: Yale University Press, 1966.

Linstant, Pradine. *Recueil Général des Lois et Actes du Gouvernement D'haïti Depuis la Proclamation de son Indépendance Jusqu'à Nos Jour* [in French]. Paris: A. Durand, 1886.

Louis, William Roger. *British Strategy in the Far East, 1919–1939*. Oxford: Clarendon Press, 1971.

Loveman, Brian. "When You Wish upon the Stars: Why the Generals (and Admirals) Say Yes to Latin American 'Transitions' to Civilian Government." In *The Origins of Liberty: Political and Economic Liberalization in the Modern World*, edited by Paul W. Drake and Mathew D. McCubbins. Princeton: Princeton University Press, 1998. pp 115–45.

Macey, David. *Frantz Fanon: A Life*. London: Granta Books, 2000.

MacIntyre, Alasdair C. *Selected Essays*. Cambridge: Cambridge University Press, 2006.

Mahoney, James. *Colonialism and Postcolonial Development: Spanish America in Comparative Perspective*. Leiden: Cambridge University Press, 2010.

Mahoney, James, and Dietrich Rueschemeyer, eds. *Comparative Historical Analysis in the Social Sciences*. Cambridge: Cambridge University Press, 2003.

Mamdani, Mahmood. *Citizen and Subject: Contemporary Africa and the Legacy of Late Colonialism*. Princeton: Princeton University Press, 1996.

Marx, Anthony W. *Making Race and Nation: A Comparison of South Africa, the United States, and Brazil* [in English]. Cambridge and New York: Cambridge University Press, 1998.

Marx, Karl. "The Materialist Conception of History (1859)." Translated by T. B. Bottomore. In *Selected Writings in Sociology & Social Philosophy*, edited by T. B. Bottomore and Maximilien Rubel. New York: McGraw-Hill, 1964.

Mayer, Nonna. "The French National Front." In *The New Politics of the Right: Neo-Populist Parties and Movements in Established Democracies*, edited by Hans-Georg Betz and Stefan Immerfall, 11–26. New York: St. Martin's Press, 1998.

Mazower, Mark. *No Enchanted Palace: The End of Empire and the Ideological Origins of the United Nations*. Princeton: Princeton University Press, 2009.

McCoskey, Denise Eileen. *Race: Antiquity and Its Legacy*. Oxford: Oxford University Press, 2012.

McCulloch, Jock. *Colonial Psychiatry and "the African Mind"*. Cambridge: Cambridge University Press, 1995.

Melas, Natalie. *All the Difference in the World: Postcoloniality and the Ends of Comparison*. Stanford: Stanford University Press, 2007.

Merriam, Charles Edward. *The New Democracy and the New Despotism*. New York: McGraw-Hill, 1939.

———. "Recent Tendencies in Political Thought." In *A History of Political Theories, Recent Times: Essays on Contemporary Developments in Political Theory*, edited by Harry Elmer Barnes and Charles Edward Merriam. New York: Macmillan Company, 1924.

Miles, Robert, Racism and *Political Action in Britain*, London: Routledge & Paul, 1979.

Miles, Robert & Phisacklea, Annie, *White Man's Country: Racism in British Politics*, London: Pluto Press, 1984.

Mills, Charles W. *The Racial Contract* [in English]. Ithaca: Cornell University Press, 1997.

Mintz, Sidney Wilfred. *Sweetness and Power*. New York: Viking, 1985.

Mitchell, James Tyndale, and Henry Flanders, eds. *The Statutes at Large of Pennsylvania from 1682–1801*, vols. 2–14. Harrisburg: State Printer of Pennsylvania, 1896.

Mitchell, Timothy. *Carbon Democracy: Political Power in the Age of Oil*. London: Verso, 2013.

Monoson, Susan Sara. *Plato's Democratic Entanglements: Athenian Politics and the Practice of Philosophy*. Princeton: Princeton University Press, 2000.

Morgan, Edmund S. *American Slavery, American Freedom: The Ordeal of Colonial Virginia*. 1st ed. New York: Norton, 1975.

Morrisroe, Vicky L. "Sanguinary Amusement: E.A. Freeman, the Comparative Method and Victorian Theories of Race" [in English]. *Modern Intellectual History* 10, no. 1 (2013): 27–56.

Mosse, George L. *Masses and Man: Nationalist and Fascist Perceptions of Reality*. New York: H. Fertig, 1980.

Mullin, Michael. *Africa in America: Slave Acculturation and Resistance in the American South and the British Caribbean, 1736–1831*. Urbana: University of Illinois Press, 1992.

Munck, Gerardo L., and Richard Snyder. *Passion, Craft, and Method in Comparative Politics*. Baltimore: Johns Hopkins University Press, 2007.

Myrdal, Gunnar. *An American Dilemma: The Negro Problem and Modern Democracy*. New York: Harper & Brothers, 1944.

Nelson, William Max. "The Atlantic World." In *The Atlantic World*, edited by D'Maris Coffman, Adrian Leonard, and William O'Reilly. Abingdon, UK: Routledge, 2015.

———. "Making Men: Enlightenment Ideas of Racial Engineering." *The American Historical Review* 115, no. 5 (2010): 1364–94.

Nesbitt, Nick. *Universal Emancipation: The Haitian Revolution and the Radical Enlightenment*. Charlottesville: University of Virginia Press, 2008.

Nobles, Melissa. *The Politics of Official Apologies*. New York: Cambridge University Press, 2008.

————. *Shades of Citizenship: Race and the Census in Modern Politics.* Stanford: Stanford University Press, 2000.

Noiriel, Gérard. *The French Melting Pot: Immigration, Citizenship, and National Identity.* Minneapolis: University of Minnesota Press, 1996.

North, Douglass C., and Robert Paul Thomas. *The Rise of the Western World: A New Economic History.* Cambridge: Cambridge University Press, 1973.

Novick, Peter. *That Noble Dream: The Objectivity Question and the American Historical Profession.* Cambridge: Cambridge University Press, 1999.

"Nunca Mas, Never Again: A Report." London: Faber and Faber, in association with Index on Censorship, 1986. Argentina's National Commission on Disappeared.

O'Donnell, Guillermo. "On the State, Democratization and Some Conceptual Problems: A Latin American View with Glances at Some Postcommunist Countries." *World Development* 21, no. 8 (8// 1993): 1355–69.

Omi, Michael, and Howard Winant. *Racial Formation in the United States: From the 1960s to the 1980s.* New York: Routledge & Kegan Paul, 1986.

Orloff, Ann Shola. *Perverse Politics? Feminism, Anti-Imperialism, Multiplicity.* Edited by Raka Ray and Evren Savci Bradford. West Yorkshire: Emerald Group Publishing Limited, 2016.

————. *The Politics of Pensions: A Comparative Analysis of Britain, Canada, and the United States, 1880–1940.* Madison: University of Wisconsin Press, 1993.

Palmer, Vernon Valentine. "The Origins and Authors of the Code Noir." *Louisiana Law Review* 56, no. 2 (1995): 363–408.

Parker, C.J.W. "The Failure of Liberal Racialism: The Racial Ideas of E. A. Freeman." *The Historical Journal* 24, no. 4 (1981): 825–46.

Paschel, Tianna S. *Becoming Black Political Subjects: Movements and Ethno-Racial Rights in Colombia and Brazil.* Princeton: Princeton University Press, 2016.

Paulo, Archdiocese of Sao. *Torture in Brazil: A Report.* edited by Joan Dassin. New York: Vintage Books, 1986.

Plato. *The Republic.* Revised ed. London: Penguin Books, 1974.

Popkin, Jeremy D. *You are All Free: The Haitian Revolution and the Abolition of Slavery.* Cambridge University Press, 2010.

Prashad, Vijay. *The Darker Nations: A People's History of the Third World.* New York: New Press, 2007.

Proudhon, Pierre-Joseph. *What is Property?* Cambridge: Cambridge University Press, 1994.

Raaflaub, Kurt A. *The Discovery of Freedom in Ancient Greece.* Chicago: University of Chicago Press, 2004.

Rabinow, Paul. "Discourse and Power: On the Limits of Ethnographic Texts." *Dialectical Anthropology* 10, no. 1-2 (1985): 1–13.

Rex, John. *Race, Colonialism and the City.* London: Routledge, 2013.

Rex, John, and David Mason, eds. *Theories of Race and Ethnic Relations.* Cambridge: Cambridge University Press, 1986.

Robinson, William I. *Promoting Polyarchy: Globalization, US Intervention, and Hegemony.* Cambridge: Cambridge University Press, 1996.

Rogin, Michael Paul. *Blackface, White Noise: Jewish Immigrants in the Hollywood Melting Pot.* Berkeley: University of California Press, 1996.

Rout, Leslie B. *The African Experience in Spanish America, 1502 to the Present Day.* Cambridge: Cambridge University Press, 1976.

Rudolph, Lloyd I., and Susanne H. Rudolph. "Surveys in India: Field Experience in Madras State." *The Public Opinion Quarterly* 22, no. 3 (1958): 235–44.

Rudolph, Lloyd I., and Susanne Hoeber Rudolph. *The Modernity of Tradition: Political Development in India.* Chicago: University of Chicago Press, 1967.

Rudolph, Susanne Hoeber. "The Imperialism of Categories: Situating Knowledge in a Globalizing World." *Perspectives on Politics* 3, no. 1 (2005): 5–14.

Santiago-Valles, Kelvin A. *"Subject People" and Colonial Discourses: Economic Transformation and Social Disorder in Puerto Rico, 1898–1947.* Albany: State University of New York Press, 1994.

Sartori, Giovanni. "Concept Misformation in Comparative Politics." *The American Political Science Review* 64, no. 4 (1970): 1033–53.

Sawyer, Mark Q. "Du Bois's Double Consciousness Versus Latin American Exceptionalism: Joe Arroyo, Salsa, and Negritude." *Souls* 7, no. 3–4 (2005/06/01 2005): 85–95.

———. *Racial Politics in Post-Revolutionary Cuba.* Cambridge: Cambridge University Press, 2006.

Schatz, Edward, ed. *Political Ethnography: What Immersion Contributes to the Study of Power.* Chicago: University of Chicago Press, 2009.

Schor, Ralph. *L'opinion Française et les Ètrangers en France: 1919–1939* [in French]. Paris: Sorbonne, 1985.

Scott, Joan Wallach. *Feminism and History.* Oxford: Oxford University Press, 1996.

Scott, Rebecca J. "Paper Thin: Freedom and Re-Enslavement in the Diaspora of the Haitian Revolution." *Law and History Review* 29, no. 4 (2011): 1061–87.

———. *Slave Emancipation in Cuba: The Transition to Free Labor, 1860–1899.* Princeton: Princeton University Press, 1985.

Seidman, Gay. *Beyond the Boycott: Labor Rights, Human Rights, and Transnational Activism.* New York: Russell Sage Foundation, 2007.

Shackford, Charles Chauncey. " 'Comparative Literature' Lecture Delivered at Cornell University." In *The Proceedings of the University Convocation.* Albany: State University of New York, 1876.

Shepard, Todd. *The Invention of Decolonization: The Algerian War and the Remaking of France.* Ithaca: Cornell University Press, 2008.

———. "Thinking between Metropole and Colony: The French Republic, 'Exceptional Promotion', and the 'Integration' of Algerians, 1955–1962." In *The French Colonial Mind: Mental Maps of Empire and Colonial Encounters*, edited by Martin Thomas, 298–323. Lincoln: University of Nebraska Press, 2011.

Sidanius, Jim, Peña, Yesilernis, and Sawyer, Mark, "Inclusionary Discrimination: Pigmentocracy and Patriotism in the Dominican Republic," *Political Psychology* 22, no. 4 (2001).

Silverman, Maxim. *Deconstructing the Nation: Immigration, Racism, and Citizenship in Modern France.* New York: Routledge, 1992.

Sivanandan, Ambalavaner. *A Different Hunger: Writings on Black Resistance.* London: Pluto Press, 1982.

———. "Race, Class and the State: The Black Experience in Britain." *Race & Class* 17, no. 4 (1976): 347–68.

Small, Stephen. *Police and People in London: A Group of Young Black People.* London: Policy Studies Institute, 1983.

———. *Racialized Barriers: The Black Experience in the United States and England in the 1980s.* London: Routledge, 1994.

Small, Stephen, and Solomos, John. "Race, Immigration and Politics in Britain." *International Journal of Comparative Sociology*, vol. 47, no. 3-4, pp. 235–57.

Solomos, John. *Black Youth, Racism and the State: The Politics of Ideology and Policy.* Cambridge: Cambridge University Press, 1988.

———. *Race and Racism in Britain.* 3rd ed. Hampshire: Palgrave Macmillan, 2003.

Spruyt, Hendrik. *Ending Empire: Contested Sovereignty and Territorial Partition.* Ithaca: Cornell University Press, 2005.

———. *The Sovereign State and Its Competitors.* Princeton: Princeton University Press, 1994.

Steinmetz, George, ed. *State/Culture: State-Formation after the Cultural Turn.* Ithaca: Cornell University Press, 1999.

Steinmo, Sven, Kathleen Ann Thelen, and Frank Longstreth, eds. *Structuring Politics: Historical Institutionalism in Comparative Analysis.* Cambridge: Cambridge University Press, 1992.

Stephens, H. Morse. "Review of the Life and Letters of Edward A. Freeman by W.R.W. Stephens." *The Annals of the American Academy of Political and Social Science* 7 (1896): 113–20.

Stocking, George W. *Race, Culture, and Evolution: Essays in the History of Anthropology.* Chicago: University of Chicago Press, 1982.

Stovall, Tyler. "Race and the Making of the Nation: Blacks in Modern France." In *Diasporic Africa: A Reader,* edited by Michael Angelo Gomez. New York: New York University Press, 2006.

Stuckey, Sterling. *Slave Culture: Nationalist Theory and the Foundations of Black America.* New York: Oxford University Press, 1987.

Thatcher, Margaret. "T.V. Interview for Granada's World in Action." Margaret Thatcher Foundation, 1978.

Thornton, John K. "African Soldiers in the Haitian Revolution." *The Journal of Caribbean History* 25, no. 1 (1991): 58.

Tilly, Charles. *Durable Inequality.* Berkeley: University of California Press, 1998.

Trouillot, Michel-Rolph. *Global Transformations: Anthropology and the Modern World.* New York: Palgrave Macmillan, 2003.

———. *Haiti, State against Nation: The Origins and Legacy of Duvalierism.* New York: Monthly Review Press, 1990.

Vitalis, Robert. *America's Kingdom: Mythmaking on the Saudi Oil Frontier.* Stanford: Stanford University Press, 2007.

———. "Birth of a Discipline." In *Imperialism and Internationalism in the Discipline of International Relations,* edited by David Long and Brian C. Schmidt. Albany: State University of New York Press, 2005.

Voegelin, Eric. *The New Science of Politics: An Introduction.* Chicago: University of Chicago Press, 1952.

Wade, Richard C. *Slavery in the Cities: The South, 1820–1860.* London: Oxford University Press, 1970.

Wallerstein, Immanuel Maurice. *The Modern World-System: Capitalist Agriculture and the Origins of the European World-Economy in the Sixteenth Century.* New York: Academic Press, 1976.

Weber, Eugen. *Peasants into Frenchmen: The Modernization of Rural France, 1870–1914.* Stanford: Stanford University Press, 1976.

Wedeen, Lisa. *Ambiguities of Domination: Politics, Rhetoric, and Symbols in Contemporary Syria.* Chicago: University of Chicago Press, 1999.

———. "Conceptualizing Culture: Possibilities for Political Science." *The American Political Science Review* 96, no. 4 (2002): 713–28.

———. *Peripheral Visions: Publics, Power, and Performance in Yemen.* Chicago: University of Chicago Press, 2008.

Weil, Patrick. *How to Be French: Nationality in the Making since 1789.* Translated by Catherine Porter. Durham: Duke University Press, 2008.

Whatley, Warren. "The Transatlantic Slave Trade and the Evolution of Political Authority in West Africa." In *Africa's Development in Historical Perspective,* edited by Emmanuel Kwaku Akyeampong, Robert H. Bates, Nathan Nunn, and James A. Robinson, 2012.

Whatley, Warren, and Rob Gillezeau. "The Impact of the Transatlantic Slave Trade on Ethnic Stratification in Africa." *The American Economic Review*, Vol. 101, No. 3, Papers and Proceedings of the One Hundred Twenty Third Annual Meeting of the American Economic Association (May 2011): 571–576.

Wieviorka, Michel. *La France Raciste*. Paris: Seuil, 1992.

William Renwick, Riddell. "Le Code Noir." *The Journal of Negro History* 10, no. 3 (1925): 321–29.

Wilson, Woodrow. *The Papers of Woodrow Wilson Vol. 2* [in English]. Edited by Arthur Stanley Link. Princeton: Princeton University Press, 1967.

———. *The State: Elements of Historical and Practical Politics*. Boston: D.C. Heath & Co., 1889.

———. "Stray Thoughts from the South (22 February, 1881)." In *The Papers of Woodrow Wilson Vol. 2*, edited by Arthur Stanley Link. Princeton: Princeton University Press, 1967.

Winters, Jeffrey A. *Oligarchy*. Cambridge: Cambridge University Press, 2011.

Wright, Winthrop R. *Café Con Leche: Race, Class, and National Image in Venezuela*. 1st ed. Austin: University of Texas Press, 1990.

Yogg, Michael R. *Passion for Reality: The Extraordinary Life of the Investing Pioneer Paul Cabot* [in English]. New York: Columbia University Press, 2014.

Zedong, Mao. *Mao's Road to Power: Revolutionary Writings 1912–1949* [in English]. Edited by Stuart R. Schram. Armonk: M.E. Sharpe, 1992.

———. *The Writings of Mao Zedong, 1949–1976*. Edited by Michael Y.M. Kau and John K. Leung. Armonk: M.E. Sharpe, 1986.

Zolberg, Aristide R. *A Nation by Design: Immigration Policy in the Fashioning of America*. New York: Russell Sage Foundation, 2006.

INDEX

A NOTE ON THE TYPE

This book has been composed in Adobe Text and Gotham. Adobe Text, designed by Robert Slimbach for Adobe, bridges the gap between fifteenth- and sixteenth-century calligraphic and eighteenth-century Modern styles. Gotham, inspired by New York street signs, was designed by Tobias Frere-Jones for Hoefler & Co.